TUTANKHAMUN AND THE TOMB THAT CHANGED THE WORLD

TUTANKHAMUN AND THE TOMB THAT CHANGED THE WORLD

BOB BRIER

OXFORD
UNIVERSITY PRESS

OXFORD
UNIVERSITY PRESS

Oxford University Press is a department of the University of Oxford. It furthers
the University's objective of excellence in research, scholarship, and education
by publishing worldwide. Oxford is a registered trade mark of Oxford University
Press in the UK and certain other countries.

Published in the United States of America by Oxford University Press
198 Madison Avenue, New York, NY 10016, United States of America.

Library of Congress Control Number: 2022943958
ISBN 978–0–19–763505–6

DOI: 10.1093/oso/9780197635056.001.0001

1 3 5 7 9 8 6 4 2

Printed by Sheridan Books, Inc., United States of America

Contents

PART III. TUTANKHAMUN'S LEGACY

Acknowledgments

I have had so much help with this book that I feel it is really a group project. Part of the reason for this is that in several chapters I was out of my comfort zone, reporting colleagues' research in areas where I had limited expertise. Fortunately, several of the researchers were willing to proof the sections where I discussed their research. Double thanks are due to Drs. André Veldmeijer and Ray Johnson, who not only proofed their sections but also provided illustrations for this book. Thanks also to Dr. Mark Gabolde, who read and corrected the section where I discuss his research on Tutankhamun's missing pectoral. Special thanks to an old friend, Dr. Peter Lacovara, who seems to know everything and proofed almost every chapter, saving me from errors several times. I was especially fortunate to be able to have several long conversations with Dr. Christine Lilyquist, who was in charge of the installation of the Metropolitan Museum of Art's Tutankhamun exhibition. Her observations were very helpful in getting an accurate perspective on a story that often seemed like *Rashomon*. Another close friend who served as proofreader and also supplied illustrations and advice about layouts was William Joy. Many of us in Egyptology are in his debt. Huge thanks go to Mary Jordan whose wonderful drawings appear throughout this book.

Thanks to George B. Johnson, who is not only a marvelous photographer but also a historian of Harry Burton. George's wonderful photographs of Tutankhamun's treasures can be seen throughout the book. Dr. Clark Haskins is yet another photographer/friend who came through in the end and provided much-needed photographs. His wife, Vickie, also helped by placing the hieroglyphs I needed within the text when my computer failed me. Anthony Marks not only let me use letters and prints in his collection but also photographed them for me. You can see why I say this is a group project. Thanks are also due to the staff of the Griffith Institute for answering all my questions and for finding the photos I needed.

My two editors, Stefan Vranka at OUP and Tom Miller at Liza Dawson Associates, helped greatly with editing and production. Helen Nicholson at Newgen Publishing UK was wonderful and helped straighten things out whenever they got tangled. A big thanks to Dr. Salima Ikram, whose early discussions were extremely helpful in guiding the direction the book took.

As usual, I forced my wife, Pat Remler, to read every word to see if it made sense. Her levelheaded comments helped nudge the book toward "readable."

Introduction

Many readers of this book will be familiar with the story of the discovery and excavation of Tutankhamun's tomb. It is a story we never seem to tire of hearing: the down-on-his-luck archaeologist who teams up with a wealthy English lord to search for a lost tomb in the Valley of the Kings. Then we have the treasures, the thousands of objects the boy-king intended to take with him to the next world—so many objects that it took the discoverer, Howard Carter, and his team ten years to clear the tomb, pack the fragile thrones, beds, shrines, and coffins, and place them on steamers to take them down the Nile to Cairo to be displayed in the Egyptian Museum. For most people, this is where the story ends—but it doesn't. There is much more to tell.

In recent years, space-age technologies have been applied to study the objects found in the tomb, yielding remarkable results. The mummy of Tutankhamun has been CAT-scanned, giving surprising new information.[1] Other studies have shown that some objects in the tomb came from outer space. A recent scan of the walls of the tomb has suggested that there may be a second tomb behind the back wall of Tutankhamun's tomb, and one highly respected scholar is convinced that it is the missing tomb of Queen Nefertiti. These are relatively recent studies, but research on Tutankhamun has been going on for decades. These studies have progressed in spurts: sometimes little happened for decades, and then there were periods of frantic activity. Now is one of those times of intense activity.

Egypt is just completing its new Grand Egyptian Museum (GEM), one of the largest in the world, and it has been decided that all of Tutankhamun's treasures will be moved from the old Egyptian Museum in Cairo to the new museum at Giza. For the first time in decades, many of Tutankhamun's possessions are being taken out of their glass display cases and are available to scholars for study. It has been discovered that many of the objects need conservation, and this is now being done at the GEM's state-of-the-art Conservation Center. Researchers are studying everything from

Tutankhamun's chariots to the sandals he wore. There are new theories about when his tomb was robbed and how he died. These are very exciting times for Tutankhamun studies, and that is partly what this book is about.

While scientific research is revealing wonderful things about the treasures found in the tomb, other studies have revealed important aspects of ancient Egyptian religion. The Egyptians were resurrectionists; they believed that the body was literally going to rise again in the next world. That's why they mummified—to preserve the body for the afterlife. But getting to the next world was going to be a difficult and dangerous journey. Malevolent deities would try to oppose Tutankhamun's passage. He would have to cross lakes of fire and go through gates guarded by demons who demanded passwords. To assist him on his journey, magical and religious texts were written on the gilded shrines that enclosed his sarcophagus. These texts have been translated and provide insights into the ancient Egyptian view of life after death. They have been overlooked for too long.

Some of these researches have been coordinated efforts, and some have been done in relative isolation. The idea behind this book is that reviewing this research will help us form a better picture of the boy-king. How did he die? Was he a frail pharaoh with a club foot, who suffered from genetic disorders caused by inbreeding in the royal family? Or was he an athlete who enjoyed hunting in the desert with his hounds and who, when he matured, led the Egyptian army into battle?

The last section of this book presents yet another aspect of the tomb that most people are not aware of: Tutankhamun's legacy. In a modest way, Tutankhamun's tomb changed the world of archaeology. Part of this legacy concerns how archaeological excavations would be conducted post-Tutankhamun. From the very beginning of the discovery, Howard Carter realized that the excavation would require not a single excavator but an entire team, each with a different skill. Photographers, conservators, engineers, translators, and draftsmen would all be needed to document and remove the thousands of items crammed into the tomb. A chemist, Alfred Lucas, devoted nearly ten years of his life to the preservation of the treasures in the tomb. The excavation and clearing of Tutankhamun's tomb would set new standards for archaeological excavations in the future. This is an important part of the boy-king's legacy. But there is another legacy of Tutankhamun's tomb, a political one rarely discussed.

When the tomb was discovered in 1922, the Antiquities Service was controlled by the French, while the British ran the government as a protectorate. Although not official, it was colonialism in practice. The Egyptians had little say in what happened to their patrimony or how their country was run. After the discovery of the tomb, there would be social upheaval in Egypt. Foreign control of the Antiquities Service would end, Egypt would decide that none of its antiquities should leave Egypt, and the Egyptians would demand self-rule. It would be too strong to suggest that the discovery of Tutankhamun's tomb caused all these changes, but the tomb certainly played a significant part. Tutankhamun and his tomb were rallying points at a crucial time in Egypt's political development. This legacy is another aspect of this book. So, in a sense, we have a play in three acts: the discovery, research, and Tut's legacy.

How Tutankhamun's Name Is Spelled

Before the play begins, I have to say something about how the main character's name is spelled. You will see Tutankhamun's name spelled several ways, and this can be confusing, but it doesn't have to be.

Many people believe that hieroglyphic writing was picture writing. This is wrong. If that were true, then the Egyptians would have always been talking about birds, legs, and snakes. The truth is that, for the most part, ancient Egyptian is an alphabetic language. All those ducks, owls, legs, and snakes represent sounds; they have phonetic value. Let's look at how Tutankhamun wrote his name.

The first three hieroglyphs were pronounced "amn." The next three are the "tut" part of his name, and the last three are the "ankh" part. We now have the three words that make up Tutankhamun's name, *amun*, *tut*, and *ankh*, but obviously they are not in the right order. The reason *amn* is written first is because it is the name of a god, Amun, and because gods are most important, their names come first in writing. We call this "honorific import." So while his mother called him Tutankhamun, when his name is written the *amun* comes first. The word *tut* means "image," and *ankh* means "life." Thus Tut's full name means something like "the living image of Amun," or perhaps "the image of Amun lives." Now remember, the point of this mini-lesson in hieroglyphics was to help explain why the boy-king's name is spelled several different ways in this book.

As we saw, the god's name was merely written *amn*, with no vowel between the *m* and the *n*. Egyptians didn't always write the vowels, so we are not sure what the missing vowel was. This is why you see the name spelled both Tutankhamun and Tutankhamen; some prefer it with a *u*, others with the *e*. In the early days of the discovery, Carter spelled it Tutankhamen, with the *e*. He often put dots between the three parts to make clear how the name was pronounced and thus wrote it Tut.Ankh.Amen. Later, because the great translator Sir Alan Gardiner preferred Tutankhamun, Carter adopted that spelling, but his three-volume work on the tomb was published as *The Tomb of Tut.Ankh.Amen.*[2]

In the United States, however, we continued to use Tutankhamen. So when I wrote *The Murder of Tutankhamen* I used that spelling.[3] Now, twenty-five years later, my colleagues have convinced me to switch to the more popular Tutankhamun. So for this book I spell the name with the *u*. When I am quoting titles of books or letters written by Egyptologists, you will see it as they used it. OK? No confusion now about spelling—either way is acceptable.

Tutankhamun wasn't Tut's only name. He actually had five. When a pharaoh became king, he was given his royal titulary of five names.[4] Three of those names are not important to us, as they are rarely used. The two important ones are those that appear in cartouches encircling the names. The word *cartouche* is French for "cartridge shell" and was used by Napoleon's soldiers in Egypt, who saw them on temple walls and thought they looked like bullets. ⬭ Tutankhamun's other name in a cartouche

is pronounced "neb-kheperu-re" and means "the lordly manifestation of Re." Usually the objects in his tomb were inscribed with both names, but sometimes only one.

Now it is time for the three-part story of Tutankhamun. First the discovery.

PART I

History of the Tomb

Wonderful things.

—Howard Carter

I

Lost but Not Found

Furnish your station in the valley,
The grave that shall conceal your corpse;
Set it before you as your concern . . .
Emulate the great departed,
Who are at rest within their tombs.

—The Scribe Ani, ca. 1400 BC

A thousand years before Tutankhamun, around 2400 BC, pharaohs were buried in pyramids in the north of Egypt. This was how they protected their provisions for the next world. It was a time when it was unimaginable that a king's tomb might be robbed. But over the centuries there were periods of lawlessness; robbers entered the pyramids and stole the treasures. A thousand years later, during the reign of King Tuthmosis I, it was clear that pyramids served as signals to robbers, showing them where treasure could be found. A different, more secure way had to be found to bury the kings of Egypt.

"No One Seeing, No One Hearing"

We know the name of the man who found the solution. He was an architect named Ineni. His tomb is not far from the Valley of the Kings, and on its walls he wrote his autobiography for the gods to see, so that they would reward him in the next life. He was an important man, "overseer of the works" for the pharaoh Tuthmosis I, an ancestor of Tutankhamun who lived two hundred years before the boy-king. Of all his accomplishments, Ineni was proudest of creating for his pharaoh a burial that would never be robbed. The key was secrecy. No more boastful pyramids. As Ineni inscribed on his tomb wall, "I inspected the excavation of the cliff-tomb of his majesty, alone, no one seeing, no one hearing. . . . It was a work of my heart, my virtue was wisdom; there was not given to me a command by an elder. I shall be praised because of my wisdom after years, by those who shall imitate that which I have done."[1] The place Ineni chose was the Valley of the Kings, and he was right. Those who came after him imitated what he had done for his king.

The Valley of the Kings is one of the most inhospitable places on earth. Nothing grows there. In summer, temperatures go past 120 degrees and the glare of the white limestone is blinding. The Valley would have been just as inhospitable during the time of Tutankhamun; that's why Ineni chose it for the burial of his king.

It was the perfect spot for a tomb to be lost. With no water and no foliage, no one would ever want to live there. With its steep cliffs and only one entrance, it could easily be guarded, and the monotonous white limestone of the Valley provided a barren landscape where tombs could be easily concealed, forgotten to the centuries.

When the Greek traveler Diodorus Siculus visited the Valley in the middle of the first century BC, the priests of Thebes told him that their lists recorded forty-seven tombs, but only fifteen remained visible; the others had been destroyed by tomb robbers.[2] Fifteen centuries later, in 1739, the English clergyman Richard Pococke sailed up the Nile and visited the Valley, but he could find only nine tombs that could be entered.[3] He was the first to publish a map of the Valley; it was a crude attempt, but it was a start. The next important excursion into the Valley would be Napoleon Bonaparte's.

Bonaparte in Egypt

When Bonaparte invaded Egypt in 1798, he brought along a group of scientists to describe the wonders of Egypt for the European world. Soon they founded the Institut d'Égypte to study the country they had just invaded. At the first meeting, Bonaparte posed rather mundane problems to the scientists: Could gunpowder be manufactured in Egypt? What was the best method for purifying Nile water? Could wine be produced there?[4] But the scientists were also free to investigate topics of their own. One of the youngest members of the expedition was Édouard Devilliers, an eighteen-year-old engineering student who came with his professor. He brought his schoolbooks along, and in October 1798 his professor tested him in Cairo and pronounced him a civil engineer. For most of the campaign Devilliers teamed up with Jean-Baptiste Prosper Jollois, a twenty-one-year-old engineer, and from their accounts, the boys forgot about constructing bridges and roads and fell in love with antiquity. Among their many accomplishments, they made the first accurate drawings of the famous Dendera Zodiac, the carved ceiling showing the constellations in the Egyptian sky, which caused a sensation in Paris. But what is more important for our story is that they carried out the first professional mapping of the Valley of the Kings, and even discovered a new tomb.

When Napoleon's army entered Egypt, there were eleven open tombs in the Valley. Exploring the Valley's remote western branch, the young engineers found a small hole in the cliff's wall and crept in. Candles in hand, they peered through the darkness and saw vivid wall paintings of a pharaoh among the gods. They didn't know it, but they had discovered the tomb of Tutankhamun's grandfather, Amenhotep III. On the tomb's floor, they found small figurines, some carved out of wood, some made from ceramic. Again, they didn't know what they had found. The ancient Egyptians believed the afterlife would be pretty much like this one, but even better. That's where the figurines that Devilliers and Jollois discovered come in: the servant statues were going to do the work. When the Nile overflowed its banks each year, all the farmers were called up by the government to dig canals from the Nile inland to irrigate the land. When in the next world your name was called, these little statues would take your place and work so that you wouldn't have to. There is even a magical spell written on the front of them that basically says: "When my name is called to work on the land, answer 'Here I am!' in my name."[5]

These little statues held farm implements in their hands, and slung over their shoulders were sacks of seeds for planting. Because these servant statues would answer for the deceased, they were called ushabtis, which derives from the ancient Egyptian word *wesheb*, which means "to answer." Devilliers and Jollois took some of these statues home as souvenirs; Devilliers's descendants still own four ushabtis that he brought back to France. The two young scientists also found a small green schist head of Amenhotep III that is now in the Louvre.[6] You can see the work of these two young engineer/ adventurers in the *Description de l'Égypte*, a monumental work that was produced by Bonaparte's savants when they returned to France and which described everything the scientists had seen.[7] It included eleven huge volumes of engravings, many by Devilliers and Jollois, including the first portrait ever published of Tutankhamun's grandfather and illustrations of some of the king's ushabtis.[8] They also published their map of the Valley of the Kings with the tomb they discovered proudly indicated (Figure 1.1).

Their hasty survey of the Valley was a remarkable achievement, considering that a war was being fought and bullets were flying as the two young engineers risked their lives to measure and record the tombs. They

Figure 1.1. Napoleon's engineers made the first accurate map of the Valley of the Kings. (Photo by Pat Remler.)

produced the first accurate diagrams of tombs in the Valley of the Kings, but they had no idea whose tombs they were. That would have to wait till their countryman Jean-François Champollion deciphered hieroglyphs twenty years later.

The Giant of Padua

In the decades after Napoleon's expedition, adventurers came to the Valley seeking treasure. The first extensive excavations in the Valley were conducted in the early nineteenth century by Giovanni Battista Belzoni, an Italian circus strongman turned adventurer. Trained as a hydraulic engineer, the six-foot-seven-inch Belzoni came to Egypt in search of riches. From 1815 to 1819, Belzoni excavated sites up and down the Nile. He was the first person in modern times to enter the Pyramid of Khephren, the second-largest pyramid in Egypt, and was also the first to enter the temple of Abu Simbel, built by Ramses the Great in remote Nubia.[9] Searching for artifacts he could remove from Egypt to sell, Belzoni first began looking in tombs of nobles near the Valley of the Kings. His account of one excursion into a tomb is the stuff of high adventure:

> This is not all; the entry or passage where the bodies are is roughly cut in the rocks, and the falling of the sand from the upper part of the ceiling of the passage causes it to be nearly filled up. In some places there is not more than a vacancy of a foot left, which you must contrive to pass through in a creeping posture like a snail, on pointed and keen stones, that can cut like glass. . . . [A]nd the Arabs with the candles or torches in their hands, naked and covered with dust, themselves resemble living mummies, absolutely formed a scene that cannot be described. In such a situation I found myself several times, and often returned exhausted and fainting, till at last I became inured to it, and indifferent to what I suffered, except from the dust, which never failed to choke my throat and nose; and though fortunately, I am destitute of the sense of smelling, I could taste that the mummies were rather unpleasant to swallow. After the exertion of entering into such a place, through a passage of fifty, a hundred, three hundred or perhaps six hundred yards, nearly overcome, I sought a resting place, found one and contrived to sit; but when my weight bore on the body of an Egyptian, it crushed it like a band-box. I naturally had recourse to my hands to sustain my weight, but they found no better support, so that I sunk altogether among the broken mummies, with a crash of bones, rags, and wooden cases, which raised such a dust as kept me motionless for a quarter off an hour, waiting till it subsided again.[10]

With this adventure behind him, Belzoni moved on to the Valley of the Kings to search for his treasure.

When the royal tombs were cut into the Valley walls, vast quantities of stone chips had to be removed and dumped outside the tombs, where they remained untouched for thousands of years. Belzoni used the mounds of chips to guide him to a tomb's location. Entrances to many of the tombs had been covered by these piles and lost. Sometimes overhanging cliffs had collapsed, falling over entrances, but also an occasional torrential rainstorm passing through the Valley had washed mud, sand, and even boulders into the entrances. As time passed, the tombs gradually filled with rubble, which hid their entrances, sometimes for centuries. Belzoni had read the accounts of ancient travelers to the Valley and didn't believe the account of the geographer Strabo, who said that when he was there, nearly two thousand years before Belzoni, he was told by the priests that there were forty-seven tombs. Belzoni could see only ten or eleven tombs when he set to work.

Employing about twenty local workmen at a time, Belzoni excavated the most likely spots, and although he uncovered several tombs, all had been plundered in antiquity. The most beautiful of these was the tomb of Seti I, father of Ramses the Great. The walls were carved with magical spells ensuring Seti's safe journey to the next world. The Book of Gates, the Book of Praising Re in the West, and the Book of What Is in the Netherworld were all illustrated with paintings of the gods who would assist Seti in defeating his enemies.[11] Above his burial chamber, an astronomical ceiling showed the Egyptian constellations against a dark blue night sky. Belzoni, bedazzled by the tomb's brilliant colors, bright as on the day Seti was laid to rest, spent a full year making paper impressions of the carved walls so that he could build a replica of the tomb for an exhibition in London. The show was a sensation, creating waves of Egyptomania throughout Europe.

Although the tomb had been plundered, Belzoni still found something in it to sell. Lying in the burial chamber was the beautiful inscribed alabaster sarcophagus in which Seti was laid to rest (see Color Plate 1). Belzoni waxed poetic about it:

> It is a sarcophagus of the finest oriental alabaster. . . . I cannot give an adequate idea of this beautiful and invaluable piece of antiquity, and can only say, that nothing has been brought into Europe from Egypt that can compare with it.[12]

He wasn't exaggerating. It is a spectacular piece.

Belzoni hauled the sarcophagus out of the tomb, got it to the Nile, and shipped it to England to sell. He offered it to the British Museum, but the £3,000 price was too high for them, so Belzoni sold it to the antiquarian John Soane. Today it is the star of Sir John Soane's Museum in London. The tomb of Seti was a great find for Belzoni; in addition to selling Seti's sarcophagus, he held a very successful exhibition of his replica tomb paintings, but Belzoni never knew that just a hundred yards away from Seti's tomb lay the greatest archaeological find ever, the tomb of Tutankhamun. Indeed, Belzoni never even knew there was a Tutankhamun.

After Belzoni, other adventurers came to the Valley of the Kings in search of treasure, and almost invariably they left disappointed. Not only didn't they find treasure, but none of them ever found the mummy of a pharaoh. For centuries the tombs had been plundered, but no one had ever found the body of a king, for surely the tomb robbers would have left it behind for it would have had no value to them. Where were the kings of Egypt?

Royal Mummies at Last

The answer to this question of where the royal mummies were came during the 1870s, when antiquities of great beauty, bearing the names of the kings and queens of Egypt, began appearing in the antiquities shops of Luxor. These rare pieces began arriving on the market at a time when Egypt had been bankrupted by building the Suez Canal and was now being administered by foreign powers, to whom the country was in debt. France was in charge of antiquities, with August Mariette as the first director of the newly formed Antiquities Service. One of Mariette's greatest contributions was his attempt to stop the looting of antiquities that had gone on for decades.

While Mariette was director of the Antiquities Service, the high-quality royal objects appearing on the antiquities market began to attract collectors and museum curators from all over the world. Even Mariette himself was forced to buy two spectacular Books of the Dead for the new Boulaq Museum before they were bought by others and left Egypt.[13] Mariette was determined to find the tomb they came from before everything was dispersed or destroyed, but he died in 1881, before he could complete his investigation. His successor, Gaston Maspero, made the search his top priority and eventually published an account of the find.[14]

Evidence pointed to the Abd er Rassouls, a family of tomb robbers living close to the Valley of the Kings. After intense questioning, one of the Rassoul brothers led Émile Brugsch, Maspero's assistant, to a high, winding path overlooking the Valley of the Kings. Chimney-like rock outcroppings lined the way through an uninhabited area about a mile from the ruined temple of Queen Hatshepsut. Near the base of one rocky outcrop, a rectangular eight-by-ten-foot shaft descended forty feet straight down. After placing a palm log across the top of the pit to anchor a rope, first Rassoul and then Brugsch descended.[15] When the young assistant squeezed through the entrance at the bottom, the first thing he saw was a huge coffin; behind it were three more coffins, and past those on the right was a corridor that ran more than seventy feet into the bedrock. Littering the length of the corridor were hundreds of small bright blue ceramic ushabtis, buried with the deceased to serve as servants in the next world. Brugsch was amazed.

> Soon we came upon cases of porcelain funerary offerings, metal and alabaster vessels, draperies and trinkets, until, reaching the turn in the passage, a cluster of mummy cases came into view in such number as to stagger me.[16]

In addition, there were canopic chests—boxes that contained the four jars in which the deceased individual's organs were placed at the time of mummification. The idea was that when it came time for resurrection, the magical spells on the jars and boxes would enable the deceased to reassemble his body so he would be complete in the next world.

The corridor opened onto a room seventeen feet square, the floor almost entirely covered with splendid coffins. Brugsch, merely an assistant at the museum, was not a great scholar, but he had attended Egyptology classes in Cairo taught by his more learned brother, Heinrich. By the dim light of his candle he began to read the names on the coffins: Amenhotep I, Tuthmosis I, Tuthmosis II, and Tuthmosis III, all kings of the Eighteenth Dynasty, ancestors of Tutankhamun. Next to them were the pharaohs of the Nineteenth Dynasty: Ramses I; his son, Seti I, whose tomb had been discovered by Belzoni seventy-five years earlier; and then Seti's illustrious son, Ramses II, better known as Ramses the Great. Up until now, no one had ever found the mummy of a single pharaoh; now Brugsch had half a dozen. But still more royalty awaited him farther back in the tomb.

There was one last room, which held the kings and queens of the Twenty-First Dynasty, the royal family whose Books of the Dead had appeared on the antiquities market. Here were the mummies of Pinedjem II, Queen Henettowey, and other members of this august family.[17] It was all very confusing to Brugsch. How had the mummies of the kings and queens of different dynasties come to be buried together? It was as if England's Norman and Tudor kings had been found together in the same burial vault. It just didn't make sense.

Eventually Egyptologists pieced the story together. By the Twentieth Dynasty, two centuries after Tutankhamun was laid to rest in the Valley of the Kings, most of the tombs in the Valley had been robbed. An official inspection of the Valley of the Kings during the Twenty-First Dynasty revealed this wholesale robbing. Rather than continue futile attempts to protect the isolated tombs, the violated bodies of the pharaohs were repaired, rewrapped, labeled with wooden tags, placed in new coffins when necessary, and removed to their secret communal tomb, which remained undiscovered for more than three thousand years.

The Deir el Bahri cache of royal mummies was the creation of Pharaoh Pinedjem II, who was so sure it wouldn't be robbed that he chose it for his tomb as well. Inscriptions on the mummies as well as one at the bottom of the shaft in black ink indicated that on the day of Pinedjem's burial the bodies of Seti I and Ramses II were interred with him, and there they remained for thirty centuries.[18]

As important and unique as the Deir el Bahri discovery was, the findings were poorly documented. After two hours in the tomb, Brugsch realized that his candle could set fire to the dry wooden coffins, so he quickly left. He then decided that the mummies, plus their ushabtis and other funerary equipment, had to be moved to Cairo as soon as possible. The inhabitants of the nearby village of Gourna had for years made their living by robbing tombs; when they learned how much they were about to lose, there was no telling what they might do. There was no time to record where each coffin was found in the tomb; not a single photograph was taken, and no drawings were made of the items in situ. Within two days, all the coffins, mummies, canopic chests, and funerary equipment were hoisted to the surface. Three hundred men then carried these treasures out of the Valley to the Nile, where everything was loaded onto the museum's steamer for their journey to Cairo. When the villagers learned of the boat's royal cargo, the women lined the banks of the Nile and wailed mourning cries, just as their ancient ancestors must have done to mark the passing of their kings.

When the royal mummies reached the museum in Cairo, they caused a sensation. Never before had anyone gazed on the face of a pharaoh; now there were a dozen. Brugsch unwrapped only one of the mummies, Tuthmosis III, the greatest of the warrior pharaohs. The mummy had been buried in the Valley of the Kings, plundered, rewrapped by Twenty-First Dynasty embalmers, and reburied in the Deir el Bahri tomb, where it suffered one final indignity at the hands of the Rassouls: they had hacked a hole in the wrappings in the area of the heart, looking for a heart scarab, a highly saleable antiquity. These large beetle-shaped amulets were placed over the heart to ensure that it would not desert the deceased. The Rassouls must have thought such a finely wrapped mummy would have a heart scarab of precious silver or gold. They didn't realize the mummy had already been robbed three thousand years earlier, and if there had ever been such an amulet, it would have been taken then.

When Brugsch and his colleagues unwrapped Tuthmosis III they became the first in modern times to see the face of a pharaoh, and what they saw was shocking. The king's body was in a horrible state. The head was separated from the body (Figure 1.2), the legs and arms disarticulated, and the feet broken off at the ankles—damage done by the ancient tomb robbers.[19] Brugsch performed a crude, quick autopsy that yielded little information, and then stopped there, perhaps fearful that he would find the other mummies in a similarly sad condition.

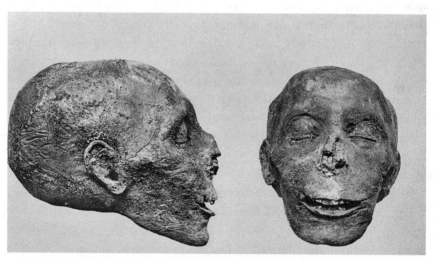

Figure 1.2. When Émile Brugsch unwrapped the mummy of Tuthmosis III, it was the first face of a pharaoh seen in modern times.

For the next few years, most of the research on the royal mummies was directed at deciphering the tags that identified the rewrapped pharaohs. Eventually most of the mummies were unwrapped at the museum, often as a social event, with visiting dignitaries present (see Color Plate 2). The kings' faces were photographed, and soon tourists were sending home postcards with the head of Ramses the Great, the pharaoh of the Exodus— probably the only face from the Bible that anyone would ever see.

Egyptologists were thrilled with the "royal cachette," as it became known, but they knew there were kings missing. Champollion had long ago deciphered hieroglyphs, and the language experts had translated the lists of pharaohs that had been carved on temple walls. They now knew the names of almost all the pharaohs, and they weren't all in the Deir el Bahri cachette. Jollois and Devilliers had found the tomb of Amenhotep III, but his mummy wasn't in the cache. And there were pharaohs of the Eighteenth through Twenty-First Dynasties who were still missing. Where were they?

A Second Royal Cache

In 1886 Maspero resigned as director of the Antiquities Service, and Victor Loret took his place. Loret decided to undertake the first comprehensive survey of the Valley of the Kings, and among his finds was the tomb of Tuthmosis III, whose mummy had already been found in the Deir el Bahri cache. It was a wonderful tomb, with spectacular paintings, but an even more important discovery was the tomb of his son, Amenhotep II.

When Loret first entered this tomb he immediately saw that it had been plundered. The floor was covered with broken ushabtis and wood fragments with the name of Amenhotep II. The tomb was littered with rubble, but Loret crawled deeper and deeper into the tomb. He saw broken models of the boats the pharaoh would need in the next world, and bits and pieces of gilded images of the king. Then the light from his candle fell on something for which he was not prepared.

> I went forward [between the two columns] with my candle and, horrible sight, a body lay there upon the boat, all black and hideous, its grimacing face turning towards me and looking at me, its long brown hair in sparse bunches around its head. I did not dream that this was just an unwrapped mummy. The legs and arms seemed to be bound. A hole exposed the sternum, there was an opening in the skull. Was this a victim of human sacrifice? Was this a thief,

murdered by his accomplices in a bloody division of the loot, or perhaps killed by soldiers or police interrupting the pillaging of the tomb?[20]

Loret wasn't very familiar with mummies, and his imagination was running away with him. What he had seen was the mummy of a prince, disturbed so soon after his burial that the oils and resins used in embalming were still liquid. The robbers had placed the body in one of the model boats, where the oils later solidified and glued the prince into it.

Loret's overreaction to his encounter with a mummy is not unusual. One of the unlabeled mummies found in the Deir el Bahri cache is known as Unknown Man E, and for years it was suggested that because he looked as if he was screaming in agony, he had been buried alive. This mummy had not been seen for a century, and some years ago it was found in its original coffin on a shelf in the Egyptian Museum in Cairo. I was allowed to remove the mummy from the coffin and do a preliminary examination.[21] All the speculation about cries of agony and being buried alive was overreaction by people not used to working with mummies. The open mouth is common with mummies. Tendons and ligaments break over thousands of years and the mandible (the lower jaw) drops, so the open mouth is natural. As a matter of fact, the examination of Unknown Man E indicated he had been buried with care.

Loret's nerves were frayed, but his adventure into the subterranean world of mummies was not yet over. Regaining his composure, he continued his descent into the tomb, eventually arriving at a burial chamber that contained a lidless stone sarcophagus. Peering over the top, Loret saw a coffin with a garland of flowers at its head and a wreath at its foot. Inside was the mummy of Amenhotep II, the first royal mummy ever found still in its original tomb.

Loret began examining the four side chambers off the burial chamber. Three small rooms contained statues of the pharaoh, vases for the sacred oils that the pharaoh would need in the next world, wood models of boats so he could journey there, and meat and fruits to sustain him for eternity. It was in one of these side chambers that Loret received his next shock:

> We passed to the rooms to the right. In the first one we entered an unusually strange sight met our eyes: three bodies lay side by side at the back in the left corner, their feet pointing towards the door. The right half of the room was filled with little coffins with mummiform covers and funerary statues of

bituminized [resin-coated] wood. These statues were contained in the coffins that the thieves had opened and rejected after having searched in vain for treasures.

We approached the cadavers. The first seemed to be that of a woman. A thick veil covered her forehead and left eye. Her broken arm had been replaced at her side, her nails in the air. Ragged and torn cloth hardly covered her body. Abundant black curled hair spread over the limestone floor on each side of her head. The face was admirably conserved and had a noble and majestic gravity.

The second mummy, in the middle, was that of a child of about fifteen years. It was naked, with hands joined on the abdomen. First of all the head appeared totally bald, but on closer examination one saw that the head had been shaved except an area on the right temple from which grew a magnificent tress of black hair. This was the coiffure of the royal princes [called the Horus lock]. I thought immediately of the prince Webensennu, thus so far unknown son of Amenophis II, whose funerary statue I had noticed in the great hall, and whose canopic fragments I was to find later. The face of the young prince was laughing and mischievous, it did not at all evoke the idea of death.

The last corpse nearest the wall seemed to be that of a man. His head was shaved but a wig lay on the ground not far from him. The face of his person displayed something horrible and something droll at the same time. The mouth was running obliquely from one side nearly to the middle of the cheek, bit a pad of linen whose two ends hung from the corner of the lips. The half-closed eyes had a strange expression, he could have died choking on a gag but he looked like a young playful cat with a piece of cloth. Death which had respected the severe beauty of the woman and the impish grace of the boy had turned in derision and amused itself with the countenance of the man.

A remarkable fact was that the three corpses, like the one in the boat, had their skulls pierced with a large hole and the breast of each one was opened.[22]

The similar condition of the three mummies in the side chamber and the one in the boat was caused by methodical tomb robbers. In their search for jewelry, they hacked at the wrappings on the head first. After quickly stripping the outer linen, they then hacked at the chest searching for the heart scarab, thus causing similar damage to all the bodies. Loret had no clear idea of the identities of the four mummies, and his judgment was certainly confused. The naked body he described as a man is clearly that of a young woman. To this day, the identities of three of these bodies remain uncertain. The one sure identification of one of the mummies in the tomb was made almost a century later and required both a surprising find in Tutankhamun's tomb and modern technology. That mummy was Tutankhamun's grand-mother; but more on that later.

After finding the three mummies, Loret's night still wasn't over. One of the side chambers had been sealed with limestone blocks, with only a small opening near the ceiling. Loret climbed to the top and with his candle was barely able to make out nine coffins, neatly arranged—six against the wall and three in front of them. That was all he could see, but that was also all he could handle. He called it a night without finding out who the nine mummies were.

Loret may have been unnerved by his nocturnal wanderings among the mummies, but he was a careful Egyptologist. In the days following his dis-covery, he carefully mapped the tomb and cleared it of all its contents. Only after this was done did he take down the wall blocking the entrance to the side chamber to determine the identities of the nine mummies, revealing that he had discovered the missing pharaohs that everyone had wondered about: Tuthmosis IV, Amenhotep III, Merenptah, Siptah, Seti II, Ramses IV, Ramses V, Ramses I, and an unidentified woman. Now most of the phar-aohs of the Eighteenth through Twenty-First Dynasties had been found.

Just as with the Deir el Bahri cache of royal mummies, these mummies in the tomb of Amenhotep II had been gathered together by a Twenty-First Dynasty king to protect them from further desecration. Written on the bandages of the mummy of Seti II was the sad story of how the convention of kings in the tomb of Amenhotep II had come to be. On the sixth day of the fourth month of winter, in the twelfth year of the reign of Pinedjem I, that king had had the despoiled royal bodies rewrapped and placed in the tomb of Amenhotep II for safekeeping, where they remained until Loret discovered them.[23]

Now almost all the Great Ones of the New Kingdom were accounted for. Tutankhamun was still missing, but no one really cared. He was a shadowy figure hardly known even to Egyptologists. He had left no tem-ples, no records of his deeds, no statues. It wasn't even clear if he had ever really existed. How was this possible?

Vanished Without a Trace

The answer to how Tutankhamun could vanish so thoroughly from his-tory lies in a city four hundred miles south of Cairo. Abydos was "the Sacred City," one of the holiest cities in ancient Egypt. This special status is due to Osiris, the god of the dead. According to an ancient Egyptian myth, Osiris was killed and dismembered by his evil brother, Set, who scattered the pieces of his dead brother up and down the Nile. Osiris's grieving widow, the goddess Isis, retrieved the pieces, reassembled them, and then, by her powerful magic, resurrected Osiris. Her husband was thus the first to conquer death, and he became the god of the dead. Tradition had it that Osiris was buried at Abydos, so it became the city to which all Egyptians wanted to make a pilgrimage to leave offerings to Osiris. The idea was that if you left an offering, Osiris would admit you to the next world when you died, and you would live forever in the west with Osiris.

Fifty years after the death of Tutankhamun, when Seti I became pharaoh, he built a temple at Abydos, the Sacred City. It was dedicated primarily to Osiris. Like many other temples in Egypt, it had a Hall of the Ancients—a list of all the kings of Egypt from the very first pharaoh, Menes, down to Seti himself.[24] This was how pharaohs showed their august lineage.

In Seti's Hall of the Ancients an entire wall is covered with cartouches encircling the names of all the pharaohs of Egypt (Figure 1.3). To the left of all the cartouches, we can see Seti and his young son (who would go on to become Ramses the Great) performing an annual ceremony. Once a

Figure 1.3. The list of kings at the temple of Abydos names seventy-six pharaohs, but Tutankhamun's name is missing. (Photo by Dr. Clark Haskins.)

year they would enter the hall, stand before the cartouches, and read their ancestors' names. There was an ancient Egyptian saying, "To say the name of the dead is to make him live again," and that is just what Seti and the young prince are doing. On the wall are all the names we are now familiar with: Zoser, the builder of the Step Pyramid of Saqqara; Khufu, builder of the Great Pyramid of Giza; Tuthmosis III, the great warrior pharaoh—they are all there, right down to Seti himself.

The names of the kings are in chronological order, so it is easy to find a particular king's name. If we want to find Tutankhamun, we go along the wall to the section listing the kings of the Eighteenth Dynasty, Tutankhamun's dynasty. We can see Amenhotep III, the great builder, the grandfather of Tutankhamun. Right after him should be his son, Akhenaten, but he's not there. Tutankhamun should be next, but he's not there either. We know that Tutankhamun was followed by King Aye, the former vizier to Akhenaten. He's missing too. The name that does follow Amenhotep III is Horemheb, a general who seized power at the end of the Eighteenth Dynasty. So the kings list goes from Amenhotep straight to Horemheb, as if Akhenaten, Tutankhamun, and Aye never existed.

When the Abydos kings list was carved, there were people still alive who had lived under the reign of Tutankhamun. There were people who remembered him. Why wasn't he included with the other kings of Egypt?

Heretic King

Nothing in Tutankhamun's tomb, or anywhere else in Egypt, states who Tutankhamun's father was, but we have a pretty good idea. He was the pharaoh Akhenaten, often called "the Heretic Pharaoh."[25] When Tutankhamun's grandfather Amenhotep III died, he was succeeded by his son, Amenhotep IV. Then everything in Egypt changed. The new pharaoh erected huge statues of himself, unlike anything ever seen in Egypt. They showed the king as deformed, with wide hips, a narrow chest, a suggestion of breasts, an elongated face, and elongated fingers and toes (Figure 1.4.[26] One of these colossal statues is on the first floor of the Egyptian Museum in Cairo. Visitors constantly wonder, "What's wrong with him?" Why was the pharaoh depicting himself as deformed?

Figure 1.4. Akhenaten, Tutankhamun's father, was the only pharaoh depicted as deformed. (Photo by Pat Remler.)

For centuries pharaohs had been depicting themselves as well-muscled warriors with broad shoulders—gods on earth. This was such a well-established tradition that sometimes it is difficult to tell one pharaoh from another by their statues if they aren't inscribed. Egyptian art wasn't supposed to change, but that is exactly what Akhenaten was doing, and that was only the beginning.

When Akhenaten first became king, his name was Amenhotep, like his father, but a few years into his rule he changed his name to Akhenaten. This was a big deal. Names were important in ancient Egypt; they meant something. Amenhotep means "Amun is pleased" and shows which god was favored by the king. Amenhotep IV changing his name is an insult to Amun. To replace it with Akhenaten is still worse. The name means "beneficial to the Aten." It takes a relatively minor god, the Aten, and elevates him above Amun, the most powerful god in Egypt at the time. Then came the last stroke, the one that condemned Tutankhamun to obscurity for three thousand years. His father, the heretic pharaoh, declared that there was only one god, the Aten, and closed all the temples in Egypt dedicated to other gods.

Think about the disruption this caused. Thousands and thousands of priests were out of jobs. And what were the ordinary people to do? They had prayed to their gods their whole lives, had been told it was crucial; what now? And if there was no Osiris, the god of the dead, was there still immortality? This is the moment where the world changed and would never be the same. Akhenaten is the first monotheist recorded in history. Prior to him, no one had ever said, "There is only one god." Akhenaten is earlier than Moses coming down from the mountain with the Ten Commandments. Remember, when Moses does come down, what are the Israelites doing? Worshipping a golden calf. They are still polytheists. Akhenaten is centuries before Christ is born, and thousands of years before Muslims proclaim "There is but one god and Allah is his name." As far as the historical record shows, monotheism begins in Egypt with Tutankhamun's father, Akhenaten.

Monotheism has shaped our world. It is only after monotheism emerged that we got deadly religious disagreements: think of the Crusades, or of jihads. Monotheism forces the practitioner into an "either-or" choice. You can't have two or three gods; there is only one true god. And if the other guy is worshipping another god, he's wrong. Almost by definition, monotheism is divisive. If you don't believe in my god, then you are wrong. Before monotheism, there was no such problem. The Egyptians fought against lots of foreign nations, but never over religion. They never said foreign gods didn't exist. They even worshipped foreign gods. When Ramses the Great was awaiting his new bride from the Hittites, he made offerings to their storm god, Bal, so that her journey would be uneventful.

Imagine, then, how upsetting the introduction of monotheism must have been for the ancient Egyptians, who had never heard such a concept, who had worshipped hundreds of gods without having to choose. And the new god was not one of the familiar, popular ones. There had been no temples to the Aten. Worse, the Aten was different from the old gods. He didn't take the shape of a man, like Osiris, or a woman, like Isis, or even an animal, like Bastet, the cat goddess. The Aten was the solar disk, an object.[27]

This new god was so strange and so unwelcome to the Egyptians that they didn't rush to join the pharaoh's new religion. They still wanted to worship their old gods. So, early in his reign, Akhenaten decided to leave

Thebes (Luxor) and found a new city in the barren desert. He was going to establish a new capital on virgin soil, where no other god had ever been worshipped. With some twenty thousand followers, Akhenaten led an exodus into the desert. Akhenaten tells us that when they were 175 miles north of Luxor, he had a vision, in which the Aten indicated to him that he was to stop and build his holy city there in the desert. Akhenaten wasn't hallucinating; he actually saw something. Several times a year, the sun rises at Amarna right over a notch in the mountains. (That is the basis for the hieroglyph for "horizon.") 📖 This is why Akhenaten named his new city Ahketaten, "Horizon of the Aten."

So, with the Aten showing him where to build, Akhenaten constructed his holy city in the desert.[28] There with his beautiful wife Nefertiti they raised a family of six girls and one boy. As I noted, names were important in ancient Egypt, so Akhenaten gave all the children names with "-aten" in them: Beketaten ("servant of the Aten"), Meritaten ("beloved of the Aten"), Nefernerfruaten ("the very beautiful Aten"), and so on. The boy he named Tutankhaten ("the living image of Aten").

The Heretic's Son

So Tutankhaten was born at Amarna and raised in the new religion, Atenism. The only god he knew was the Aten, and he grew up isolated from the rest of Egypt. As soon as Akhenaten decided to build at Amarna, he erected boundary markers to establish the city limits. On these markers, inscriptions proclaimed that Akhenaten would never leave the precincts of his new city, and as far as we know, he never did. One consequence of the pharaoh being absent from the rest of Egypt was that he could no longer lead the army in battle or attend to the details of governing, but he didn't seem to care. He was a religious mystic, an absentee ruler devoted solely to his new religion, and Egypt suffered.[29]

When Akhenaten died in the seventeenth year of his reign, circa 1334 BC, several decisions had to be made. First, who would be the new king? There seems to have been only one possibility, for there was only one male child of Akhenaten: his ten-year-old son, Tutankhaten. But Tutankhaten wasn't fully royal; his mother was not Queen Nefertiti. One good guess is that his mother was Kiya, the second, minor wife of Akhenaten.[30] So to cement his claim to the throne, little Tut was married to his fully royal half-sister, Anhesenpaaten, who was about the same age as her half-brother. It was a bit later, when the Aten religion was abandoned, that their names were changed to Tutankhamun and Ankhesenamun.

The next question was whether the new rulers should continue following the new religion or go back to the old religion and return to Thebes. Not all the people who had followed their king to the new city were happy. For the ten years that the followers of the new religion had lived in the city, they had been isolated from the rest of Egypt. They hadn't seen their families and friends who stayed behind. And now with the leader of the new religion dead, its future was uncertain. It was quickly decided that they would return to the old religion and move back to Thebes. Soon after this decision, Amarna was abandoned. Later, the entire city was dismantled and its blocks reused as filler in later building projects. So the main reason Tutankhamun vanished without a trace is that his father was the heretic pharaoh who had tried to vanquish all the gods of Egypt. Anything or anyone associated with him was erased from history. That is why in the Hall of the Ancients at Abydos we didn't find the names of Akhenaten, Tutankhamun, or Aye. They were all tainted with the heresy of Atenism. After Tutankhamun's death his name was chiseled off all his statues, and he was omitted from all the kings lists, as if he never existed. The same went for his teenage wife, Ankhesenamun. Her tomb has yet to be found—if there is one.

The famous statue of Akhenaten's wife Nefertiti was discovered by German archaeologists excavating at Amarna just before World War I. It was left behind in the sculptor's studio when Amarna was abandoned. No one wanted it; no one wanted souvenirs of the seventeen years of turmoil. So at the end of the nineteenth century when lost tombs of the pharaohs were being discovered, when the Deir el Bahri cache was discovered, and when the second cache of pharaohs was discovered by Victor Loret in the tomb of Amenhotep II, no one was thinking about Tutankhamun because no one knew about him. That all changed when Howard Carter came on the scene.

2

Preferably a Non-Gentleman

At about the time when Loret was discovering the second cache of royal mummies in the Valley of the Kings, a teenage artist named Howard Carter was copying inscriptions on tomb walls at a site several hundred miles away. Carter came from a family of artists. His father made his living painting portraits for wealthy patrons. His children—Howard was the youngest of eleven—inherited their father's talent, and several became artists. For years Howard's father had been the portrait painter for Lord Amherst's family, so as a young boy Howard had accompanied his father to Didlington Hall, the family seat that housed Lord Amherst's collection of Egyptian antiquities. Amherst was an early patron of the Egypt Exploration Fund, the British society recently formed to excavate and record the monuments of ancient Egypt. One of its excavators, in need of an artist to help copy images painted on the tomb walls at Beni Hasan, in Middle Egypt, wrote to Lady Amherst, asking if she knew of an artist. He suggested the artist be a "non-gentleman," as such a person would make fewer demands than a person of high breeding and thus some expenses could be saved.[1] Young Howard had almost no formal schooling and fit the bill perfectly. Lady Amherst recommended the seventeen-year-old boy. Carter spent the summer in the British Museum copying tomb paintings as practice for his first job and in October 1891 he boarded a steamer bound for Alexandria.

First Drawings

Carter quickly proved to be capable, hardworking, and able to live happily in the simple surroundings of the archaeological camp at Beni Hasan. He had been hired to copy tomb paintings because they were in danger of

being lost to vandalism and the elements. Here around 2000 BC, seven centuries before Tutankhamun was born, the governors of the region carved
their tombs into the cliffs of the west bank of the Nile. They are large, pil-
lared tombs, and on the walls ancient artists painted scenes of daily life. We
see people working in the fields, troupes of female acrobats, flocks of birds
in the marshes, desert foxes. These scenes in the tombs of the nobles are a
sharp contrast to the tombs of the kings. No portrayals of daily life in the
pharaohs' tombs. Their tombs in the Valley of the Kings are covered with
religious scenes. So copying daily life scenes was young Howard's introduction to Egyptology, and he acquitted himself well. His paintings have a
charm that is surprising for a teenager (see Color Plate 3). He must have
been pleased when the publication of the Beni Hasan tombs came out and
"Mr. Howard Carter" was credited for the drawings.[2]

He also worked that year at El Bersha, another series of nobles' tombs,
copying the paintings in the tomb of Djhotyhotep, a tomb famous because
of its depiction of a colossal thirty-eight-ton statue being hauled by 170
men pulling on ropes. Carter's drawing is still admired today (Figure 2.1).[3]
It is a wonderful scene. One man stands on the statue clapping his hands,
rhythmically exhorting the men to pull on the ropes. Another is on the sled
on which the statue rests. He is pouring oil on the ground to lubricate the
sled. These are not slaves; they are volunteers. It is an event of great civic
pride in which all are happy to participate. The hieroglyphs even say that
the frail leaned on the strong so they could take part.

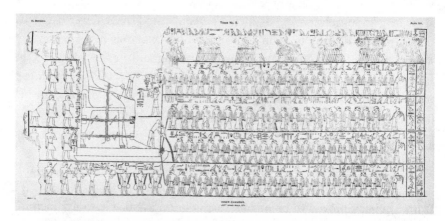

Figure 2.1. The tomb of Djhoutyhotep is the only one depicting a colossal
statue being moved. The scene is now destroyed, but we have Howard Carter's
drawing of it.

The next year, young Howard was sent to learn the rudiments of excavation techniques from Flinders Petrie, who was excavating at Amarna; these skills would later serve him very well. Petrie is a legend in Egyptology. He is often viewed as the founder of modern Egyptology. Trained as a surveyor, as a young man he went out to Egypt to survey the Great Pyramid of Giza. Living frugally in an abandoned tomb on the Giza plateau, he produced plans of the pyramid that are so accurate, they are still quoted today. Petrie discovered that the Great Pyramid is so level that the elevation from one corner of the pyramid to the other never varies by more than half an inch. Then there are the stories of Petrie's frugality. A young trainee camping out on one of Petrie's excavations noticed that there was no toilet paper. Afraid to ask the great man about it, he approached Lady Petrie and inquired. The answer: "Oh, Sir Flinders and I use potsherds."

Petrie may have used broken pottery fragments in lieu of toilet paper, but he was one of the first in archaeology to realize that pottery could also be extremely useful in figuring out which cities came first in history. For example, if the site of one ancient city has only undecorated pottery and another nearby site has pots with decoration, it is a good bet that the decorations were an innovation and thus that city is more recent. Then take it one more step. If another ancient city had pots with handles *and* decorations, well, that's another innovation, so that city is probably older than pots with decorations but no handles. These kinds of conclusions seem obvious today, but in his time, Petrie was the only one looking at broken pots. Everyone else was looking for the beautiful objects.

The Young Excavator

When Howard arrived at Petrie's Tel el Amarna excavation for training, Petrie didn't know the young artist well enough to trust his work, so he put him to work at a site where he couldn't do too much damage. Years after Carter had become famous, Petrie remembered young Howard:

> Howard Carter came as a lad of seventeen to join me in order to do some excavating for Mr. Tyson Amherst. His interest then was entirely in painting and natural history, and I little thought how much he would be enabled to do. To keep his work distant, I left him to the clearing of a temple site. There he found the broken statues of the queen, torsos and masses of chips from them.[4]

This is one of those curious quirks of history where the paths of two great men cross and neither realizes the significance. Petrie, though still a young man, was by then the most skilled excavator in Egypt, and had begun uncovering early clues to the life of Tutankhamun at his Amarna excavation. Neither Petrie nor Carter could have had any idea that a quarter of a century later, Carter would discover the tomb of Tutankhamun and become the most famous Egyptologist of all time. Indeed, as Carter worked on the site at Amarna, he probably handled objects inscribed with Tutankhamun's name but had no idea who Tutankhamun was. Undoubtedly, he heard Petrie and others discussing who this mysterious figure could have been, but he certainly couldn't have imagined that he would forever be linked with the now famous boy-king.

After his training with Petrie, Carter went on to other excavations, working the next few years at Queen Hatshepsut's temple at Deir el Bahri, across the Nile from Karnak Temple. When Howard reported for work, he didn't know it, but he had landed on the royal road of Egyptology. Deir el Bahri was a choice piece of property that was to play a leading role in the rediscovery of important ancient Egyptian history.

The name Deir el Bahri means "Place of the Northern Monastery" in Arabic. More than a thousand years after Queen Hatshepsut died, Coptic Christian monks used her temple as a monastery. Eventually Hatshepsut was lost to history and the site became known not for the queen but for the monastery that had once been there. By the time Napoleon's savants were surveying Egypt's monuments in 1798, the temple was so covered in rubble that they didn't even mention it. Hatshepsut was rediscovered by Jean-François Champollion, the decipherer of hieroglyphs. When he visited Deir el Bahri in 1829, he was the first to be able to read the hieroglyphs on the walls, and he immediately realized something strange was going on. At almost every other temple, we see only one king, the one who built the temple. Here, Champollion saw that there were two kings. One he had seen on other monuments: Tuthmosis III, a great warrior king. The other, "lesser king," as he called him, was one he had never seen, King Hatshepsut—and he was shown walking in front of the great Tuthmosis III. Champollion also noticed that in many places, Hatshepsut's name had been chiseled out and replaced with another pharaoh's name. Sometimes it was Tuthmosis III, sometimes his father, Tuthmosis II, and sometimes his grandfather, Tuthmosis I. What was going on? That was the situation when nineteen-year-old Howard arrived for work in 1893.

The excavation was under the supervision of the great Swiss archaeologist Édouard Naville and took several years. As more and more walls
were revealed, the situation got stranger and stranger. King Hatshepsut was
a she. Everyone had a theory about what had happened three thousand
years ago. Some felt that Hatshepsut had led a palace coup, taken power,
and kept Tuthmosis I, II, and III in captivity. Then she was overthrown and
the rightful names were restored on the temple walls. As far-fetched as this
sounds, there was some reason to believe it. Pharaohs never put the names
of previous kings on their temples; the king who built a temple wanted all
the credit for building it. Why would Tuthmosis III do it differently?

Today we know what happened, but it wasn't easy to figure it out.
Hatshepsut had been married to her half-brother, Tuthmosis II, and was
thus Queen Hatshepsut. When Tuthmosis II died, the only heir was his son
(Tuthmosis III) by another wife, and thus Tuthmosis III became king of
Egypt. The problem was that he was young, not even a teenager. So Queen
Hatshepsut became regent, ruling in the place of her stepson. All evidence
is that this was agreeable to everyone concerned. After several years of
ruling, Queen Hatshepsut declared herself King Hatshepsut, wore all the
regalia of kingship, including the false beard, and continued running the
country. Thus, for several years there was a co-regency, with both Tuthmosis
III and Hatshepsut as kings, and this is what confused Champollion and
everyone else.

Soon after Tuthmosis III came of age, Hatshepsut died, so Tuthmosis
ruled on his own and went on to be a great military pharaoh. Several
years after he came to power on his own, it was decided that it should not
be recorded that Egypt had been ruled by a woman. Carvers were sent
throughout the country to erase her name everywhere they found it. At
Deir el Bahri, her name was replaced by those of Tuthmosis I, II, and III
to show the "legitimate lineage." This, of course, was not known when
Howard Carter arrived to copy the inscriptions. At this stage, figuring out
archaeological puzzles was still above his abilities, but he could certainly
appreciate the scenes on the walls.

Deir el Bahri was Hatshepsut's mortuary temple, a place where after
her death, priests would make offerings for the well-being of her soul. In
Hatshepsut's time the temple was called *djser djseru*, "Holiest of Holies." On
the walls Hatshepsut depicted the events during her reign of which she was
proudest. Most important was a trading expedition she sent to the land of
Punt, in the south, along the Red Sea. She showed the ships arriving, being

greeted by the queen of Punt, and returning home loaded with incense, exotic animals, and other commodities. This is the earliest depiction of an expedition to sub-Saharan Africa—a very early ethnographic study.

Another very important scene was the bringing of her two obelisks from the Aswan granite quarries to Karnak Temple for erection. We see Hatshepsut's two obelisks end to end on a barge towed by two dozen ships. It is the only representation we have from ancient Egypt of how obelisks were moved.

Howard worked copying the scenes and inscriptions at Deir el Bahri till the project was completed.[5] These were his formative years, when he grew from "just an artist" to an archaeologist. Today, the people who copy the scenes and inscriptions on temple walls are called *epigraphers*. Like Carter, they are skilled artists, but most are Egyptologists as well: they have degrees in Egyptology and can read and translate hieroglyphs. This is an important combination of skills because if a hieroglyph or word is damaged, they will probably be able to figure out what was once there. In Carter's day, they just copied. However, it wasn't *just* copying. Carter's technique was to trace the scene on the wall and then transfer it to graph paper, square by square, to reduce the scene to a size suitable for reproduction in a book. The final step was inking the pencil drawing for publication. Carter could do all this, and do it very well, perhaps better than anyone else of his time. I say this because of something one of the greats of Egyptology said about Carter's work.

Ricardo Caminos was a very well-respected epigrapher. He was also a bibliophile, and I will never forget seeing his library for the first time. In Cairo, there are still old-time bookbinders, and their services are very inexpensive. Ricardo had all his books rebound in leather, even paperback novels. Anyway, Ricardo's assessment of Howard Carter's work at Deir el Bahri is worth quoting: "I know of few epigraphic drawings which so effectively convey the feeling of the sculptured wall. That is epigraphy at its best."[6] (See Color Plate 4.)

Carter's skills as an artist were also appreciated by Naville, who repeatedly praised his artistic abilities.[7] However, Naville saw even greater possibilities for Carter beyond copying walls. He realized Carter had organizational skills and could supervise workmen at the site. Soon Carter was telling large teams of workmen where to dig and where to dump the rubble; he was becoming an archaeologist. Naville so appreciated Carter's excavation skills that he asked the Egypt Exploration Fund to send out another artist to relieve Carter of his copying duties. Carter arranged for his brother Vernet to come; Vernet was also a talented artist, but he didn't take to the Egyptian climate and worked with his brother for only a season.

Carter had several styles of drawing, as shown in a biography of one of the Amhersts' daughters.[8] The Amhersts had seven daughters, and one became a famous historian of gardening, writing an important book on the subject.[9] While Carter was working at Deir el Bahri, he was also doing some illustrations for her book. Carter's illustrations are so realistic that at first glance they look like photographs (Figure 2.2).

Under Naville's tutelage, Carter learned more and more excavation techniques, and soon he was capable of supervising excavations on his own. By the age of twenty-five, Carter was working for the Antiquities Service. The following year he was appointed chief inspector of Upper Egypt. This was a very important position. He was responsible for a large area that now includes more than ten World Heritage sites—Luxor Temple, Karnak Temple, the Valley of the Kings, and others. His accomplishments included constructing iron doors on tomb entrances to prevent vandalism and theft, installing electric lights in the tombs so tourists could see the wall paintings, and restoring temples. Carter seems to have had a special interest in

Figure 2.2. Carter's illustration for Alicia Amherst's *History of Gardening in England* is almost photographic and shows a style totally different from his Egyptian work. (Photo by Pat Remler.)

preventing thefts and recorded one incident that verges on a Sherlock Holmes story.

Detective Carter

Carter had prepared the tomb of Amenhotep II (the one with the royal mummies that had unnerved Victor Loret) for tourism. He placed the king's mummy in its sarcophagus, displayed some of the objects Loret had found there, and installed an iron gate so the tomb could be locked at night. In spite of these precautions, on November 20, 1901, the tomb was broken into, the mummy damaged, and some of the objects stolen. Carter's report shows just how determined he was to track down the criminals.

> Nov. 28th 1901.—The following day I again went to the tomb of Amenophis II. . . . It had been reported to me formerly by the parquet that the padlock of the tomb had been stuck together and made to look all right by means of little pieces of lead paper. . . . I found more small pieces of lead paper beneath the door and a little round piece of resin, probably from a sont-tree. This piece was the exact size of the socket for the tongue in the padlock and gave me a small clue; for on 11th Nov., it had been broken into, the lock being forced by a lever and made to look all right by the means of resin that stuck it together, the material and methods in both cases being exactly the same.
>
> I must add before going on further that I had grave suspicions against Mohamed Abd El Rasoul in the case of the Yi-ma-dua tomb, and I watched this man whenever possible, he being a well-known tomb plunderer and his house being quite near the tomb. . . .
>
> I carefully compared the footprints in both tombs and found them to have a strong resemblance. In both cases, *the footprints, being prints of bare feet, are of one person only.* . . . I then took photographs, to scale as near as possible, of the foot marks of bare feet, and measured them up very carefully.
>
> During the meantime, the spoor-man tracked footprints from Biban El Moluk to the village of Goorneh and to the house of Soleman and Ahmed El Rasoul. These men were arrested. . . .
>
> 30th Nov. 1901.—I went to the parquet and . . . requested leave to inspect the footprints of Mohamed Abd El Rasoul. This I did at Markaz, and found them to agree totally with my photographs and with the measurements which I had taken in the tomb of Amenophis II and Yi-ma-dua. The measurements agree to the millimeter.[10]

Carter got his man.

One of Carter's duties as chief inspector was to supervise excavators, and many of them really did need supervision. This was an era when with a little money and not much knowledge, foreigners could obtain permission to excavate. If they found anything, the Antiquities Service kept half and the excavator got to take the other half home to his museum or university. This is how the Germans obtained the famous bust of Nefertiti: at the end of their excavation season at Armana the finds were divided into two groups and the Egyptian official picked the group without the Nefertiti bust, so the Germans brought Nefertiti home to Berlin. Theodore Davis was a wealthy American lawyer and businessman who wintered in Egypt on his house-boat, *The Bedouin*, a rather elaborate affair complete with piano, crystal chandelier, butler, and staff of a dozen. Davis was a self-made man who left home at fifteen to become a "looker" for the railroad, which was expanding west. Lookers were sent to scout the land to see which pieces of land had minerals or timber and would be the best for the railroad to purchase. It was not an easy job, as it involved carrying a hundred-pound backpack into the wilderness, camping out in subfreezing temperatures in winter, and enduring mosquitoes in summer. After a couple of years of this, Davis apprenticed to a lawyer in Iowa and at the age of twenty was admitted to the bar. Later he moved to New York to make his fortune. This was the era of the "robber barons." Through a series of very suspicious stock and land deals Davis made a fortune. Three times he was hauled before congressional investigations, and each time he was castigated but served no jail time. (He was a master at bribery.)[11]

An American Millionaire in the Valley of the Kings

While wintering in Egypt, he decided it would be nice to excavate, but needed someone experienced to see him through the process. When Carter heard that Davis was interested in excavating, he suggested that he could arrange a concession in the Valley of the Kings for him, and when Carter's duties as chief inspector permitted, he would supervise the work. Carter had found a broken ushabti of Tuthmosis IV and was sure his undiscovered tomb must be near. Davis thought it would be exciting to search for the lost tomb of a pharaoh and signed on. In their first year of serious excavation they found the plundered tomb of Tuthmosis IV. Many of the funerary objects had been left behind by the ancient robbers, including beautiful blue ushabti figures and part of the pharaoh's chariot, decorated with battle scenes. Davis was thrilled with his discovery and paid for the publication of the findings in a lavish book that included drawings by Carter of scenes on the chariot.[12]

While they were excavating the tomb of Tuthmosis IV, they found a scarab in the rubble outside the tomb with Queen Hatshepsut's name on it. Carter believed that Hatshepsut's tomb had to be near. He was right. The entrance to Hatshepsut's tomb had been found earlier by Napoleon's savants, but it was filled with rubble washed into it by the occasional thunderstorm that sent rocks and boulders careening through the Valley. The savants tried to enter it but gave up after twenty-five yards. They, of course, had no idea whose tomb it was. In the decades following Napoleon's expedition, the tomb simply disappeared under more rubble washed through the Valley. Once Davis and Carter rediscovered the entrance, Carter began systematically clearing the tomb, but it was not easy. Hatshepsut's tomb is the longest in the Valley, about 250 yards, and descends to a depth of 100 yards. When Carter and his workmen reached about 100 yards, the air was so hot and foul that their candles melted and went out. Carter ran wire into the tomb so he could have electric lighting and pressed on.

When he reached the burial chamber, it too was blocked and had to be cleared. The oxygen level was so low that he had to rig up a pump to bring air into the tomb via a zinc pipe. Still the air was so bad that Carter could only work one or two days per week in the tomb, but finally he cleared the burial chamber of rubble. His reward was two beautiful sarcophagi, one for Hatshepsut and one for her father, Tuthmosis I.[13] When the queen who would be king built her tomb in the Valley of the Kings, she moved her beloved father's body and sarcophagus to her tomb so they could spend eternity together. Once again Theodore Davis paid for a lavish book describing the finds and illustrated it with Carter's beautiful drawings (see Color Plate 5).[14] These early explorations of the Valley of the Kings gave Carter an intimate knowledge of the terrain, which would serve him well when he began his search for Tutankhamun.

Not all the finds in the Valley were royal. Occasionally a commoner was given the honor of being buried in the Valley; one was Mahepri, a general in the pharaoh's army. His tomb had been discovered before Carter and Davis had teamed up, but in a niche outside the tomb, Carter discovered a small wooden box with Mahepri's name on it. (The name Mahepri means something like "lion upon the field.") Inside the box were two gazelle-skin loincloths, which were worn while outside in the summer heat. The leather covered your private parts, but in other areas the leather was slit to create a net so air could circulate. Carter found these before Davis had arrived in Egypt for the season, but when Davis returned to Luxor, Carter invited Davis to his house, where he presented him with the box and loincloths.

With Davis was Emma Andrews, Davis's constant companion. Every year Davis brought Emma with him to Egypt to live with him on his boat, *The Bedouin*. It was a strange situation; she was clearly his mistress, but she was also the cousin of Davis's wife, who stayed home at the Davis mansion in Newport, Rhode Island. But it was even a bit stranger than that. Emma also lived with them in the house in Newport. Anyway, Emma was quite impressed with the loincloths, saying, "They are the most wonderful work I have seen in Egypt."[15] You might wonder, how can a loincloth be the best thing produced in ancient Egypt? But you can judge for yourself; you just have to go to Boston.

Theodore Davis was always generous with his finds, and he gave one of the loincloths to the newly founded Egyptian Department at the Boston Museum of Fine Arts. It's not the most beautiful object ever produced in Egypt, but you have to wonder, "How'd they do that?" If you look closely, you see that it looks like little tiny diamonds have been cut out of the gazelle skin to make the netting. At the time the loincloth was produced, ancient Egyptian craftsmen had only bronze knives, and bronze doesn't take a sharp edge. But here is another possibility: obsidian. Obsidian is volcanic glass, and we know that ancient Egyptian embalmers used obsidian blades. They are sharper than any surgical steel scalpels used today. Still, you look at the kilt in wonder. I think this is what Emma Andrews experienced when she saw it at Carter's house.

The second kilt was just as wonderful, but I say *was* because it has disappeared. Davis gave the second kilt to Chicago's Field Museum, where it was labeled as the earliest Masonic apron ever found. The Masons had always claimed ancient Egyptian origins, which is a big stretch, but to claim Mahepri's kilt was a Masonic apron is an even bigger stretch. Still, that claim may have led to its disappearance. More than a hundred years ago, the apron was stolen from the museum and has not been seen since. Perhaps it was whisked off to some Masonic lodge, where it may still lie today, unrecognized for what it is.

The Carter-Davis team had been quite successful, discovering two royal tombs and some lesser things as well, but Carter's work for the Antiquities Service led to a breakup of the duo. After being responsible for the antiquities of Upper Egypt, Carter was transferred to the north to become inspector of Saqqara, one of the largest archaeological sites in Egypt, covering several hundred acres. Beneath the sands are hundreds and hundreds of underground tombs; aboveground are several pyramids, including the first ever, the Step Pyramid of Saqqara. Even at the beginning of the twentieth century, before tourism was a multimillion-dollar business, Saqqara was visited by thousands of tourists each year.

During the time Carter was stationed at Saqqara, Davis continued his excavations in the Valley of the Kings. Early on, he spoke to James Quibell, who was now the new chief inspector at Luxor, about his plan to excavate a small strip in the Valley between two existing tombs. Quibell explained that the area was too small to expect a tomb, but Davis said he just wanted to be thorough. Later Gaston Maspero, the director of antiquities, was asked his opinion, and he agreed with Quibell. Still, Davis persisted, saying that he would feel better knowing the area had been completely excavated. Both Maspero and Quibell knew he couldn't do any harm, and they gave him permission to clear the area. So the workmen began clearing a huge pile of limestone chips that was the result of the two known tombs in that area having been carved out of the mountain. It was difficult going, as there was always danger of the thirty-five-foot-high pile collapsing. Davis visited the site each morning to supervise the men and see the progress. One morning he arrived and saw there was excitement. The *reis*, the overseer of the workmen, told Davis that they had discovered a step cut into the bedrock, indicating there might be a tomb.

Tutankhamun's Great-Grandparents

Several days later Davis visited the site with Arthur Weigall, who was going to replace Quibell as inspector of Upper Egypt. The clearing now revealed the top of a doorway; there was definitely a tomb there. A guard was stationed outside for the night, Maspero was alerted, and the next day Davis was given the go-ahead to clear the tomb. The day after that, Weigall and Davis rode together on donkeys to the tomb to decide how to proceed. There were thirteen steps leading down into the bedrock, and at the end was a stone and mortar wall going up to the ceiling, with an eighteen-inch gap at the top. They peered into the darkness, but all they could see was a long descending ramp leading farther into the bedrock. A small boy was lifted up to the gap and lowered by ropes to the other side, so he could report back what he saw. After a minute, the frightened boy returned with a green scarab covered with gold foil, the yoke of a chariot, and a gilded wood staff of authority.

It was clear they had found an important tomb, but it had been robbed. The yoke, scarab, and staff had probably been dropped on the ramp when the robbers removed them from the burial chamber and later discovered they were only gilded and not solid gold. This had a modern parallel during the 2011 Egyptian revolution. The Egyptian Museum in Cairo was broken into during the night and the thieves took some Tutankhamun objects, but smashed others and left them behind when they discovered they were merely gilded and not solid gold.

Still, even though the tomb had been robbed, it could be very important— so important that the Egyptian police couldn't be trusted to guard it. Weigall would return later to sleep at the tomb. But in the meantime, Davis and Weigall returned to *The Bedouin*. Davis invited several Egyptologists in the area over for a sumptuous dinner, and the conversation was undoubtedly about whose tomb it was and what they might find the following day when they took the wall down and entered the burial chamber.

The next morning a small group of excited archaeologists accompanied Davis and Emma to the tomb. There they met Weigall, who had slept there accompanied by Joseph Lindon Smith, an expedition artist who had worked on many digs and was known for his beautiful paintings of temples and tombs. When Maspero arrived, the workmen began taking down the wall while the group waited outside. It was slow going, as each rock had to be examined to see if there was a plaster seal that might indicate whose tomb it was or when the tomb had been robbed and resealed by the necropolis officials. Finally, with the wall down, Weigall and Smith went down the thirteen steps and down the ramp, where they were confronted by another stone wall, again breached at the top. The two peered through and then returned above to report to Maspero and Davis. Both looked stunned. "Extraordinary, wonderful," Weigall sputtered. And Smith blurted out, "There's everything down there but a grand piano."[16]

Smith stayed up top while Maspero and Davis, accompanied by Weigall, made their way down, carrying candles. When they reached the wall, the three men removed some of the stones at the top so that Davis could squeeze in. Then Weigall helped Maspero go through the opening, but it was not easy, as Maspero was quite portly. When all three were in the burial chamber, they began to look for the name of the occupant. Davis spotted a large coffin that was covered in bitumen—as part of the burial ritual, often pitch was poured on the coffin. Going around the coffin was a band of hieroglyphs. Davis called Maspero over to translate. Maspero handed Davis his candle, and by the flickering light he found the name Yuya: the father-in-law of Pharaoh Amenhotep III. Excited, Davis leaned closer with the candle to see the inscription, but was pulled back by Maspero—he had almost ignited the pitch-coated coffin!

The three had had enough excitement for the time being and made their way out of the tomb into the glaring sunlight to tell the others what they had seen. On their way out, Davis brought with him a papyrus scroll that he had spotted in the descending corridor. When later unrolled, it turned out to be Yuya's beautiful Book of the Dead, intended to help him on his journey to the next world. Davis later published it in a separate volume with a complete translation by Édouard Naville.[17]

Workers were now sent down to remove the rest of the wall and then electric wires were run all the way to the burial chamber so they could get a better look at what they had discovered. There were *two* sets of beautiful nested coffins, one for Yuya and one for his wife, Tuya. But that was only the beginning. There was a spectacular chariot, the first complete chariot ever found in the Valley. Archaeologists had seen plenty of depictions of them on temple walls, where pharaohs were shown victorious in battle, but none had ever been found before. There was more: chairs, beds, linen boxes, everything the couple would need for the next world. It was the most spectacular find ever in the Valley of the Kings. In a letter to his wife, Weigall wrote breathlessly:

> In the middle of the room were two enormous sarcophagi of wood inlaid with gold. The lids had been wrenched off by plunderers and the coffins inside had been tumbled about so that the two mummies were exposed. . . . All round . . . were chairs, tables, beds, vases . . . [It] looked just as a drawing

room would look in a London house shut up while the people were away for the summer. But with this terrifying difference—that everything was in the fashion of 34 centuries ago . . . Maspero, Davis and I stood there gaping and almost trembling.[18]

Yuya and Tuya were the parents of Queen Tiye, who was a commoner but married pharaoh Amenhotep III, who was Akhenaten's father. Thus, Yuya and Tuya were Tutankhamun's great-grandparents. We know a bit about their daughter Tiye, because we have the wedding announcement. Twenty-five years before the birth of Tutankhamun, Egypt was ruled by the great King Amenhotep III. Egypt was at its most prosperous, trade was booming, the Egyptian army was strong. Kingship was matrilineal in Egypt; a pharaoh became king by marrying the "right woman," a woman with pure royal blood. Amenhotep III, however, was secure in his claim to the throne because his father had publicly proclaimed him as his successor, so his wife did not have to be of royal blood for him to become king. To commemorate his marriage to Tiye, he ordered scarabs carved to announce the marriage.

Scarabs are a purely unique Egyptian creation. They were carved in the shape of a beetle, *Scarabaeus sacer*, from which the modern name *scarab* comes. The Egyptians were especially fond of puns, and the hieroglyph for beetle 🪲 (*kheper*) also means "to exist." So, if you wore a scarab amulet, your continued existence was assured.

Amenhotep III had about a hundred scarabs about the size of your fist carved to commemorate his marriage. These were sent to rulers of foreign lands, like telegrams used to be sent. On the bottom of each stone scarab was an inscription:

> . . . the king's great wife, Tiye, may she live,
> The name of her father is Yuya
> The name of her mother is Tuya
> She is the wife of a mighty king.[19]

Anyone reading between the lines would get the message: Tiye is a commoner, but everyone had better accept her as Amenhotep's wife.

The discovery of Yuya and Tuya's tomb created a sensation around the world. The illustrated magazines of the day ran stories about the treasures, newspapers published articles, and Egyptologists were thrilled. Davis was perhaps pleased most by the fact that his tactic of methodically clearing the Valley floor had been vindicated. The professionals had been sure that nothing would be found where Davis wanted to dig, but Davis was right. From now on, his method was the one used in the Valley, including by Carter when years later he got his turn to search for Tutankhamun.

After the discovery, Maspero generously offered Davis some of the objects in the tomb, but Davis graciously refused. He felt the discovery was too important to be divided and everything should stay in Egypt. So all the treasures of the tomb of Yuya and Tuya were sent to Cairo's new Egyptian Museum, where they were displayed in the Theodore Davis Room.

The Egyptian Museum in downtown Cairo is a wonderful Beaux Arts building completed in 1902; it served as a setting in the 1934 classic Boris Karloff movie *The Mummy*. Going through the museum is a trip back in time. There are glass cases from the 1930s, handwritten labels, and hardly any high-tech displays. The Tutankhamun objects were on the second floor, up a grand stone staircase.[20] Tour groups often spot what they think is the Tutankhamun display. There is a spectacular chariot, nested gilded coffins, endless pieces of furniture —but it's not Tut's. These are the objects from the tomb of Yuya and Tuya that Davis discovered.

Because he was working in the Valley of the Kings, Davis had a special excavation contract with the Antiquities Service. Usually an excavator paid for the excavations, and in return got a portion of the finds. Davis's contract did not grant him any of the finds. He was not a treasure hunter; his rewards were all up to Maspero's generosity. Davis never received the credit he deserves for his work in the Valley. Not only did he excavate responsibly and make important discoveries, he also promptly published his findings in a series of well-illustrated books. Relatively recently John Adams wrote the first biography of Davis, and here readers can see the remarkable Theodore Davis in action.[21]

Davis had now discovered three important tombs in the Valley of the Kings: those of Tuthmosis IV and Hatshepsut with Carter, and that of Yuya and Tuya pretty much by himself. Now Davis needed a trained archaeologist to continue his excavations in the Valley, and he hired twenty-two-year-old Edward Ayrton. The son of a diplomat, Ayrton was born in China, and at nineteen traveled to Egypt to excavate with Petrie. Like most of Petrie's disciples, he was well trained, and he served Davis well.

Davis had already discovered the tomb of Yuya and Tuya, the great-grandparents of Tutankhamun. Soon he would come even closer to Tut.

The joke among archaeologists was that Theodore Davis discovered a tomb every year. Actually, he discovered more. He excavated for just under ten years (1903–1911) and found more than a dozen tombs. We can get an idea of his achievements in the Valley by looking at the numbering system for the tombs. The tombs were first numbered by John Gardner Wilkinson, one of the pioneers of modern Egyptology. Educated at Oxford, Wilkinson abandoned traditional careers and spent much of his life in Egypt, studying the tombs. He lived in Egypt just after Champollion's decipherment of hieroglyphs, so he was one of the earliest to be able to determine which tomb in the Valley of the Kings belonged to which pharaoh. In order that the tombs could be better studied and more easily referred to, Wilkinson thought they should be numbered. So in 1827 he took a bucket of paint, walked through the Valley, and at the entrance to each tomb he assigned a number. These painted numbers are still visible but usually go unnoticed by tourists as they enter the tombs. In Wilkinson's time there were twenty-eight tombs visible. As later adventurers and Egyptologists worked in the Valley, more tombs were discovered, so by the time Theodore Davis arrived, there were forty-two tombs known in the Valley, numbered KV-1 through KV-42, with KV standing for Kings' Valley. Thus, when he and Carter discovered their first tomb, that of Tuthmosis IV, it was given the number KV-43. By the time Davis ceased his excavations, his last tomb was numbered KV-61—an amazing achievement. The number KV-62 would later be assigned to Tutankhamun's tomb, but that was still a bit in the future. However, Howard Carter was about to return to the scene.

Incident at Saqqara

Egypt was still being governed by foreigners, and it was the accepted view that Europeans were superior to anyone on the African continent, including Egyptians. This attitude contributed to what in Egyptology is known as the Saqqara Incident. One day a party of inebriated French tourists tried to enter the Serapeum, the tomb where the sacred Apis bulls were buried. Some in the party hadn't purchased the necessary ticket, and when the local guard rightly stopped them, they pushed their way in. Carter was called and the group became more rowdy, attacking the guards. Carter told the guards to defend themselves, which they did. In this era of colonialism, a native touching a European was unheard of, and the French group complained to their countryman Gaston Maspero, the director of antiquities, claiming that the guards had assaulted them. Soon the matter became one of national pride, debated in the local newspapers. Maspero was a good man who knew the truth, but he asked Carter to smooth things over by expressing his regrets to the French consul. Carter refused and took the side of his guards, demanding that the French be punished. Maspero told Davis about the situation, and Davis wrote to Carter, urging him to apologize. Carter said no. Maspero felt he had no option but to come down hard on Carter. He transferred Carter to Tanta, a small industrial town with no significant antiquity sites. Carter resigned (Figure 2.3).[22] He didn't know it, but he had just taken his first step on the path to Tutankhamun.

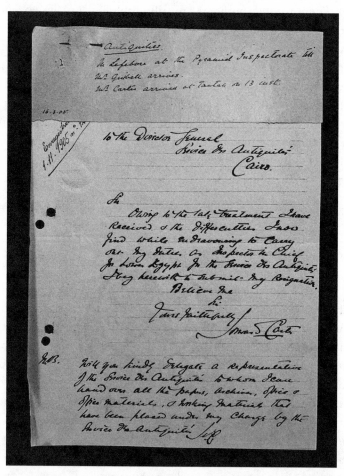

Figure 2.3. Carter's letter of resignation, which ultimately led to the discovery of the tomb of Tutankhamun. (Photo by Anthony Marks.)

Out of a job, Carter returned to Luxor, where he had friends from his old days as chief inspector and where there was a bustling tourist trade. He made ends meet for three years by selling his beautiful watercolors of scenes on tomb walls to tourists. To help Carter, Davis paid him to make drawings of the Yuya and Tuya treasures for his publication of that tomb. Carter also made commissions by selling antiquities, which was legal in those days. His wasn't an easy life, but he managed.

After the discovery of Yuya and Tuya, Davis put Ayrton to work clearing the next part of the Valley that had to be systematically excavated. It was not a promising spot, but again Davis wanted to be thorough. On January 7, 1907, Ayrton found a step cut into the Valley floor, followed by thirteen more. This tomb would become known as KV-55, and no tomb has caused more controversy.

Tutankhamun's Father?

At the bottom of the steps was a doorway that when cleared revealed another set of steps ending in a wall built of large limestone flakes. The wall had been constructed three thousand years ago to reseal the tomb, which had been entered in ancient times—a familiar story. Behind the wall was a descending passage filled nearly to the ceiling with limestone chips to deter robbers. A small crawl space at the top suggested it hadn't worked; the tomb probably had been plundered. All present adjourned for the night. In the morning, the passage could be cleared a bit, electric lights could be run into the tomb, and a proper examination could be made.

Half a dozen accounts of the opening of the tomb have survived, and none agree on what happened. The next morning everyone wanted to see what Davis had discovered, so the cast of characters was large, but not quite so large as Joseph Lindon Smith says. As he describes it in his memoir, several of the men present went down to see what was there. They placed a plank on top of the chips so they could wriggle deeper into the tomb. Maspero, crawling on top of the plank, encountered a gilded wood panel, but couldn't make out exactly what it was and because of his girth could get no further. He asked Smith, an artist, to squeeze into the tight space and draw the panel, which he did with great difficulty. When Maspero saw the drawing, he told Smith that his drawing was of great importance because

Maspero could read the cartouche of Queen Tiye, the daughter of Yuya and Tuya, mother of Akhenaten and grandmother of Tutankhamun.

Smith then relates that Maspero told him:

> To repay you for your great assistance. . . . I am going to permit you to slide along the end of the plank and find out what are the conditions in the passage leading down into the tomb chamber.[23]

There are many things wrong with Smith's account. First, Maspero was not there. Neither was Howard Carter, whom Smith places at the scene. Second, none of the other accounts put Smith among the first group to enter the tomb. It is all Smith's fantasy. To be fair, the account was written fifty years after the events took place, but this is not an isolated event: Smith's accounts are usually wrong on the details and almost always place him in the center of things.

What is certain is that Weigall, Davis, and Ayrton first went in together. They did indeed see a gilded wood panel nearly eight feet high, and carved on it was a relief of Queen Tiye worshipping the solar disk, the Aten. Davis was thrilled that they had discovered Queen Tiye's tomb. When they finally reached the burial chamber, they encountered other gilded wood panels. They had never seen anything like this and weren't really sure what they had found. In fact, it was a shrine that once enclosed the coffin of the queen. Only when Carter later discovered Tutankhamun's tomb would there be a clear parallel. The wood panels were extremely fragile and the very thin gold leaf was flaking off everywhere, coating the floor with gold flecks; the flecks were also suspended in the air, sticking to the trio's clothing.

In the center of the burial chamber was a beautiful coffin, inlaid with glass and semiprecious stones. It had been badly damaged by water seeping in from the ceiling and by rocks falling from above. The lid had cracked in two, but down the center was a gold band with a funerary inscription. The cartouche, identifying the occupant, had been carefully removed. When the archaeologists removed the lid, revealing the mummy, it was surrounded by thick gold sheets, and around its head was a gold "crown" in the shape of a vulture, one of the protective deities of the pharaoh. Like the coffin, the mummy had been damaged by the water that had seeped into the coffin from above; little soft tissue remained, and the wrappings crumbled when touched. The mummy once had a necklace of gold beads, but the stringing had broken long ago, though the beads were still in the coffin (Figure 2.4).

Things in the burial chamber were disorganized, but this was not an ordinary plundered tomb. Robbers don't leave behind gold crowns or sheets

Figure 2.4. The damaged coffin in KV-55 may have held the body of Tutankhamun's father.

of gold around a mummy. The reason for the disorder had to be something else. Along with the coffin and the shrine were four spectacular alabaster canopic jars, used to hold the internal organs of the deceased when they were removed at the time of mummification. Each jar's lid was a sculpted head of a beautiful woman. The jar bottoms were undecorated; the inscriptions they once bore had been erased.

Finding the tomb of Queen Tiye was exciting. When, later in the day, Davis heard that there were "two surgeons" who happened to be in the Valley of the Kings, he asked them to examine the bones of the mummy. They both concluded they were the bones of an old woman. This is when things get interesting. Weigall later sent the bones to Dr. Grafton Elliot Smith, professor of anatomy at the Cairo School of Medicine. Smith had been making the first systematic study of the royal mummies and was the first trained anatomist to examine these bodies. Smith's reply to Weigall shocked everyone, especially Davis.

Are you sure the bones you sent me are those which were found in the tomb? Instead of the bones of an old woman, you have sent me those of a young man. Surely there is some mistake.[24]

Smith was right and the "two surgeons" were wrong. It's not even close.

There are many indicators of the sex of skeletal remains—the pelvises are different, the supraorbital ridges (the area of the eyebrows) are more pronounced in males, the orbits (the area around the eyes) are shaped differently, et cetera, et cetera. There is no doubt the skeleton was that of a male.[25] How could the surgeons have gotten it so wrong? I have thought about this quite a bit. It is possible that they were not surgeons but just ordinary tourists in the Valley, and when Davis sent out an "Is there a physician in the house?" request, they thought it would be fun to see a mummy and responded. Davis would have told them he had just found the tomb of Queen Tiye, and they obligingly said it was an old lady.

If the mummy is a male, who is it? This has been debated for the last hundred years, and still not everyone agrees. From various skeletal indicators, Smith estimated the age at twenty-five years plus or minus five years, so no matter what, he was a young man. If a vote were taken today among Egyptologists, I think the majority might say it's Akhenaten, the heretic father of Tutankhamun. But this is far from certain, and there is a problem with this attribution. From the skeleton, it would seem as if the bones belong to a young man, thirty at most, and Akhenaten probably had to be at least thirty-five at the time of death, given what we know about his life.[26] The other candidate is a shadowy figure, a half-brother of Akhenaten named Smenkare. We just don't know.

Within KV-55 the excavators found "magical bricks" inscribed to protect the mummy of Akhenaten. Although the cartouche on the coffin was removed, the titles that remain suggest it was made for Akhenaten. Also, the mummy had an elongated head, typical of that depicted in art of the Amarna period. How did canopic jars for a female, the mummy of Akhenaten/Smenkare, and the funeral shrine of Queen Tiye all come to be in the same tomb in the Valley of the Kings? Here there is a consensus.

At the end of the Amarna period, when Akhenaten died, it was decided to abandon the new city, Akhetaten, and return to Thebes. What about the royal burials at Akhetaten? You couldn't just leave them behind for robbers. KV-55 seems to have been the answer. Gather up what can be gotten in the royal tombs, take everything to the Valley of the Kings, and rebury everything quickly in an empty tomb. It may have even been done secretly; the Aten was no longer in favor. Who could have authorized such a thing? Tutankhamun—he was king now, and these were the remains of his father or uncle and grandmother. So while Davis thought he had discovered the tomb of Queen Tiye, he had found something even better: the reburial of the royals of the Amarna period. But Davis didn't see it that way. He was not happy when Smith told him he didn't have the tomb of Tiye. When Davis published the findings in one of his sumptuous volumes, it was titled *The Tomb of Queen Tiyi.*[27] He did permit Smith to contribute a brief two-page description of the bones, stating they are those of a male.

When Smith published his own book on the royal mummies he presented his detailed analysis of the bones and concluded the individual was Akhenaten. In addition, he thought that the unusual shape of the skull was due to a pathological condition, hydrocephalus. Smith was probably wrong here. With hydrocephalus there is an excess of cerebral fluid on the brain that can build up and cause pressure on the cranium, causing it to distort and the walls to thin in some areas. In the skull found in KV-55, one doesn't see the thinning, and the skull is quite elongated, not globular as in hydrocephalus. The shape of the skull, called the *cephalic index*, is unusual, but still at the high end of the normal range. I don't think any pathology is involved in its shape.

Davis had now discovered two tombs directly connected to Tutankhamun: the tomb of Yuya and Tuya, Tutankhamun's great-grandparents, and now KV-55, which housed a close relative from the Amarna period, possibly Tut's father. As Davis and Ayrton continued their excavations in the Valley, they continued to inch closer and closer to Tutankhamun. Almost by chance, they discovered a first clue, lodged under a rock, that Tutankhamun might be buried in the Valley of the Kings. It was a faience cup bearing Tutankhamun's name.[28] In 1907 they came upon a small pit containing the remains of what appeared to be an ancient meal. Mixed with the duck bones, cups, wine jars, and floral garlands were mummy wrappings bearing Tutankhamun's name. Davis wasn't sure what he had found, but clearly he didn't think it very important. The floral pectorals were the kind worn around the necks of those who attended social events. These were made by cutting out a large collar shape from a piece of papyrus and then sewing flowers to it (Figure 2.5). Davis used to hand a floral pectoral to visitors and ask them to try to rip it apart, to show how strong the papyrus was even after three thousand years.

Herbert Winlock, a young excavator for the Metropolitan Museum of Art, visited Davis and saw the cache. Realizing it was important, he asked

Figure 2.5. A pectoral worn by one of the mourners at the funeral of Tutankhamun. (Photo by Pat Remler.)

if he could have it for the museum, and Davis happily gave the material to him. Years later, Winlock was excavating near Deir el Bahri and discovered the embalmer's cache of a man named Ipy, and it is probably then that he first realized what Davis had discovered: another embalmer's cache.[29] At the time of mummification, there are often materials left over—wrappings, natron (the substance used to dehydrate the body), and so forth. Because they are associated with the dead, these things are sacred and can't just be thrown out. So often a small pit was dug and the extra material buried. Much of what Davis had found matched the embalmer's cache of Ipy. There were jars filled with natron, bandages, and animal bones (at the time of burial, the family gathered together near the tomb for a last meal, and that's what the bones are from). Davis had found the extra embalming material and the remains of the last meal from Tutankhamun's burial.

Winlock went on to have a distinguished career, first as an excavator, then as head of the Egyptian Department of the Metropolitan Museum of Art, and finally as director of the museum. He didn't publish Davis's find of the cache till 1941, well after the discovery of the famous tomb.[30] Today these finds can be seen at the Metropolitan Museum of Art. They are in a small side room in the Egyptian collection. There is hardly ever anyone there, but this is real history. Imagine who wore those pectorals—Ankhesenamum, Tut's widow; Aye, Tutankhamun's vizier, who would succeed him as king of Egypt; Horemheb, the general who would become pharaoh and end the dynasty. You can almost reconstruct the entire meal they ate—there are the duck bones and broken wine jars. After the meal, the servants gathered everything, dug the small pit, and buried it all, where it remained for three thousand years till Davis discovered it.

Even the bandages tell a story. All cloth in Egypt was linen, made from the flax plant; there was no cotton in ancient Egypt. When a person was mummified, yards and yards of linen were needed for the wrappings, and this was usually supplied from the bed linens of the deceased. The old sheets were taken and torn into strips suitable for wrappings. Sometimes if the person was wealthy you can see "laundry marks"—inscriptions in ink instructing the servants where the sheet went, perhaps "on the bed of so-and-so" or something similar. Occasionally these ink inscriptions merely gave the quality of the sheet: "fine" or "very good." Tutankhamun's bandages are interesting for two reasons. First, they often bear his name and the year the inscription was put on, for example, "Year 8 of the reign of Tutankhamun." So from the bandages alone, we know that he must have ruled for at least eight years. Second, because bandages were made by tearing sheets, there is always a ragged edge, sometimes two. This is true for most of Tutankhamun's bandages also, but some have *two* finished edges. These are the only ones that have been found with two finished edges. This means that these bandages were specially woven for the funeral of the king. No expense was being spared. It was a find far more important than anyone knew at the time. When Davis found these remains, he was standing just a hundred yards from the intact tomb of Tutankhamun.

"The Valley of the Tombs Is Now Exhausted"

Davis had now found two direct bits of evidence that the tomb of Tutankhamun was somewhere in the Valley of the Kings. First he had found the faience cup with Tutankhamun's name on it, and now he had the embalmer's cache. But he was not done. In 1909 he made his last Tutankhamun discovery. Davis found a small unfinished tomb containing an ushabti figure and some gold foil with the name of Tutankhamun, and he concluded that he had found the plundered tomb of Tutankhamun. He published his findings in one of his beautiful books, and in the preface to the description of the Tutankhamun finds, Davis concluded, "I fear the Valley of the Tombs is now exhausted."[31] He would soon give up his concession to excavate in the Valley of the Kings, opening the door to Carter.

But Carter couldn't excavate by himself. He didn't have the means to fund an excavation. He would need a wealthy patron. This role was filled by George Edward Stanhope Molyneux Herbert, Fifth Earl of Carnarvon, in Wales. Carnarvon, a wealthy aristocrat and collector, had a passion for breeding racehorses and racing automobiles, and also had the unfortunate distinction of being in one of the world's earliest near-fatal automobile crashes. Carnarvon had one of the first cars registered in England and in 1901 took it to Germany. He was driving through the countryside when he nearly ran into two bullock carts in the middle of the road. He swerved to avoid them, and two of his tires hit a rock and blew out, flipping the car upside down. Fortunately, it landed in a ditch, not on the road, or Carnarvon would have been crushed. As it was, his wrist and jaw were broken, he had a serious concussion as well as other injuries, and he suffered from poor health for the rest of his life. Later, he went to Egypt to recuperate, and decided it would be great fun to excavate.

Carnarvon obtained permission to excavate, but was given a not very promising area on the west bank of Luxor. In his first two years of excavation, Carnarvon dug where there were many known but plundered tombs of the private citizens of Thebes of three thousand years ago. He found one lost tomb, the tomb of Tetiky, a mayor of Thebes during the Eighteenth Dynasty. The tomb had been thoroughly robbed, but still the wall paintings were worth recording, and there were some interesting servant statues that had been left behind by the thieves.

In another tomb, Carnarvon found a writing board that would become known as the "Carnarvon tablet." It had an interesting historical text on it, telling of the expulsion from Egypt of foreign invaders known as the Hyksos. The tablet was written in hieratic, a cursive form of hieroglyphs, and at the time of its discovery Carnarvon had no idea of its meaning.

When he left Luxor at the end of the excavating season, he merely left the tablet in a basket in the office of the chief inspector of antiquities with no explanation. Later, when it was published it caused quite a stir in the world of Egyptology, because it dealt with a period of Egyptian history for which there were very few records.[32] This is partly because the Egyptians never recorded defeats, so they certainly weren't going to have accounts about a time when they had been invaded and conquered. Still later, when the great scholar Sir Alan Gardiner published the complete text and declared that it was a true historical document rather than a fanciful tale, it created a sensation.[33]

Carnarvon's finds during his first two years were not as spectacular as Theodore Davis's in the Valley of the Kings, but they were enough to keep Carnarvon interested in continuing his excavations. He realized, however, that he needed a skilled excavator to assist him, and Maspero suggested he hire Carter. Maspero was trying to make amends for the way he had treated Carter at Saqqara. Thus the Saqqara Incident and a very early automobile accident brought Carter and Carnarvon together. Now they were both on the path to Tutankhamun; they just didn't know it. As soon as they joined forces, they made some impressive finds. They found three tombs that had been reused for multiple burials and discovered a total of sixty-four decorated coffins and an ivory game board with pieces for a game called Hounds and Jackals. Carnarvon would have been given a share of these coffins, and while they weren't fine enough for his personal collection of Egyptian antiquities, they could be sold to museums around the world and thus help pay for the expenses incurred while excavating.

During these early days of supervised excavating in Egypt, there was also a lively, legal trade in antiquities, and Carter served as his patron's intermediary, often buying the finest pieces from the licensed antiquities dealers in Luxor. One purchase was three beautiful stone plaques from bracelets belonging to Amenhotep III, Tutankhamun's grandfather. These had probably been plundered from the king's rubble-filled tomb by recent tomb robbers. They can be seen today in the Metropolitan Museum of Art.

When pharaohs built temples, they had an equivalent of our ceremony of laying the cornerstone. At the four corners of the future temple they dug pits and buried miniature building implements and magical amulets to ensure that the project would go well. Carter and Carnarvon discovered the foundation deposit for the mortuary temple of Queen Hatshepsut, again an important find. After three years of excavating with Carter, Carnarvon felt that he had made enough finds to publish his discoveries, and he paid for the publication of a summary of his five years' work.[34] He hired specialists to write chapters describing different aspects of his discoveries, with Carter contributing several essays.

From their time collaborating, it was clear that the two men worked well together. Carter had assisted Carnarvon in only the last three of his five years of excavating, but in the preface to his book, Carnarvon gives credit to Carter for all five years: "Mr. Howard Carter has been in charge of all operations; and whatever successes have resulted from our labours are due to his unremitting watchfulness and care in systematically recording, drawing, and photographing everything as it came to light."

Carter and Carnarvon were planning their next season when the door to Tutankhamun opened. Theodore Davis, convinced that there was nothing left to find in the Valley of the Kings, gave up his concession. The year was 1914; Carter and Carnarvon pounced and obtained the concession. Carter was convinced that Tutankhamun's tomb, still undiscovered, was in the Valley of the Kings. Now the two began the hunt in earnest, convinced that somewhere beneath the tons of limestone chips that littered the Valley floor, Tutankhamun was waiting for them.

They began modestly, beginning in a surprising place, the tomb of Amenhotep III in the remote western spur of the Valley. The tomb had been investigated by Napoleon's savants, but it was so filled with hard-packed rubble that they quickly gave up. More recently Harry Burton, assisting Theodore Davis, had investigated, but he too quickly gave up the enterprise. Now Carter had decided to see what he and Carnarvon could find. Perhaps the idea was that in the rubble there might be more plaques. Or, more likely, they felt they shouldn't begin with large-scale investigations because there were rumblings of war with Germany and they might have to stop suddenly. Regardless, Carter's decision soon paid off.

They began by clearing the piles of debris in front of the tomb, and after a few days, Carter, knowing what to look for, spotted the intact foundation deposits. Surprisingly, the miniature objects were inscribed for Tuthmosis IV, the father of Amenhotep III. Carter deduced that the tomb had been originally begun by Tuthmosis IV but taken over and completed by Amenhotep III. Inside the tomb they found a number of damaged royal objects among the debris. They uncovered several damaged but still beautiful servant statues that are to this day in the Carnarvon collection at Highclere Castle. They worked for a month and then stopped; war was on the horizon. Carnarvon left for England, and Carter worked as a civilian in the British intelligence office in Cairo.

The hope among the British was that the war would be over soon—"home by Christmas"—but that was not to be, as the conflict dragged on for four years. Although Carter worked in Cairo, he was still able to make trips to Luxor. During one of his periodic visits, at the height of anti-German sentiment, the German dig house at Luxor was blown up. It is part of the lore of Egyptology that Carter had a hand in it, but this is far from established.

Carter had a small salary from the intelligence work, but eventually they no longer needed his services. He made ends meet by making drawings of scenes on the walls at Luxor temple for Alan Gardiner, who wanted to publish a monograph of both text and scenes. Gardiner paid him a fair salary, and Carter enjoyed resuming his role as an archaeological artist. He was also able to make some money by dealing in antiquities. During the war years there were virtually no foreigners in Luxor, and he had his pick of the choice pieces from the dealers at very reasonable prices. When the war finally ended, Carter reconnected with his patron, whom he had not seen in two years. It was time to search in earnest for Tutankhamun.

In Egypt things changed after the war. Pierre Lacau replaced Maspero as director of antiquities, and while he too was a Frenchman, he did business quite differently. Less friendly than Maspero, he was a stickler for regulations; more important, he felt that all major finds should stay in Egypt. Carter discussed with him possible future sites for excavation, mentioning Tel el Amarna. Lacau unhesitatingly said no. He thought that should be reserved for the Antiquities Service itself, and if not the service, perhaps a well-established museum or university, but certainly not a private individual like Carnarvon.

Lacau's attitude was a sign of the times. Egyptian nationalism was growing, and in 1918 Saad Zaghloul, leader of the nationalist movement, brought a delegation to discuss the situation with Sir Reginald Wingate, Britain's high commissioner for Egypt. Zaghloul demanded self-rule for Egypt; Wingate refused and arrested Zaghloul. Rioting spread throughout Egypt, and this was the backdrop for Carter and Carnarvon reopening their work in the Valley of the Kings.

They intended to follow Davis's technique of excavating every inch of the Valley down to bedrock. Carter thought that a triangle of unexcavated land just below the tomb of Ramses VI might be promising, but the tomb of Ramses VI was popular with tourists and clearing that area would have required closing the tomb, so the triangle would have to wait.

The 1919 season brought no results, but the 1920 season turned up something quite interesting. On February 26 a cache of thirteen large alabaster jars was found in the debris near the tomb of Merenptah. The vessels had green- and yellow-colored wax applied to their surfaces, forming floral designs. These jars bore the names of Merenptah and his father, Ramses II. Once used during the reign of Ramses, they had been reused for the embalming and burial of the son. Because they had contained sacred oils, natron, and other items used in the burial of the king, they had been ritually buried in the Valley of the Kings. Lacau permitted Carnarvon to keep six of the jars, a fair division given the circumstances.

The next season Carter intended to return to the area in front of the tomb of Ramses VI, but because of tourism he couldn't close the path to the tomb, so he moved on to a different part of the Valley, though with no success. At this point, it seems that Carnarvon had decided that there was little chance of finding anything in the Valley, and in the summer of 1922 he asked Carter to visit him at Highclere. Carnarvon explained his position, but Carter countered that there was still that one patch in front of the tomb of Ramses VI that had not been cleared. Carter even offered to pay for the excavation himself and allow Carnarvon to keep anything they found. Carnarvon was moved by Carter's arguments and agreed to pay for one more season; this would be their last chance at finding Tutankhamun.

3
Wonderful Things

On November 1, 1922, Carter began what he knew might be his last season of excavation. Finally, he was working at the undisturbed triangle of land just below the tomb of Ramses VI. The first order of business was to clear away the ancient workmen's huts. The workmen who built the tombs in the Valley of the Kings had lived in a village on the far side of a very high ridge on the other side of the Valley. It was a long walk from the village, up one side of the ridge and then down the other into the Valley, so sometimes they spent the night in temporary circular stone huts near where they worked. Family members would be sent at various times of the day to bring food to them. The village, today called Deir el Medineh, was a tightly controlled community. There was a wall surrounding their houses and only one gate for entering or leaving the community. The members of this community of painters, carvers, and plasterers were often in close proximity to treasures of the pharaohs, and they were watched very closely.

Because the Valley was never inhabited and until recently rarely visited, the huts these workers slept in were still present, so Carter recorded them for posterity and then they were dismantled so the team could excavate down to bedrock. After a day of clearing, on November 4, one of the workmen discovered a step cut into the valley floor. It was a very good sign. Normally steps were cut into the bedrock for about twenty feet, and then the tomb was hollowed out of the limestone horizontally. The clearing continued, and by the evening of November 5 they had uncovered twelve steps, revealing the upper part of a doorway with the royal necropolis seal still in place (Figure 3.1). Carter knew he had almost certainly discovered a king's tomb, but he couldn't determine which king. Through a small hole near the top of the doorway, he could see that the passage behind the plastered door was filled with rubble to deter tomb robbers. There was a chance

Figure 3.1. The seal of the royal necropolis, with Anubis, god of mummification, above bound captives. (Griffith Institute.)

the tomb might be intact. What bothered Carter was the narrow stairway, only about six feet wide; the entrances to other royal tombs were considerably wider. Somehow able to keep his excitement in check, he had the workmen fill in the stairway with sand and rubble and cabled his patron, Lord Carnarvon, who was still in England: "At last have made wonderful discovery in Valley; a magnificent tomb with seals intact, recovered same for your arrival; congratulations." We know that Carnarvon suspected they had finally found Tutankhamun, because when he received Carter's telegram he called Alan Gardiner to ask if he thought it could be Tutankhamun's tomb. Gardiner, always the cautious scholar, told Carnavon that he really couldn't say; excavating was not his specialty.

Carter waited nearly three weeks for Carnarvon, who finally arrived in Alexandria on November 20 accompanied by his daughter Lady Evelyn. Carter went to Cairo to meet them and the three took the train to Luxor. We can only imagine the conversation.

When they arrived in Luxor the stairway was cleared again, and this time Tutankhamun's cartouche was revealed on the lower part of the sealed door. When the door was removed, the excavators could see a narrow path through the rubble, almost certainly made by ancient robbers. The tomb had been entered before.

Word of the discovery spread throughout Luxor to the other teams that were excavating, and then throughout the world. Newspapers ran speculative articles about the king inside and what treasures the tomb might contain. At this point no one really knew, but one French newspaper, *Le Pèlerin*, ran an imaginative drawing of what the scene would be like when the wall was taken down and Carter and Carnarvon went inside (see Color Plate 6).[1]

November 23 was devoted to clearing the thirty-foot-long descending passage that led to the tomb. Strewn among the limestone chips were alabaster jars, pottery, and workmen's tools. Finally they reached a second plastered door. There was clear evidence of the door having been breached and then resealed. Carter made an opening in the upper left corner of the doorway to insert a candle for testing the air inside. One can do no better than to let Carter's words describe the scene:

> At first I could see nothing, the hot air escaping from the chamber causing the candle flame to flicker, but presently, as my eyes grew accustomed to the light, details of the room within emerged slowly from the mist, strange animals, statues, and gold—everywhere the glint of gold. For the moment—an eternity it must have seemed to the others standing by—I was struck dumb with amazement, and when Lord Carnarvon, unable to stand the suspense any longer, inquired anxiously, "Can you see anything?" it was all I could do to get out the words, "Yes, wonderful things."[2]

The room into which Carter peered was packed with all the possessions Tutankhamun would need in the next world—chariots, statues, game boards, linens, jewelry, beds, chairs, even a throne; they were all piled on top of each other. The ancient robbers had apparently been caught in the act or frightened away, for little had been disturbed. The tomb was virtually intact.

It had been a long day, and the tension of not knowing what they would find had exhausted everyone. The tomb was closed, guards were posted, and the small team left. On the twenty-seventh they returned to remove the wall they had breathlessly peered through. Electric lighting was brought into the tomb, and for the first time they could see the magnitude of what they had discovered. The room they had first looked into by candlelight was about twenty-six by thirteen feet and packed with objects the likes of which no one had ever seen before (Figure 3.2). There was a set of three

Figure 3.2. The Antechamber before any of the treasures had been moved.

waist-high funerary couches made of gilded wood decorated with the heads of animals, which had been used for rituals performed on the mummy of Tutankhamun. Against the north wall were two life-sized guardian statues protecting something behind the wall, almost certainly the Burial Chamber. The room they had entered was merely the tomb's Antechamber.

Now that they were inside the room, with good lighting, Carter and Carnarvon could see a smaller room carved through the west wall of the Antechamber that was about fourteen by nine feet in floor area and eight feet high; this would become known as the Annex. It too was packed with treasures.

Forming the Team

Carter and Carnarvon now understood the immensity of the task ahead of them. In front of them were hundreds and hundreds of objects, many in extremely fragile condition, and who knew what was behind the wall? It could be room upon room filled with more treasures. It was an incredible discovery, but also an incredible responsibility. Every object had to be recorded in place before it could be removed, and sometimes it would have to be conserved in the tomb before it could even be moved. It was going to take years to excavate the tomb properly. Very quickly Carter realized he would need help.

Fortunately for Carter, with a discovery as glamorous and historically important as this, everyone was eager to take part in the excavation. Carter's main source of help came from New York's Metropolitan Museum of Art. They had a large, experienced team already in Egypt and offered whatever assistance Carter needed. In the end, they supplied several members of Carter's team; perhaps the most crucial was Arthur C. Mace. Mace had decades of excavation experience, but more important, he was known as a superb conservator with great patience. He had been on the Metropolitan Museum's team when they discovered the tomb of Lady Senebtisi at the city of Lisht.[3] One of her garments, a bead girdle, consisted of more than ten thousand beads. The threads on which the beads were strung were rotted, so Mace heated wax and poured it over the beads to keep them in place so that the garment could be removed from the tomb. Later the beads could be restrung, and then the wax could be reheated and removed. While he was working at Lisht, Mace's in-laws were concerned that their daughter might not have all the amenities she needed, so they sent out a Bechstein piano to the village of Lisht that was delivered by baggage camels. This became part of the folklore of excavation stories, and the one biography we have of Mace is titled *The Grand Piano Came by Camel.*[4]

Mace's conservation experience served him well. When the clearing of the tomb began, he set up a conservation lab in a nearby tomb in the Valley where he worked tirelessly on Tutankhamun's fragile treasures. In addition to his conservation skills, Mace could write well, which was good because Carter had received little formal schooling; his letters are full of spelling and grammatical errors. After the first season of excavation, Carter and Mace quickly produced the first volume of the three-volume set describing the discovery and excavation. Mace did most of the writing, producing a fascinating archaeological classic. A grateful Carter happily shared the spotlight, putting Mace's name on the title page along with his.

The other member of the Metropolitan Museum's team whose name appears on the title page is Harry Burton. Burton was also an excavator, but Carter really didn't need excavators. This was a discovery where no digging was going to be needed. Everything was there, in a clean tomb. Carter needed Burton for his photographic skills, which were considerable. The plan was to photograph every object in situ before it was moved. The tomb of Tutankhamun would become the most thoroughly photographed excavation site in history. New standards were being set for future expeditions. Burton had considerable experience photographing fragile objects and knew just how important it was to record them before they were moved. Sometimes they could disintegrate before your very eyes. In a *New York Times* account, Burton told of just such an experience:

> I remember, when we were clearing a series of XVIIth Dynasty tombs, which had been infested with white ants, the preliminary photographs were literally the only record of most of the wooden objects found. The coffins appeared to be in perfect condition, but when touched they collapsed into dust.
> There was one very attractive small wooden statuette of a girl in one of these tombs, which appeared to be quite sound. It was standing quite alone, and after the general view of the chamber had been taken, the camera was turned on to it. I intended to expose a plate for two minutes, but after it had been exposed for one and three-quarters minutes the figure suddenly collapsed, and nothing remained but a small heap of dust. I immediately switched off the beam of light, put a cap on the camera, and went off to develop the plate. Fortunately the negative turned out to be quite good, and, although the statue no longer existed, we had a complete record of it. This is only one of many similar cases.[5]

Over the course of the ten years it took to excavate Tutankhamun's tomb, Burton produced thousands of beautiful photographs that are still used today by scholars. He even went to Hollywood for a brief course on how to operate a movie camera. Because of his visit to Hollywood, we have vintage film of Carter and Mace taking the objects from the tomb.

Carter knew that he would need someone to assist Mace with the conservation of the fragile objects, and he asked Alfred Lucas to come on board. Lucas was a chemist working in Cairo at the Government Assay Office, but he had already displayed a deep interest in archaeology, helping at several excavations. After his work on the Tutankhamun excavation, he published a book, *Ancient Egyptian Materials*, and became a consulting chemist for the Antiquities Service.[6]

Carter was assembling an all-star team. For any inscriptions that needed to be translated he had Alan Gardiner, who literally wrote the book that some of us still use in our hieroglyph classes.[7]

One of the first members Carter enlisted for his team was Arthur Callender, a retired engineer living not far from Luxor. He had worked for the Railway Service and had all kinds of skills that Carter rightly thought might be needed. A heavy sarcophagus might have to be moved, shrines taken apart, complex objects dismantled and later put back together. As soon as Carter found the stairway, he asked Callender to come on board, and he did. He was there when they first peered through the wall and would later prove especially useful when moving large objects in small spaces.

As the team was being assembled, Carter went to Cairo to have a strong iron grille fabricated to serve as a door to the tomb. He also bought thirty-two bales of calico, and more than a mile of wadding and surgical bandages to wrap the fragile objects. Carter now had the discovery of a lifetime and full financial backing. He bought a Ford motorcar to make travel to the Valley easier. This all took about two weeks, but finally they were ready to get to work. It was Carter's hope that now they would finally learn more about who this mysterious King Tutankhamun was.

Today, Tutankhamun is the most famous pharaoh of ancient Egypt, but when Carter discovered his tomb it wasn't even known that he was a boy-king. One popular song rushed out to capitalize on the sensational new find was "Old King Tut Was a Wise Old Nut" (Figure 3.3). The cover of the sheet music featured an old geezer with a wineglass in hand. Even among Egyptologists, little was known about Tutankhamun. When Carter made the discovery, two histories of ancient Egypt were available, both written by the same remarkable man, James Henry Breasted. Trained as a pharmacist, Breasted soon realized that Egyptology interested him more than dispensing drugs, so he left for Germany to study hieroglyphs. The Europeans were far ahead of America in offering formal courses in Egyptology, so Breasted studied with Adolph Erman, the great philologist, and was the first American awarded a doctorate in Egyptology. His main interest was translating ancient Egyptian texts—all of them.

At the turn of the century Breasted began his incredible one-man campaign to translate all the historical records of ancient Egypt: every battle account, every religious procession, every coronation. For eleven years he roamed up and down the Nile, translating inscriptions on temple and tomb walls, often risking his health. His diary for November 14, 1906, reads:

> We are at work at 6:00 AM, and the sun is long down before we stop. I spent yesterday on a ladder, copying from a glaring wall upon which this fierce sun

Figure 3.3. Before the objects in the tomb had been carefully examined, no one (certainly not the author of this song) knew that Tutankhamun was a boy-king.

was beating in full force; and I rose this morning with one eye swollen shut. Even with dark glasses, I sometimes find work on a sunlit wall impossible.[8]

After his exhaustive project, Breasted published his five-volume *Ancient Records of Egypt.* In his eleven years of research he had found only one monument from the reign of Tutankhamun: the tomb of Huy, Tutankhamun's viceroy to Nubia.[9] Later, when Breasted wrote his six-hundred-page *History of Egypt* he devoted less than a page to Tutankhamun.[10] There simply wasn't more to say. So as the team began clearing the Antechamber, there was great excitement and anticipation that Tutankhamun would finally be revealed.

There were several wooden chests in the Antechamber, and there was hope they would contain papyri, shedding light on Tutankhamun's reign, but no luck. They held mostly clothes, which were extremely difficult to preserve. Mace sent daily reports to his wife that almost always included details of the difficulties they faced.

> [January 6] Just now we are working on a box which contains garments and shoes all covered with beadwork. The cloth is so rotten you can hardly touch it, and the beads drop off the shoes if you look at them. Moreover resin has run out and glued all the shoes together, so you can imagine what a job it is.[11]

Tutankhamun: Warrior King

The clothes that were giving Mace such difficulty were contained in a chest of great beauty but also of considerable historical interest. The wooden chest has scenes painted on all four sides. The two long sides show Tutankhamun as a military leader, defeating the enemy. Egypt was almost constantly in a state of war. The idea was for the army to march out (unprovoked) each year, beat up a neighboring country, and return with everything that wasn't nailed down—cattle, slaves, gold—and let the enemy know that they had better send tribute the next year, or the Egyptians would be back. War was good business and contributed considerably to the economy of Egypt. All this was possible because of the Nile.

Each July, the Nile rose and overflowed its banks, depositing rich topsoil from the south, fertilizing the land. Inundation was a near-magical event to the ancient Egyptians. They didn't know the cause, but first the Nile turned brown because of the topsoil suspended in the water. Then it turned green with the slower-moving vegetation that was floating on the top. Finally it rose thirty feet. Pure magic. This phenomenon is what made Egypt great, and they knew it.

To make the most of this wonderful bounty, the farmers dug irrigation canals to bring the water and topsoil inland, creating as much farmland as possible. The Egyptians could now grow more food than they needed, and this is what enabled them to have a standing army, a military made up not of farmers but of professionals. Egypt could feed an extra twenty thousand or so men who didn't contribute immediately to the economy but in the end would make a great contribution to Egypt's coffers. This is in stark contrast to modern military forces, who are viewed as a necessary drain on reserves. Our armies do not bring in income.

Other countries didn't have a chance against Egypt's professional army, and Egypt prospered. The pharaoh was expected to physically lead his men in battle; he was not a figurehead, and Tutankhamun's painted wooden chest shows him in battle.

Did Tutankhamun ever really go into battle? We can't be sure (see Chapter 12 for Tutankhamun as warrior). For much of his reign he was a child. What is important is that he is showing himself in battle, which is quite different from the path taken by his father, Akhenaten. Akhenaten had vowed never to leave his holy city at Amarna, and as far as we know he never did. So he obviously couldn't be the leader of the army, and all indications are that the army suffered. We have no records of battles, but we do have records of Akhenaten's foreign ambassadors writing to their king, pleading for him to send the military, as Egypt was no longer respected abroad.[12] These pleas went unanswered. Akhenaten simply wasn't interested in the military.

Tutankhamun's painted chest is like a campaign poster. It tells us what his reign is going to be like. The pharaoh is again leading the army in battle against Egypt's traditional enemies.

The clothes that the chest contained had to be conserved, but so did the chest. The paintings were in danger of flaking off, so Mace and Lucas applied a thin wax coating so that the images wouldn't be lost. But once Mace conquered one challenge, another popped up. Mace was constantly writing home, describing the next problem to be solved.

> [January 8] I spent most of the morning in the tomb melting wax and treating a footstool covered with beadwork that was in a very bad condition, and a shoe composed entirely of beads. I think I'll get them up all right, but the amount of restoration work ahead of us is appalling. . . . I am lucky to have such a nice chap as Lucas to work with, as we spend almost all our time together in our tomb workshop.[13]

The Gold Throne

Carter thought the Gold Throne was the most beautiful of all the objects removed from the Antechamber. Indeed, after everything was cleared out of the tomb and shipped to Cairo and he had time to reflect, he declared it "the most beautiful thing that has yet been found in Egypt." (He hadn't seen the Gold Mask yet.) For two pages he talks about its beauty, how re-laxed the figures on the backrest are, but he doesn't give it its due when it comes to what it reveals about Tutankhamun. He acknowledges that it is of the Amarna period, and even wonders about the erased cartouches on its backrest, but doesn't trumpet how much he learned from it.

It had been known for decades that Tutankhamun had something to do with the Amarna revolution. The early mentions of him were from Tel el Amarna, Akhenaten's holy city in the desert. But the throne makes clear that Tutankhamun is Akhenaten's successor, and even introduces his wife, Queen Ankhesenamun. Perhaps even more important, of the thousands of objects found in Tutankhamun's tomb, the Gold Throne confirms our sus-picions about why he vanished without a trace. He was a central part of the Amarna revolution.

The throne isn't solid gold; it is wood covered with sheet gold and decor-ated with semiprecious stones, colored glass, and ceramic inlays. It is, indeed, an object of striking beauty. Lord Carnarvon felt it was "one of the most marvelous pieces of furniture that has ever been discovered." It was displayed on the second floor of the Egyptian Museum in Cairo, along with the other Tutankhamun treasures.[14] There it vied for attention with Tut's Gold Mask, the solid gold coffin, and the life-sized wooden statues of the boy-king. Even with that stiff competition, there was always a crowd around the throne.

Almost everyone is drawn to the event depicted on the backrest (see Color Plate 7). It shows two youthful figures, and the hieroglyphs make clear who they are: Tutankhamun, Lord of the Two Lands, and Ankhesenamun, the Great Wife, Mistress of the Two Lands. The young king is shown in a relaxed pose; he's lounging, with his arm on the top of the throne. Ankhesenamun has a shallow bowl in one hand and the other hand is touching her hus-band's shoulder; she is anointing him with oil. This is as far as it goes for the average tourist; time to move on to another treasure. But if you look carefully, the throne tells a far more interesting story.

First there are the cartouches containing their names. When you look closely, you can see that they have been altered. The names Tutankhamun and Ankhesenamun have replaced something else that was there before.

The next clue is the scene itself, especially the relaxed position of the king. With the exception of a brief twenty-year period surrounding Tutankhamun's life, you can search all of Egyptian history and you won't find such a relaxed pose. The scene is very unusual. The kings and queens of ancient Egypt were gods on earth, not ordinary people, and they were not shown as ordinary people. It is a little bit like how the English treat their queen. You never see a photo of Queen Elizabeth having breakfast with her family. Newspapers aren't even permitted to quote the queen. For the kings and queens of Egypt, everything was an official, stylized portrait. There was no lounging.

The next unusual feature is the rays of the sun behind the young couple. The rays end in hands, some holding ankhs, the symbol of life. We are being told that the god Aten, the solar disk, gives life to all of Egypt. This representation was seen only during a period of about twenty years in all of Egypt's three-thousand-year history. This is the reason Tutankhamun vanished without a trace—because he was associated with the Aten and one of the great religious upheavals in history.

If we look on the side of the throne, we will see the name Aten written in hieroglyphs. Our brief hieroglyph lesson in the Introduction, where we learned how to read Tutankhamun's name, will help us here. There's a large cartouche, so it's the king's name, but it doesn't say Tutankhamun (see Color Plate 8). There's another name. Whose name is in the cartouche?

The bottom two groups of hieroglyphs are the same, *tut* and *ankh*; only the top group is different. If we sound it out, we get *atn* or Aten if we put in a guess as to the vowel that isn't written. So the name reads Atentutankh. We know that the Aten was a god, and we know it is written first because it is a god. So if we rearrange as we did for Tutankhamun, we get the name Tutankhaten. That is the name that was first placed on the backrest of Tut's golden throne. And the replaced cartouches that now say Tutankhamun and Ankhesenamun? They originally said Tutankhaten and Ankhesenpaaten. All the names on the throne originally said that. The reason we have Tutankhaten on the side is that the workers sent to change the names missed it. These were the original names of the royal couple, given to them when they were born during the heyday of the religious revolution. The throne must have been made for Tutankhaten shortly after he became king and just before the revolution was officially over and his name changed to Tutankhamun.

So the Gold Throne is an important historical document throwing considerable light on Tutankhamun and his times. He succeeded the heretic pharaoh Akhenaten, and was thus probably his son. He was the pharaoh during the time of transition back to the traditional gods. We are also introduced to his wife, Ankhesenamun. But we can learn a bit more about her from another beautiful object found in the Antechamber: the Gold Shrine.

The Gold Shrine

Another important historical document found in the Antechamber was a small gold-covered wooden shrine that once housed a statue of Tutankhamun. Only a foot and a half high, it is actually a model of a full-sized shrine, not unlike the ones nested inside each other in the Burial Chamber. When Carter opened its tiny doors, he saw two little recessed sandal prints on gold sheeting on the floor of the shrine, where a statue of Tutankhamun, stolen by thieves in ancient times, once stood. The outside of the shrine is carved with eighteen scenes of Tutankhamun doing all the things he loved. In one he is hunting marsh fowl with his bow (see Color Plate 9), Ankhesenamun holding his next arrow. She brings flowers to Tutankhamun and ties a necklace around his neck. The king pours perfume on his queen's hands; they are almost always touching (see Color Plate 10).[15] The royal couple in a variety of relaxed, daily-life poses is a holdover from the Amarna period, rarely seen in other periods. As noted earlier, the daily life scenes we see in the art books are from the tombs of the non-royals. Kings and queens are almost always shown in formal poses. This is a portrayal of a young couple devoted to each other, engrossed in each other. This is not a hastily fashioned funerary object commissioned for his tomb; it is a love letter written in gold. We are learning more about Tutankhamun than Carter acknowledged.

Conservation of all the fragile objects was slow going for Mace and Lucas, and their pace determined what the others could do. Carter and Callender would come in and determine which object should be moved next, and if it didn't need conservation, they would supervise its removal from the tomb after Burton had photographed it in situ. But when it came to moving fragile objects, it was up to Mace and Lucas. For example, Burton might photograph a wooden chest in place and then have to wait for Mace to remove the top layer of objects it contained. Once that was done, Burton could photograph the second layer of clothes, or whatever was in the chest. This would be repeated till the chest was empty. To keep the pace as swift as possible, Lucas would often postpone conservation work in the lab they had set up in the tomb of King Seti II. They would stabilize pieces so they could be moved out of the Antechamber and then stockpile them for future conservation. After two months, the Antechamber was nearly empty and everyone was wondering what they would find behind the wall flanked by the two guardian statues. Carter and Carnarvon decided to secretly find out.

The Break-in

Sometime before the official taking down of the wall, Carter, Carnarvon, and Lady Evelyn returned to the tomb at night and made a small hole at the bottom in the wall leading to the Burial Chamber. Then the three crawled through to see what treasures awaited them.[16] They must have been confused at first, not fully understanding what they were seeing. When they crawled through the hole it would have seemed as if they were in front of another wall of solid gold. Actually, almost all the space in the Burial Chamber was taken up by a huge gilded wooden shrine, leaving only about eighteen inches between it and the Burial Chamber walls. The doors to the shrine, once sealed with an ebony bolt, were open, but they could see that inside was another, smaller shrine with its bolt and seal still intact. Tutankhamun was inside, waiting for them. The three left through the hole they had entered, and then concealed the break-in by placing some baskets against the wall to hide the entry point.

We know about the break-in from several sources. One is a diary kept by Lord Carnarvon's brother, Mervyn Herbert. He tells of driving to the official opening with Carnarvon (who was called Porch) and his daughter Evelyn:

> Porch and Evelyn and I started in this Ford and after we had been going a few minutes, he said that it would really be alright and he could quite well get me in while the tomb was being opened. Then he whispered something to Evelyn and told her to tell me.
>
> This she did under the strictest promise of secrecy—this is a thing I would never give away, in any case, and it is one which I think ought not to be known, at any rate, for the present. Here is the secret. They had both already been into the second chamber! After the discovery they had not been able to resist it—they had made a small hole in the wall (which they afterwards filled up again) and afterwards climbed through.[17]

Later in the diary entry, Herbert says that Carnarvon was nervous at the official opening late that day because he was afraid their entry might be discovered.

Mervyn Herbert's diary isn't the only evidence of the break-in. There is photographic evidence of it. Some of Burton's photos don't make any archaeological sense unless we think about the secret entry. They were published in the first volume of Carter's three-volume work. Plate XLI shows the tomb nearly empty, except for the two guardian statues and a basket and some reeds propped up against the wall leading to the Burial Chamber (Figure 3.4). What is that basket doing there? Why hasn't it been cleared? The answer is that it is concealing the hole through which Carnarvon, Carter, and Lady Evelyn crawled. A second photo looks absolutely insane to anyone familiar with excavation techniques. It was taken on February 1, the day Carter officially broke through the wall. Taking down the wall involved hammers, crowbars, and heavy stones being moved. Why hadn't the guardian statues been moved to safety? When Carter broke through the wall, he built a small platform on which he and Callender stood during the procedure. The position of the guardian statues determined where this platform had to go—between the statues, right in front of the secret entrance, concealing it (Figure 3.5). Carter knew how strange this looked

Figure 3.4. Carter and Carnarvon concealed the hole from their secret entry with baskets propped against the wall. (*L'Illustration.*)

Figure 3.5. Why haven't the guardian statues been moved to a safe spot? (*L'Illustration.*)

and, in his book, mentions the guardian statues. He says that the tomb had been completely cleared, every last bead gathered "with the exception of the two sentinel statues, left for a special reason."[18] He never elaborated on what that special reason was.

With the official entry to the Burial Chamber completed, Carter could announce what he already knew: Tutankhamen was undisturbed inside the large gilded shrines. He could also announce the "discovery" of the Treasury, another side chamber, off the Burial Chamber that also was packed with treasures. The work for this season was over; the excavation of the Burial Chamber would have to wait for the next year.

Carter Alone

Things had gone relatively smoothly, but tragedy struck at the end of the season and would affect all future work on the tomb. While in Luxor, Carnarvon had been bitten by a mosquito. When he returned to Cairo, in preparation for sailing to England, the bite became infected, and on April 5, 1923, Lord Carnarvon died. It was a terrible loss in several ways. For Lady Carnarvon and Lady Evelyn it was a family tragedy. For Carter it was the loss of a patron and friend who had been a great help to him in navigating personal interactions with the public and with the administration. Carter was despondent, but he still had to pack all the objects from the Antechamber for shipment to Cairo.

More than six hundred objects were removed from the Antechamber. And this is where all the linen and cotton Carter had bought in Cairo was consumed. In the end there were eighty-nine boxes of artifacts that were further enclosed in thirty-four heavy wooden crates for extra protection. From the Valley of the Kings it was slightly more than five miles to the Nile, where a steamer sent by the Antiquities Service awaited the treasures of Tutankhamun. There were three ways the artifacts could make the journey to the steamer: on the backs of camels, by human portage, or via a Decauville railway. Carter took the railway option.

A Decauville is a very narrow-gauge railway frequently used in excavations in Egypt where large amounts of sand and earth had to be moved. There is no engine; the carts filled with sand are moved by workers pushing them along the tracks, and this is how Tutankhamun's treasures made their way to the Nile. Of course, five miles of track were not laid at once. Rather, a kind of relay was formed by fifty workers. About a hundred yards of track were put down, and the carts were pushed along to the front, while other workers brought the now unoccupied tracks at the back to the front, where they were laid down. The whole process of leapfrogging took fifteen hours, and there were no mishaps.

It had been a very successful season, but one punctuated by a great tragedy that left Carter without his patron. Carter expressed some disappointment in the archaeological finds, but that may have been because of the sadness he was feeling. He had hoped to discover more about Tutankhamun, but as he put it, "We are getting to know to the last detail what he had, but of what he was and what he did we are still sadly to seek."[19] With hindsight we can see that this is too harsh a judgment. Carter was revealing quite a bit about the missing pharaoh.

4

Locked Out

The second season of excavating Tutankhamun's tomb should have been easier than the first. Carter had a skilled team in place that worked very well together, and he now knew what to expect. He knew what condition the objects were in, and he also had a good idea of what the Burial Chamber was like. He would be working without Carnarvon, but had a support system of friends and colleagues. The first major task was to dismantle the largest, outermost shrine that nearly filled the Burial Chamber.

It was difficult because of the confined space, but also because Carter had to deal with dry, brittle wood. When the ancient workers first assembled the shrine in the Burial Chamber, the wood was fresh and strong and they could pound the panels into place. Still visible on the walls of the shrine were ancient instructions for assembling the shrines. On the front of the side panels was the hieroglyph 𓂀, meaning "front," and on the rear was the hindquarters of a baboon, 𓃻 meaning "rear." These hieroglyphs matched those on the roof of the shrine that aligned accordingly—the ancient equivalent of "insert tab A into slot A." In addition to the assembly instructions, there were also hieroglyphs for the workmen telling them how to orient the shrines in the burial chamber. The intention was that the doors would open to the west. The ancient Egyptians believed that the next world was in the west. When someone died it was said that "he went west." The deceased were called "westerners," and Osiris, the god of the dead, was Lord of the West. So it was important that the doors faced west. Toward the top of the shrine are the hieroglyphs for "west" in the front and "east" in the back. But somehow, while assembling the shrines, the workmen became disoriented and got it backward. When Tutankhamun resurrected, he would have walked into this world rather than the next.

With great difficulty Carter dismantled the outer shrine (Figure 4.1), but they couldn't remove it from the burial chamber. There just wasn't enough room to maneuver the large pieces through the hole in the wall they had created to enter the Burial Chamber, so they left them leaning against the wall until they could enlarge the hole at the end of the excavation. With the first shrine dismantled, Carter decided to open the doors to the still-sealed inner three shrines. He carefully cut the cords securing the bolts, removed the seals, and opened the doors. When the doors to the innermost shrine were opened, the team could see that it was almost completely filled with a beautifully carved sarcophagus. Inside they were certain they would find nested coffins, and inside the innermost one would be Tutankhamun, waiting for them.

They set to work taking apart the three remaining shrines, which took the better part of three months. The shrines were wood but covered with a fragile thin coating of gesso, to which the gold foil was attached. It was a difficult operation. Once the shrines were dismantled, the sarcophagus was

Figure 4.1. Carter had great difficulty dismantling the large shrine that surrounded Tutankhamun's sarcophagus. (*L'Illustration.*)

at last revealed. It was carved from a single block of yellow quartzite, and a beautiful winged goddess stood at each corner, protecting Tutankhamun with her outstretched arms. The lid was made of pink granite painted to look like the yellow quartzite of the base (something like a precursor to faux marble); in the rush to prepare Tutankhamun's burial, something must have gone wrong and the original lid broke, so a lid of pink granite was substituted. But here too the stonemasons had a problem. The second lid developed a crack, which they concealed with plaster and paint.

The haste with which Tutankhamun's tomb was prepared in ancient times made Carter's job more stressful. The crack in the lid of the sarcophagus made it difficult to lift in one piece without breaking. But eventually Carter and Callender figured it out. Block and tackle were brought into the Burial Chamber, and ropes and iron clamps were placed beneath the lid so that it could be hoisted. The sarcophagus was one of the last barriers between Howard Carter and Tutankhamun.

The word *sarcophagus* has an interesting origin. It is made up of two Greek roots: *sarkoma*, "flesh," and *oisophagus*, "eat." When the Greeks first entered Egypt in the third century BC, they discovered that these stone boxes contained emaciated mummies who looked as if their flesh was gone. So they called the stone boxes "flesh eaters."

Carter hoped that Tutankhamun would be the best-preserved royal mummy ever. He was quite familiar with the mummies from the Deir el Bahri cache, and many of them looked as if they were merely sleeping, especially Seti I (Figure 4.2) and Ramses the Great. These mummies had been wrapped and unwrapped, plundered by tomb robbers, and moved from place to place, but they still looked quite good. He could only imagine the beauty of Tutankhamun, who had been slumbering undisturbed for thirty-three centuries. He planned the lifting of the sarcophagus lid for February 12.

The raising of the lid would be another milestone in the excavation, so Carter prepared a list of invited guests for an official lifting. He sent the list to Pierre Lacau, the director of the Antiquities Service, who forwarded it on to Morcos Bey Hanna, the Egyptian minister of public works. Carter also planned that on the following day, the wives of his collaborators would be invited to see the result of removing the lid.

The actual raising of the lid was scheduled for 3:00 p.m., and on that day Carter had lunch with his colleagues and friends in a vacant tomb in the

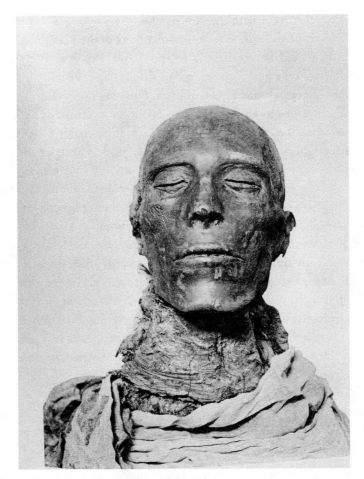

Figure 4.2. The mummy of Seti I was one of the best preserved of all the royal mummies.

Valley. It should have been a joyous occasion, but Carter was agitated. He had just received a sheaf of paper from Morcos Bey giving Carter instructions as to the program for the tomb for the next few days. Morcos Bey was flexing his muscles and Carter didn't like it, but he should have seen it coming.

When the tomb was first discovered, newspapers from around the world dispatched reporters to cover the story. Carter and Carnarvon had found themselves in the middle of a media frenzy, constantly bombarded with requests for interviews. Carnarvon made the very bad decision to give the exclusive rights to the Tutankhamun story to the *Times* of London. Carter and Carnarvon would talk to no other members of the press, and Burton's photographs would be given only to the *Times*. This way, they thought, they could work in peace. As everyone should have imagined, the press was furious, especially the Egyptian press. This was *their* country, and *they* were not being given any information about their tomb, while England was. Even worse, the team controlling the excavation, making the decisions, were all foreigners. Between the first and second seasons of excavation, these sentiments had been percolating in Egypt. Times were changing, but many of the Egyptologists excavating in Egypt didn't want to admit it, and those who did were fighting the change. A former colleague of Carter's, Arthur Weigall, warned him, but Carter didn't listen.

Weigall had once served as inspector of antiquities for Luxor and knew Carter from early times. When he left Egypt and his job as inspector, he became one of the best archaeological writers of the time. In the introduction to one of his books he made the wonderful statement that "it is the job of the archaeological writer to make the dead come alive, not put the living to sleep." When Carter discovered the tomb, Weigall was in England, and the *Daily Mail* sent him to Luxor as their correspondent. Weigall expected to be welcomed as an old friend by Carter, but Carter, in the middle of the *Times* debacle, rebuffed his former colleague.

Weigall, who clearly understood the political climate in Egypt, wrote Carter a letter telling him that times had changed, pretty much predicting the way things would go:

> You and Lord Carnarvon made the initial error when you discovered the tomb thinking that the old British prestige in this country is still maintained and that you could do more or less what you liked, just as we all used to do in the old days. You have found this tomb, however, at a moment when the least spark may send the whole magazine sky-high, when the utmost diplomacy is needed, when Egyptians have to be considered in a way to which you and I are not accustomed. . . . You opened the tomb before you notified the Government representative, and the natives all say that you therefore have had the opportunity of stealing some millions of pounds' worth of gold of which you talked. . . . You two are being held up to execration of the most bitter kind and already before I left London I was told of the intense feeling which you had aroused.[1]

Weigall, of course, had his own interests. He was one of the journalists shut out by Carnarvon's decision, but that doesn't mean he was wrong. Soon after his letter, Weigall joined with other journalists in opposing Carter and Carnarvon's contract with the *Times*. So when the Egyptian government began to assert itself before the lifting of the sarcophagus lid, Carter knew why. Still, there was great excitement when the group took the short walk to the tomb to see the lid lifted.

Everyone watched in silence as the one-and-a-half-ton lid rose and was swung aside. First there was puzzlement at what they saw as they peered into the sarcophagus, but quickly the situation became clear. Indeed, there was a coffin inside, but it was covered by linen shrouds that had turned brown over the centuries. Slowly, carefully, Carter and Mace rolled back and then removed the shrouds, revealing the most beautiful anthropoid coffin anyone had ever seen (see Color Plate 11). Carter described the situation:

> A gasp of wonderment escaped our lips, so gorgeous was the sight that met our eyes: a golden effigy of the boy king, of most magnificent workmanship filled the whole interior of the sarcophagus . . . enclosing the mortal remains of the king.[2]

They left the tomb awed by what they had seen, leaving the lid still suspended from the block and tackle. Things were about to get very bad.

Early on the morning of the thirteenth, when the wives were to view the tomb, Carter received notice that the minister had forbidden them from visiting the tomb. Indeed, the tomb was to be put under Egyptian guard to ensure that no unauthorized persons would enter. Carter was furious. He rushed over to the Winter Palace Hotel, where Gardiner and Breasted were staying, to discuss the situation. Others quickly joined the discussion. In the end, Carter tacked up a notice at the hotel saying that he could not work under such conditions and was closing the excavation. The government responded by taking control of the tomb, essentially locking Carter out.

At a time when anti-foreign sentiment was growing, the French director of antiquities, Pierre Lacau, sided with the Egyptians. He was aware that this was Egypt's patrimony, and he felt that the best pieces from all excavations should remain in Egypt. He had made this clear to other foreign excavation teams, including the Metropolitan Museum of Art's, well before the discovery of Tutankhamun's tomb. Lacau's progressive idea was viewed by Egyptologists excavating in Egypt as a threat to their careers. Many were sponsored by museums and universities, where decisions about their funding were made by trustees. How could they convince trustees to fund a season of excavation if they weren't going to bring something back for the museum?

The archaeological community in Luxor was shocked by Carter's closing of the tomb and the government's subsequent move to take control of it. Letters were sent back and forth between Egyptologists, lawyers for both sides, and anyone else Carter thought might help. Carter's friends knew he was a difficult man and were afraid of what he might say in anger. The debate went on for weeks, and several of his colleagues tried to mediate with the government on Carter's behalf. Morcos Bey conceded that Carter might be permitted back in the tomb if he agreed to relinquish all claims to objects from the tomb, but tempers flared again when Carter's lawyer referred to some of the officials as "thieves" because they had broken the locks on the tomb to inspect it. Things were heating up.

It was decided that Carter would go to America on a lecture tour while his colleagues in Egypt tried to work things out. It was a way of getting Carter out of the picture so that cooler heads could prevail, and it was also a way for Carter to make some much-needed income from lecture fees. But Carter wasn't so easily silenced. Before his lecture tour, he prepared a small pamphlet that he had printed in England that has become known as the *Statement* (Figure 4.3).[3] It was never intended for public circulation, and we don't know how many copies Carter had printed; my guess is about seventy-five, as they are quite rare. The *Statement* had two purposes. First, it allowed Carter to vent his anger. Second, he could give it to people who he thought could help his cause and get him back into the tomb.

It is of course written from Carter's viewpoint and must be read with that in mind. However, it contains documents that require little interpretation. Carter includes his excavation agreement with the Antiquities Service, letters written between him and officials, and letters written by his colleagues. The publishing of these confidential letters written by friends, without asking their permission, put a severe strain on several of these relationships.

Articles 8–10 of the excavation concession show why Carter and Carnarvon expected to keep part of the finds:

8. Mummies of the Kings, of Princes, and High Priests, together with their coffins and sarcophagi, shall remain the property of the Antiquities Service.

9. Tombs which are discovered intact, together with all objects they may contain, shall be handed over to the Museum whole and without division.

10. In the case of tombs that have already been searched, the Antiquities Service shall, over and above the mummies and sarcophagi intended in Article 8, reserve for themselves all objects of capital importance from the

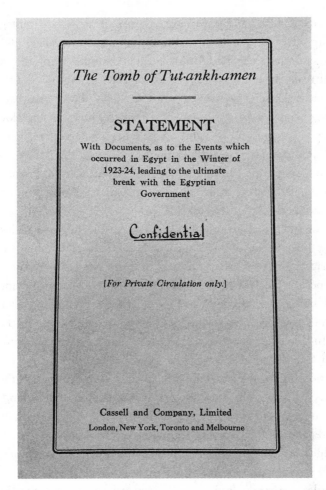

The Tomb of Tut·ankh·amen

STATEMENT

With Documents, as to the Events which
occurred in Egypt in the Winter of
1923-24, leading to the ultimate
break with the Egyptian
Government

Confidential

[*For Private Circulation only.*]

Cassell and Company, Limited
London, New York, Toronto and Melbourne

Figure 4.3. Carter wrote the *Statement* to present his case that he was being mistreated by the Egyptian Antiquities Service.

point of view of history and archeology, and shall share the remainder with the Permittee.

As it is probable that the majority of tombs as may be discovered will fall within the category of the present article, it is agreed that the permittee's share will sufficiently recompense him for the pains and labour of the undertaking.

From Article 8, it is clear the excavators could not expect Tutankhamun's mummy, sarcophagus, or coffins. No problem there. Article 9 presents a problem. Any tomb that is intact goes "without division" to the Antiquities Service. There is a precedent for this. When Theodore Davis discovered the intact tomb of Yuya and Tuya, Tutankhamun's great-grandparents, Maspero generously offered Davis some of the finds, but Davis realized they should all stay together and declined. But was Tutankhamun's tomb discovered intact? Not really. It had been robbed at least twice, and in the first volume of the three-volume excavation account, Carter and Mace made this clear.[4] Gold rings wrapped in a piece of linen were found on the floor of the Antechamber, suggesting the thieves had been interrupted as they were robbing the tomb. There was the tunneling through the rubble used to fill in the staircase and descending passageway. There was the resealed wall at the bottom of the steps and the one between the Antechamber and the Burial Chamber. All pointed to break-ins.

Carter and Mace also explained that the reason they had such difficulty removing the contents of boxes and chests in the Antechamber was that the thieves had thrown things everywhere and the objects were later replaced by necropolis officials with little care. So there was plenty of evidence that the tomb had been "searched," and thus Carnarvon could expect a division of the finds to "recompense him for the pains and labour of the undertaking." Indeed, Carnarvon and Carter discussed just what they might expect, and Carnarvon even promised several museums that he would give them something from the tomb. Thus in more agreeable times they might have expected something. Now, however, that seemed unlikely, and it wasn't clear if Carter would ever get back in the tomb to complete the work.

After reprinting the concession agreement, the *Statement* gives a glimpse of the negotiations during the first season of excavation. Much of the back-and-forth concerns the unfortunate agreement with the *Times*. That agreement made everybody look bad: Carter and Carnarvon, the *Times*, and the Antiquities Service, which seemed to be agreeing with the decision to exclude the Egyptian press. The local press wanted to know why Mr. Merton, the Luxor correspondent for the *Times*, was the only press member permitted into the tomb. Something had to be done. The letters between Carter and the Antiquities Service show one attempted solution. Carter would give his daily bulletin to Merton to send in the evening, and the Egyptian press would get it the next morning. Because of the time difference between Cairo and London, they would for all practical purposes be getting the news at the same time with respect to going to press. The European press, however, objected because it still left them out; they would have to get the news via the *Times*.

Later in the negotiations, Carter put Merton on the list of members of his team—to explain why he alone among reporters could enter the tomb. The Antiquities Service countered by demanding a list of all members of Carter's team and reserving the right to remove anyone they did not see as fit—perhaps Mr. Merton? Carter refused to provide the list. This gives an idea of how the situation had deteriorated, for it seems perfectly reasonable for the Antiquities Service to ask for a list of those working on an excavation in their country. At this point the focus shifted from the newspaper agreement to something much more basic: who controls Tutankhamun's tomb?

As Carter was working on dismantling the large shrines in the burial chamber, the Antiquities Service was placing on display in the Egyptian Museum in Cairo the objects removed the previous season from the Antechamber. The museum would be issuing a new guide to its collections that would include the Tutankhamun objects.[5] Carter went ballistic, fuming that he and Lady Carnarvon (now replacing her deceased husband as permittee) had the sole right to publish the objects. Further, how could the Egyptians put the objects in the museum guidebook when it wasn't clear that the objects belonged to them? Carter argued that since the tomb had obviously been robbed, there would be a partition of the finds, as specified in their contract. How did the museum know they would end up with the objects being listed in the catalogue? Again, not an argument Carter could win easily. It is difficult to claim that the Egyptian government did not have the right to describe objects found in their country that were on display in their national museum. So this was the atmosphere that started the chain reaction in which Carter was informed he couldn't invite the wives, Carter shut the tomb, Egypt locked out Carter, and Carter sailed off for his American lecture tour.

Even while he was touring, there were new problems for Carter to deal with. Winlock, the Metropolitan Museum's excavator in Egypt, had been given power of attorney by Carter and tried to help resolve the difficulties, but he quickly found himself dealing with a totally new problem. The Egyptian authorities had entered and inspected Tomb No. 4, which Carter and the team had used for storage of antiquities, and discovered a beautiful life-sized wooden head of Tutankhamun as a youth. It had been packed in a Fortnum and Mason crate, but it had never been mentioned in Carter's records of the finds, nor in the volume describing the contents of the Antechamber. Carter's detractors quickly suggested he was intending to steal it. Winlock cabled Carter, who was now in London, telling him that it looked bad. Perhaps he had purchased it at Amarna for Lord Carnarvon's collection the year before? Carter cabled back that the head was part of the Tutankhamun finds of the first year and had been discovered in the rubble in the descending passage.[6] The answer was accepted, but while Carter was in England, he had a chance to stir the pot once again.

The British Empire Exhibition for 1924 was a celebration of the British Empire's achievements and would take place at Wembley, an exhibition site in north London. There would be displays of the crafts of England's colonies, new inventions, and an amusement park with rides, not unlike those at America's Coney Island. Carter heard that there was going to be a replica of Tutankhamun's tomb filled with copies of the treasures he had discovered. He quickly concluded that the replicas must have been made from Burton's photographs, which were his property, and he asked his lawyers to get a cease-and-desist writ to prevent the show from opening. Carter's proprietary instincts were rearing up again, but the truth was that the replicas were not based on Burton's photos. Arthur Weigall had been an advisor to the exhibition, and he had been able to obtain his own photos of the objects as they were being brought out of the tomb. Such photos became a series of postcards quite popular with tourists at the time. Consequently Carter let the matter drop.

The North American tour was a great success. Carter visited the largest cities in the United States and Canada, and everywhere he went he was welcomed enthusiastically. In New York he lectured at Carnegie Hall to a crowd of twenty-five hundred, and he thanked the Metropolitan Museum for all their help. The lecture was repeated at the Museum of Natural History.[7] He also gave a smaller, informal lecture for the Metropolitan Museum to help them with their fundraising, and later did the same for Breasted in Chicago. He was not a brilliant lecturer, and the Americans had difficulty with his accent, but everyone was thrilled to be hearing firsthand about the discovery, and Burton's photographs illustrating the lectures were wonderful.

He gave a private lecture for President Calvin Coolidge and friends, and at Yale he received an honorary doctorate (the only such recognition he would receive, as none was ever awarded by his native England). Everywhere he went—Pittsburgh, Worcester, Hartford, Boston, Cleveland, Columbus, Buffalo, Washington, D.C., Cincinnati, Detroit—he was a rousing success, which was good for his spirits (Figure 4.4). The lectures also gave him

Figure 4.4. Carter in Washington, D.C., for one of his lectures. (Peggy Joy Library.)

considerable income that he could use in the future. The U.S. schedule was exhausting, and it was the same in Canada—Toronto, Montreal, Ottawa all welcomed him with open arms.

As Carter was lecturing to overflowing crowds, Winlock back in Egypt, was negotiating for Carter's return to the tomb, with some success. For the most part, the Antiquities Service realized that Carter was the best man for the difficult job of clearing the tomb. He had carried out the very complex jobs of dismantling the large shrines and lifting the cracked sarcophagus lid with no mishaps. Further, he had assembled an all-star team that worked well together. Almost everyone wanted to find a way to go forward and get Carter back in the tomb. Eventually, Winlock hammered out an agreement that could work. He presented it to Carter in a realistic manner, pointing out to him that in Cairo he had a reputation for being a difficult person. Under the terms he had negotiated, Carter and Lady Carnarvon would relinquish all claims to a division of the finds and pay the excavation expenses, and Carter would keep his mouth shut and not call officials "thieves" or "bandits." Though this would have given Carter had a way back into the tomb—and Winlock could put an end to his unwanted role as negotiator—Carter's response to the proposal was to reject it out of hand and suggest he would rather retire from archaeology.

To be fair to Carter, when he received Winlock's proposal, he was alone in Detroit, exhausted from a demanding lecture tour, and had no one with whom he could discuss the proposal. Later, when the tour was over and he had two weeks to rest in New York and had the staff of the Metropolitan Museum to advise him, they eventually guided him to the idea that it was possible that he would be returning to the tomb he had discovered. But he was not there yet.

While he was recovering in New York, copies of his newly printed *Statement* arrived. As mentioned before, he had included private correspondence from friends without their knowledge. Some of the letters contained criticisms of Pierre Lacau, the Egyptian ministers, and colleagues. In an appendix to the *Statement*, Carter had included correspondence from Winlock of the Metropolitan Museum that the museum's administrators considered quite damaging to them, and they asked Carter to remove it. As a result, several of the few surviving copies of the *Statement* have the appendix cut out.

After his two weeks in New York, Carter returned to England to discuss the situation with Lady Carnarvon. Carter had a deep sense of loyalty to friends, especially to Lord Carnarvon. Now with his patron gone, that loyalty transferred to his widow. If they were to continue working in the tomb, Lady Carnarvon would have to renew the concession in her name and continue paying the expenses. Carter was protective of her rights to a portion of the finds, as stipulated in their contract, and was not going to give them away without her informed consent.

When they discussed the situation at Highclere Castle, Lady Carnarvon was certainly willing to renew the concession and pay to continue the work. She was also quite willing to give up her rights to a division of the finds. Unlike her husband, she was not a lover of Egyptian antiquities.

As a matter of fact, she asked Carter to arrange to sell the lord's collection. Carter now felt he could return to Egypt and negotiate the return to work.

In Cairo, he spoke with several ministers and officials in the Antiquities Service. Everyone expressed the sentiment that Carter was the best man for the job and they all wanted him to return. Yes, they would renew Lord Carnarvon's concession in Lady Carnarvon's name so long as she was willing to pay for the excavation. The one major change in the concession agreement was that she would be giving up all rights to a division of the finds. Carter, however, obtained an informal concession for his new patroness. The Antiquities Service promised to be generous in awarding Lady Carnarvon duplicate objects that were not important to keep in Egypt for scientific reasons—quite a coup for Carter.

The petty sticking points now disappeared. Of course, the museum in Cairo could describe the Tutankhamun objects in the new guidebook. Of course, neither Carter nor any member of his team would call Egyptian officials "bandits." Excitedly, Carter cabled Lady Carnarvon with the news. He was so sure the agreement would go through that he asked her to wire some funds so he could open the excavation in the Valley.

Carter arrived in Luxor to find everything pretty much in order, but his team had changed. Carnarvon was gone, of course, but now Carter would no longer have Mace either. After the second season, Mace, who had been so helpful as a conservator, took ill and was never again able to help on the excavation. However, he still had Callender, Lucas, and Burton. Because of all the political upheaval, they would have a short season, but at least conservation of some remaining objects such as the two guardian statues would be completed and the objects shipped to Cairo.

Relationships with the authorities improved considerably. Carter was permitted visitors to the tomb, journalists were accommodated, and in all it was a successful season. Unfortunately, this would also be Callender's last season. He had had a disagreement with his old friend Carter over finances. At the beginning of the first season, Carter had agreed to pay Callender £50 per season. When the second season ended early because of the disputes, he gave Callender only part of the amount. Callender felt this was wrong, and lawyers became involved; although Callender returned for one last season, it would be his last, and the friendship was over.[8] Their final cooperative effort came at the end of the season when they traveled to the museum in Cairo to help unpack the crates of antiquities they had sent. That meant Carter would not have Callender by his side when he attempted the most difficult of all maneuvers—the removal of the three coffins nested inside the sarcophagus.

5

Face-to-Face with Tutankhamun

It was not until October 1925 that Carter began to remove the three coffins nested inside the sarcophagus. He no longer had Mace and Callender
to assist, so it was going to be him and Lucas the chemist with Burton
photographing. Removing three coffins tightly fitted one inside the other
was a difficult task that occupied much of the 1925–1926 season. Imagine
three very tightly fitting Russian nesting dolls; add to that the fact that they
are three thousand years old and weigh hundreds of pounds, and you have
an idea of what Carter was facing.

The lid of the outer coffin had four silver handles, two on each side, that
proved strong enough to raise the lid. The second, anthropoid coffin, six feet
eight inches long and equally beautiful, was now revealed under its own
shroud. It too bore floral wreaths. These wreaths were an important part of
the burial ritual. There was even one that was called the "wreath of victory"
and symbolized the deceased's victory over death, when he would resurrect
in the west. This second coffin gave Carter his first inkling that the mummy
might not be in the condition hoped for. Some of the inlays in the decoration on the surface had fallen out, indicating that there might have been
some moisture in the coffin and that the wood might have deteriorated. It
was not an easy situation. In any event, they had time to think about what
to do. Work had to be stopped to await Burton's arrival in Egypt so he could
take photographs, documenting everything, including the position of the
wreaths and the condition of the shrouds.

Burton arrived in Luxor on October 15, and by October 17 he had taken
his photographs, so Carter could remove the shroud and floral wreaths.
Because of the delicate condition of the second coffin, it was decided to

remove the entire coffin rather than just the lid. But the coffin was nestled tightly inside the bottom of the outer coffin. How could they lift it out? Carter's solution was to insert steel pins in the outer coffin and hope the wood was strong enough to hold the pins while the coffins were lifted out of the sarcophagus. He tested by tugging on the pins and they felt secure. It was another gutsy move. Carter didn't want the pins to support all the weight, so he slipped straps beneath the bottom of the outer coffin, to take some of the weight off the steel pins. Slowly the pulleys lifted the outer coffin, with the second coffin still inside it, out of the sarcophagus. It was going well, but as they hoisted, the ensemble felt far too heavy, much more than expected. It was quickly lowered onto planks set across the stone sarcophagus. They had done it, but where was all that weight coming from?

Again, Burton photographed, and when he was done, Carter removed the second set of shrouds and wreaths. For the first time they could see clearly what the coffin looked like. Tutankhamun's likeness was staring back at them from three thousand years ago (see Color Plate 11).

Unlike the first coffin, this second coffin had no handles to raise the lid, and it fit inside the outer one with less than half an inch to spare on either side. The lid was attached to the bottom by silver pins with gold heads, but there was so little space between the two coffins that the pins could not be removed. The tight fit was an anti-theft device devised by the officials responsible for Tutankhamun's burial. It was not going to be easy for thieves to get at the jewels on the mummy of the dead pharaoh. It was a real problem for Carter too. They had the fragile second coffin, which for some unknown reason was very heavy, and little room to maneuver. Carter was looking for the solution that would do the least damage, and felt a tremendous responsibility. He wrote:

> It may be, under the strain of such operations as these, that one is too conscious of the risk of irreparable damage to the rare and beautiful object one desires to preserve intact. . . . Everything may seem to be going well until suddenly, in the crisis of the process, you hear a crack—little pieces of surface ornament fall. . . . What action is needed to avert a catastrophe?[1]

Carter studied the problem for two days before he came up with a plan. There was not enough space between the two coffins to pull out and remove the pins in the second coffin, but they could be pulled out a quarter of an inch. Strong copper wires were passed around the protruding quarter of an inch of pins to support the second coffin. Next, Carter screwed strong metal eyelets into the edge of the outer coffin to support it. Then, using his pulleys and an ingenious system of ropes, rather than lifting the second coffin out, he lowered the outer coffin back into the sarcophagus while keeping the second coffin suspended by the ten stout wires. Once the outer coffin was inside the sarcophagus, planks were quickly set across the sarcophagus and the second coffin lowered onto them.

It was another bold move. There was no guarantee that the fragile wood of the second coffin could support its own weight, but it worked. It is clear why the Antiquities Service wanted to get Carter back into the tomb. Who else would be willing to attempt such a feat with so much at stake? Certainly no one in the Antiquities Service was stepping up to volunteer. Something similar had happened 350 years earlier in Rome. Pope Sixtus V wanted the Vatican obelisk to be moved a quarter of a mile to the new St. Peter's Basilica, and like Carter's situation, it wasn't clear how to do it. Michelangelo was asked to do the job. He refused with a simple question: "And if it breaks?" Carter had done what no one else was willing to do (or try to do) and had done it superbly.

When everyone had recovered from the tension, they had to think about how to raise the handle-less lid of the second coffin. Carter now had room to extract the gold-headed silver pins holding the lid to the bottom, but even with the pins out, he still had to figure out how to lift the lid without handles. Where do you grip it? How heavy was it? By now Carter knew that metal eyelets would probably hold in the ancient wood. Further, if placed properly, they would only leave small holes in an undecorated part of the wood that could later be filled in. So Carter screwed in four metal eyelets where they would not damage the decoration. The eyelets were attached to the tackle, and the lid rose easily into the air. It was quickly placed on a tray waiting for it beside the sarcophagus. They could now look inside the second coffin. Beneath a linen shroud, they could just make out a third coffin.

Burton took his photos, and then Carter and Lucas carefully removed the fragile shroud and floral wreaths. Now they could see the last coffin clearly. This third, innermost coffin, was the reason for the unexpected weight. It was solid gold, weighing nearly 250 pounds. Nothing like this had ever been seen, and everyone was shocked. Usually when you see gold on coffins, shrines, or boxes, you are looking at a thin layer of sheet gold placed over wood. Not here. Tutankhamun had had a brief reign and was a minor king.

He ruled when Egypt was just beginning a comeback, not when it was on top. If he had a gold coffin, think about what Ramses the Great had, or any of the other Great Ones of ancient Egypt.

The solid gold coffin was an astounding revelation, so astounding that at least one seasoned Egyptologist didn't believe it. When James Henry Breasted heard Carter was talking about having revealed a solid gold coffin, he wrote to his wife that Carter was wrong: "Of course we all are familiar with the fact that Carter does not know the meaning of the English language. There can be no doubt that the coffin is wood overlaid with gold."[2] Breasted was wrong, dead wrong. But there was no need for his deprecating tone about Carter. Here too, Carter's relationship with a collaborator had soured. Breasted had earlier asked Carter for five of Burton's photos that had been already published, to use in his *History of Egypt*. Carter supplied them, but to Breasted's surprise he charged him for the photos. Such pettiness, on both sides, seems even smaller when we think about Carter's achievement—not just the discovery, but the successful clearing of the tomb. Everything was difficult; even the gold coffin would present problems no other archaeologist had ever seen. Still, Breasted never forgave him.

The features of the gold coffin were obscured by a black coating, the remains of sacred unguents that had been poured over it at the time of Tutankhamun's burial. The liquids had run into the bottom of the second coffin, rising along the edges and filling the spaces between the two coffins. Over the centuries the oils had solidified, essentially gluing the two coffins together. Separating them would be a real problem. The only good thing was that the solid gold lid was not sealed by the oils to the gold bottom and, with its handles, could be lifted. Carter fully expected that when the lid was removed he would see the king he had been searching for all these years. He was right. He later wrote about encountering Tutankhamun for the first time:

> At such moments the emotions evade verbal expressions, complex and stirring as they are. Three thousand years and more had elapsed since men's eyes had gazed into that golden coffin. Time, measured by the brevity of human life, seemed to lose its common perspectives before a spectacle so vividly recalling the solemn religious rites of a vanished civilization. But it is useless to dwell on such sentiments, based as they are on feelings of awe and human pity. The emotional side is no part of archaeological research. Here at last lay all that was left of the youthful Pharaoh, hitherto little more to us than the shadow of a name.[3]

Carter was clearly moved by his first encounter with Tutankhamun, but he felt obliged to dismiss his strong emotional experience as having no place in archaeological research. He was a complex man, more complex than most realize.

While moved by the experience, he was also disappointed. Tutankhamun was not in good condition. The oils that had been poured on the gold coffin had also been ritually poured on the mummy of the boy-king, causing considerable damage. The mummy was blackened and was solidly stuck to the bottom of the gold coffin by the unguents. Carter's first meeting with Tutankhamun was not face-to-face; the famous Gold Mask was concealing the pharaoh's features. But there were consolations. Carter could see numerous pieces of jewelry that had been buried on the king—pectorals, rings, magical amulets, gold bands with inscriptions. It was fabulous, but many objects were stuck in the congealed oils. How would they get Tutankhamen, the Gold Mask, and the other treasures out of the coffin? Carter's hope was that heat could soften the hardened oils. So the two nested coffins, still one inside the other, with Tutankhamun's mummy still stuck to the bottom of the gold coffin, were brought out of the tomb and into the hot Egyptian sun, hoping that would soften the oils. After several hours, nothing had happened. Lucas and Carter would have to come up with another idea.

They were able to remove the Gold Mask by using heated knives to soften the resins, but that didn't work for separating the coffins or getting Tutankhamun out of the gold coffin to which he was stuck. It was decided that the examination of the king would have to take place while he was stuck in the coffin. Unfortunately, Carter chose the wrong man for the job.

Tutankhamun's Worst Nightmare

Carter had considerable experience excavating artifacts of all kinds, but mummies were a different thing altogether. Almost always, if a mummy is found on an excavation, an outside expert is called in to work with the mummy. People respond to mummies differently than they do to other artifacts. Mummies are the bodies of once-living individuals who died thousands of years ago, and often people are not sure how to react. This is the case now, and it was the case in Carter's time. One difference between now and then, however, is that we now have a fairly well-developed discipline called mummy studies; there are experts. In Carter's day, who was qualified to examine a mummy and who wasn't was not clearly defined.

Dr. Douglas Derry, professor of anatomy at Cairo University, was given the responsibility of working with the body. Assisted by Dr. Saleh Bey Hamdy, director of sanitary services in Alexandria, Derry began unwrapping the mummy of Tutankhamun on November 11, 1925. Other attendees were Pierre Lacau, the director of the Antiquities Service, and several other officials. Burton was, of course, present to document the event (Figure 5.1).

Examining Tutankhamun's mummy was slow going and took nearly a week. The unguents poured on the mummy had caused a chemical reaction with the bandages, darkening them by a slow spontaneous combustion. Because the bandages could not be unrolled in such a state, Lucas brushed heated wax over the outer layer so that when the wax cooled, it could be cut away in a large piece. Derry made a longitudinal incision and peeled

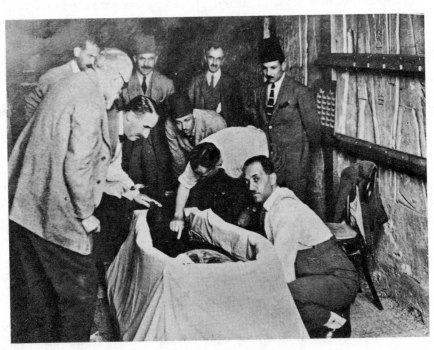

Figure 5.1. High officials present at the unwrapping of Tutankhamun's mummy. (Photo Griffith Institute)

back the first layer to reveal amulets and jewelry incorporated within the wrappings. Over the next few days, as the layers of bandages were removed, Burton would photograph the position of amulets and jewelry, and then Carter would remove them. Then another layer of bandages could be removed and the process repeated.

They started by peeling away layers of bandages on the lower part of the mummy, eventually revealing Tutankhamun's gold sandals (see Color Plate 12). Then the arms were bared, and on the following day rings were removed from the pharaoh's hands and bracelets from his arms. As this was going on, the mummy of Tutankhamun was being removed from the coffin in pieces. The biggest problem was the torso, which was firmly glued to the bottom of the gold coffin.

First Derry tried to chisel the mummy free, and then he switched to heated knives, both operations causing considerable damage to the already fragile body. Finally, in desperation, he cut the mummy in half at the third lumbar vertebra so it could be removed in sections. Derry's treatment of the mummy shows how carelessly the physical evidence that might have revealed the cause of Tutankhamen's death was treated. Carter had little idea of how much information could be gained by a careful examination, so he abandoned the mummy to Derry's rough handling. If Tutankhamun's throne had been stuck in the unguents, I doubt Carter would have permitted it to be sawed in half. The unguents would have been chemically analyzed and a solvent devised to free the throne without damage. Not so for poor Tutankhamun. The mummy was in bad shape when Derry started to work on it, but it was in far worse condition when he finished.

The King Is a Boy

There were some benefits to the rough treatment Tutankhamun's mummy received. Tutankhamun's arms and legs had become disarticulated from their joints, so Derry could clearly see the tops and bottoms of the long bones. This enabled him to estimate the approximate age of death for Tutankhamun. In young people, the ends of the long bones, the epiphyses, are loosely connected by cartilage that becomes bone as the person ages. This is one of the reasons young people are more flexible than old folks—cartilage flexes, bones break. We know the average age at which the epiphyses join to the long bones, and the degree of this union is a reliable criterion of age. In the case of Tutankhamun, the kneecap could easily be lifted to examine the lower end of the femur, the longest bone in the body. The union of the tip of the lower end of the femur with the main shaft takes place at about the age of twenty. Here Derry could see cartilage; the union was not yet complete. Tutankhamun was under twenty years of age. At the top of the femur is the great trochanter—the part that fits into your hip and is what is replaced when you need a hip replacement. This part unites with the shaft at around eighteen or nineteen years of age. Here the head of the femur was solidly fixed to the neck of the bone, but Derry could still just see the line of the union. Derry concluded Tutankhamun was less than twenty but over eighteen at the time of death. His estimate was accurate and still holds today.

There were other age indicators that Derry used, most of them still standard today. One was the eruption of the molars, which follow a fairly predictable schedule. So it is not surprising that Derry would want to confirm his other observations with the state of Tutankhamun's molars. In the appendix to Carter's second volume on the excavation, Derry observed, "The right upper and lower wisdom teeth had just erupted the gum and reached to about half the height of the second molar. Those on the left side were not so easily seen but appeared to be in the same stage of eruption."[4] This all makes sense and would again place the boy-king's age between eighteen and nineteen at the time of his death. But how did Derry examine the molars? If we look at the photos of Tutankhamun's head, we can see that his mouth was closed (Figure 5.2). You can't see the molars. X-rays would have done it, but Tutankhamun was not X-rayed till decades later. Again, how did Derry examine the molars? The answer is that he cut the skin that is around the mandible, pulling down a semicircular flap so he could look inside from the bottom. Then, using some of the readily available black sticky stuff from the coffins, he glued the flap back up and never told anyone.[5] There were lots of things Derry did to the mummy that he never mentioned—like the damage done to the head in removing it from the Gold Mask.

Part of the reason for the rough treatment of Tutankhamun's mummy is Derry's background—he was an anatomist. Anatomists dissect bodies, they don't preserve them. In an era before mummy studies, even Derry didn't realize how much information is contained in a mummy. Still, he knew he

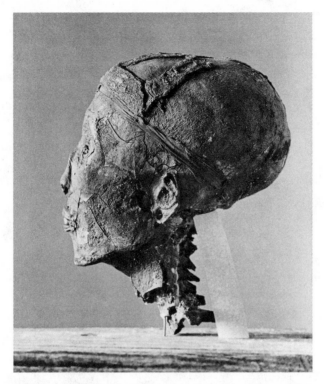

Figure 5.2. The head of Tutankhamun is almost exactly the same shape as that of the mummy found in KV-55. (Courtesy of the Metropolitan Museum of Art, Department of Egyptian Art Archives.)

had manhandled the body, and he covered it up. I should point out that my trouble with Derry is about how he mistreated the body. As an anatomist, he was quite good and his observations about Tutankhamun's age and so on have held up over the years.

After Derry was done with his examination, the Antiquities Service decided that because Tutankhamun was the only pharaoh ever found undisturbed in his tomb, he should remain there. So the body was reassembled on a wooden litter filled with sand in such a way as to conceal the damage done (Figure 5.3). The arms are crossed, hiding the cut across the lumbar region. But if you look closely, you can see that the bones are disarticulated; this is, clearest at the shoulders. The tray was put inside the outer coffin and then lowered into the sarcophagus, where it remained for more than half a century, undisturbed.

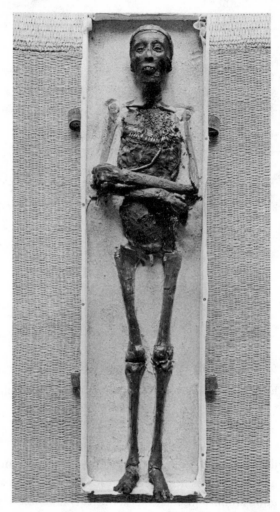

Figure 5.3. After the mummy was removed from the coffin, the parts were reassembled on a sand tray. (Courtesy of the Metropolitan Museum of Art Archives.)

Derry was also able to establish that Tutankhamen was about five feet six inches in height, slight of build, with no obvious cause of death ascertainable. Interestingly, the two guardian statues from the Antechamber are almost exactly six feet six inches tall.

With Tutankhamun out of the gold coffin, Carter and Lucas could proceed with the very difficult task of separating the gold coffin from the second coffin, to which it was still solidly stuck.

A Dangerous Maneuver

Lucas determined that considerably more heat would be required to separate the two coffins. The coffins were now resting on the two trestles across the sarcophagus, so they were lifted and suspended from the block and tackle. Then they were turned upside down, with the concave part toward the ground—like carrying a canoe. Extreme heat was going to be applied, and the hope was that one coffin would slide out from the other. But the heat couldn't be applied directly; the wood of the outer coffin or the gold of the inner one couldn't survive the heat that would be needed. So the gold coffin was protected with zinc plates and wet blankets were placed on the other coffin. A series of Primus paraffin lamps were turned on full blast to provide the heat. After a few hours there was movement: the gold coffin was beginning to slide downward and separate from the second coffin. The lamps were turned off, and for the next hour gravity did the work—the coffins separated enough so that the wood shell of the second coffin could be pulled from the bottom of the gold coffin. Both coffins, now separated, were still covered in the tar-like coating of ancient oils, which would take months to remove. When tourists at the Egyptian Museum see the gold coffin and the second coffin, they appreciate their beauty, but have no idea what an effort it was to restore them to their original glory.

As we have seen, Carter was working with a greatly reduced team, but he was very fortunate to have Lucas assisting. Lucas, the chemist, could determine at what temperatures the different substances would melt, and so know how much heat could be applied. Further, he could analyze the oils and figure out that acetone would dissolve the oils and not damage the coffins. He also determined that applying melted wax to keep the inlays in place would not damage anything and was reversible.

With the mummy back in the sarcophagus and the coffins separated, the drama was over. There would be no more difficult logistical maneuvers—no fragile shines to dismantle, no cracked lids to raise, no coffins stuck together with resin. Even the press frenzy subsided. The discovery and clearing of the Antechamber had created one kind of interest—in the treasure. The Burial Chamber created a different kind of interest. Here the focus was on the mummy. Tutankhamun would finally be revealed. There was the bonus of the solid gold coffin, but "King Tut" was the star. The public now knew for certain that they had a boy-king who died tragically early. The hubbub had subsided, and Carter liked it that way. He could do what he did best: work in peace and quiet.

6

Final Clearance

It was now four years since the discovery of the tomb, and despite the political distractions, Carter being locked out, and other problems, a great deal had been accomplished. The Antechamber had been completely cleared and its treasures conserved and shipped to Cairo. Although work inside the Burial Chamber had been completed, it was far from empty. The large shrines had been dismantled, but the larger panels were still leaning against the walls of the Burial Chamber. The panels had to be crated before they could be moved, and then the hole in the wall Carter and Carnarvon had made to enter the Burial Chamber would have to be enlarged to get the panels out. That would be the last step in clearing the tomb. The Burial Chamber also still contained the sarcophagus and, inside it, the outer coffin containing Tutankhamun on the sand tray.

Carter's job was made more difficult because of visitors to the tomb. While he was working, tourists were permitted to visit two days a week, but because the lid of the outer coffin was in place, most never knew Tutankhamun was inside. With the shrine panels leaning against the walls, they would leave with a feeling that this was a work in progress, history in the making.

The tourist season began in earnest in late November, so Carter arrived in September, knowing he could get a few months of work in before tourists would be admitted. Then, on the two days each week the tomb was open for visits, he would turn to conservation of the objects. It was a schedule that worked.

The Treasury

On October 23, 1926, Carter entered into his diary: "The first outermost coffin containing the King's Mummy, finally rewrapped, was lowered into the sarcophagus this morning. We are now ready to begin upon the investigation of the Store Room"—that is, the Treasury.[1] Carter says the mummy was "rewrapped," but it wasn't. It was so disarticulated that rewrapping would have been extremely difficult, so it was merely reassembled on a sand tray, as we have seen.

The job remaining for Carter and Lucas was to clear the two storage rooms. The one off the Antechamber later became known as the Annex, and the one off the Burial Chamber became known as the Treasury. Both were crammed with fragile objects that would have to be photographed, removed, conserved, and then sent to Cairo. It would take years, but Carter and Lucas were patient men. They begin with the Treasury.

Early in the discovery, Carter had boarded up the Treasury to protect its contents while they were working on the Antechamber and the Burial Chamber. Now with the boards removed, he could peer in and see a statue of Anubis, god of mummification, guarding the Treasury (Figure 6.1). In ancient Egypt, jackals were associated with death and mummification. There is a practical reason for this. The digestive system of the jackal lacks the enzymes that break down animal proteins, so jackals don't like fresh meat. They prefer their meat predigested by bacteria, so they prowl cemeteries, looking for rotting meat. When the ancient Egyptians saw jackals in cemeteries, they associated them with death, and the jackal became an important part of the Egyptian pantheon.

Not every jackal god was Anubis, the god of mummification. There was also Wepwaat, who guided the deceased to the next world. His name is composed of two words: *wep*, "open," ᗄ and *waat*, "road," ⚊ because he was the "opener of the ways." Then there was Duamutef, one of the four sons of Horus, who guarded the internal organs of the deceased. But the main jackal was clearly Anubis, who presided over mummification and set the process of immortality in motion. During mummification, a priest wearing a jackal mask represented the god. So it was appropriate that looking out of the Treasury, protecting the king's mummy, was a life-sized Anubis sitting on his shrine.

Figure 6.1. A life-sized statue of Anubis, the jackal god of mummification, guarded the Treasury.

The purpose of mummification was to preserve the mummy for resurrection in the west. Contrary to what many occultists believe, the Egyptians did not believe in reincarnation. They believed you were on earth only once and then you resurrected in the west. This wasn't just a spiritual resurrection; it was physical, so you would need your body—all of it. But the internal organs were a problem. Because the internal organs are so moist, they would decay if left inside the body. So, at the time of mummification, the internal organs were removed, covered in a naturally occurring compound called natron—basically salt and baking soda—that would dehydrate the organs. So long as there is no moisture, bacteria will not act on them and the tissue will last indefinitely.

Once the internal organs were dehydrated, they were placed in four special vases called canopic jars. Often the lids of the jars were fashioned like the heads of the sons of Horus. There was Duamutef, who was jackal-headed (see Color Plate 13); Qebesenuf, falcon-headed; Hapi, baboon-headed; and Imsety, human-headed. In early books on Egyptology, it was often said that there was one jar for each organ (liver, stomach, intestines, and lungs), but this doesn't really make sense, for you have more than four organs. What about the spleen? Gallbladder? The Egyptian embalmers simply fit whatever they removed into four jars.

In antiquity and throughout the Middle Ages, it was believed that the ancient Egyptians were the most advanced in the study of anatomy because they practiced mummification. Not so. In anatomy class in medical school you make a large abdominal flap in the cadaver so you can clearly see the relative position of the organs, the blood vessels, and so on. The ancient Egyptians, however, because they wanted to keep the body as intact as possible, removed the internal organs through a three-and-a-half-inch incision on the left side of the abdomen. Then they reached inside and blindly cut out whatever they could feel. You don't learn much anatomy that way.

In 1994 I mummified a human cadaver in the ancient Egyptian style to figure out how the embalmers did it.[2] I was working with a colleague, Ron Wade, who was director of the State Anatomy Board for Maryland. I had just about finished the evisceration and asked Ron, "Where's the gallbladder?" He replied, "It came with the liver." I simply hadn't seen it. I suspect the same was true of the ancient embalmers. There is no Egyptian word for "gallbladder," probably because they didn't know it existed.

There was a similar situation with the kidneys. When I examine ancient Egyptian mummies, quite often the kidneys are still in place. Why? Because they didn't know they were there. If you have already taken out the stomach, liver, intestines, et cetera, and reach inside the abdominal cavity through the three-and-a-half-inch incision, the body cavity will feel empty because the kidneys are behind a thick smooth membrane, the peritoneum. Many embalmers simply didn't know they were there. They didn't have anatomy classes. No one would give up his body for medical science; everyone wanted to be immortal.

So mummification wasn't what many people think. It was a bit haphazard, with whatever organs that came out through the small incision being placed in the four canopic jars. Tutankhamun's canopic set was unique. They were enclosed in a spectacular gilded wooden shrine with four goddesses (Isis, Nephthys, Neith, and Selket) spreading their arms, protecting the king's internal organs (Figure 6.2). Unlike the huge nested shrines that surrounded the sarcophagus in the Burial Chamber, there was plenty of room to take the canopic shrine apart, revealing the container for the pharaoh's organs. It was quite something.

Figure 6.2. A canopic shrine protected the chest that contained Tutankhamun's internal organs.

Carved out of a single block of alabaster was not jars but a canopic chest (Figure 6.3). Once again, around the chest were the four protective goddesses. The lid of the chest was tied to the chest by a rope that bore the seal of the royal necropolis—Anubis above nine bound captives. The nine prisoners represent the nine traditional enemies of Egypt, sometimes called the Nine Bows, including the Assyrians, Nubians, and Hittites. If you look at a statue of a seated pharaoh, frequently under his feet will be the Nine Bows.

Inside, the alabaster shrine was carved to form four square chambers, each with a lid in the shape of a pharaoh's head. Although the chambers seemed intended to hold the internal organs, when the lids were removed the truth was revealed: the compartments were only five inches deep, and

Figure 6.3. The canopic chest was carved out of a large block of alabaster. (Photo by George B. Johnson.)

did not take the place of the four traditional canopic jars. Rather, inside each compartment was a beautiful miniature gold coffin, each a tiny replica of Tutankhamun's second coffin (Figure 6.4). Inside the four coffinettes, wrapped in linen, were the internal organs of Tutankhamun. The miniature coffins, like the full-sized coffins, had oils poured over them as part of the funeral ritual.

Almost all the objects in the Treasury related to Tutankhamun's quest for immortality. Some, such as the canopic chest containing the internal organs, were involved in the mummification of the deceased king, but preservation of the body was only the first step toward immortality. Other objects were intended for the time after resurrection, when the king would be living in the west. The most numerous of these items were the miniature servant statues. The Egyptians believed that the next world was going to be pretty much like this one, and because the daily life of ancient Egyptians centered around agriculture, they viewed the next world also as primarily agrarian. The deceased would have to plant the fields and maintain irrigation canals, so they had hundreds of little servant statues, the ushabtis, buried in their tombs to do their bidding. Because these little statuettes were funerary, they

Figure 6.4. Four miniature coffins contained Tutankhamun's internal organs. (Courtesy Metropolitan Museum of Art, Department of Egyptian Art Archives.)

were shaped like mummies, but their hands protruded from the bandages, holding farm implements, so they could still work. As noted in Chapter 1, on the front of these little statues was a magical spell to make them come to life: "When my name is called to work on the land, answer 'Here I am' in my name . . ."

During Tutankhamun's time, it was common for the deceased to have 365 servant statues, one for each day of the year. Sometimes the number was even larger, with an extra overseer ushabti for each ten workers. The quality of these statues varied, depending upon what a person could afford. For the

poorer Egyptians, they were simple affairs made out of clay, with few rec-
ognizable features and no hieroglyphs. Some of the larger ushabtis for the
wealthy Egyptians were made of faience, a ceramic material that was fired in
a kiln; these were often beautiful works of art. Tutankhamun's are extraordinary. All of his ushabtis are individual sculptures, in either wood or stone,
with the features of the boy-king. Carter found 413 of them in the Treasury,
and more would be found later when the Annex was excavated. Each little
worker had his own farm implements, ready to serve the king, On the soles
of the feet of six of the statues are hieroglyphic inscriptions. One reads:
"Made by the king's scribe, the General, Min-Nekht, for his lord, the Osiris,
the King, Neb-Kheperu-Re, justified." Tutankhamun is called "the Osiris"
because like Osiris in the myth of Isis and Osiris, he will resurrect and live
forever. The phrase at the end, "justified," refers to the ancient Egyptian belief that before you entered the next world you would be judged to see if
you had been a good person, worthy of being admitted to the next world.

The deceased had to enter the Hall of the Double Truth, where he
would be judged by a tribunal of forty-two gods. Here he had to "separate
himself from his evil-doings" by making a "negative plea."[3] He would deny
having done a long list of specific wrongdoings: "I have not diverted the
irrigation canal," "I have not cursed the gods," "I have not slaughtered the
divine cattle," and so forth. If he passed the test, the gods would declare
him "true of voice" and he could be admitted into the next world. Thus
Tutankhamun, on his ushabtis, is called "True of Voice."

Several ushabtis were given by other officials. The inscription on the
bottom of another one reads: "Made by the servant who is beneficial to
his lord, Neb-Kheperu-Re, the Overseer of the Treasury, Maya." Clearly,
Tutankhamun had officials who were dedicated to him even after his death.

An Unexpected Tragedy

Hidden among all the traditional funerary items in the Treasury was one
that no one expected. In a simple wooden box were two miniature wood
anthropoid coffins, coated with black resin, suggesting there had been a
funeral for the contents of these coffins. Inscriptions on the outside of the
coffins didn't give any indication of what was inside. One of the first to spot
them was Alan Gardiner, who noticed them from a distance when he peered

into the Treasury. He wrote to his wife, Heddie, that he couldn't tell if they were mummies of babies or servant statues.[4] There were no names, merely the designation "Osiris," as if inside were the unnamed dead (Figure 6.5). But what could these miniature coffins contain? The coffins were sealed with the stamp of the royal necropolis, indicating a royal burial. When the seals were broken and the coffins opened, two even smaller gilded coffins were revealed. Inside them were two neatly wrapped miniature mummies. One was slightly more than a foot long, and the other was approximately ten inches. Carter removed the wrappings from the smaller of the two and was shocked to find a human fetus (Figure 6.6). Carter quickly realized the

Figure 6.5. Two mysterious miniature coffins were found inside the Treasury. (Courtesy Metropolitan Museum of Art, Department of Egyptian Art Archives.)

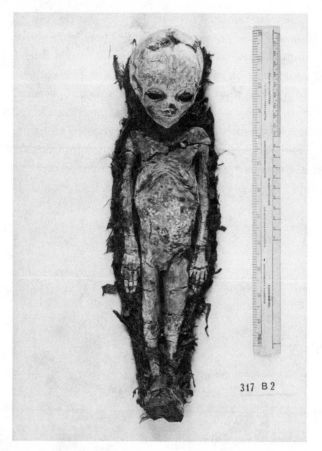

Figure 6.6. The larger bundle contained a seven- or eight-month-old female fetus, probably a miscarriage of Ankhesenamun. (Courtesy Metropolitan Museum of Art, Department of Egyptian Art Archives.)

significance. These two fetuses were almost certainly the miscarriages of Tutankhamun's teenage wife, Ankhesenamun. If they had lived and continued the royal line, the history of the end of the Eighteenth Dynasty might have been quite different. Because they were never born, they weren't given names, so on their coffins they were merely called "Osiris."

Carter was not a mummy person; he usually left mummies to others. I have always wondered: why did he unwrap the little mummy? He didn't have to unwrap it. He could have had it X-rayed, and he would have known what was inside without damaging the fetus. He just didn't think.

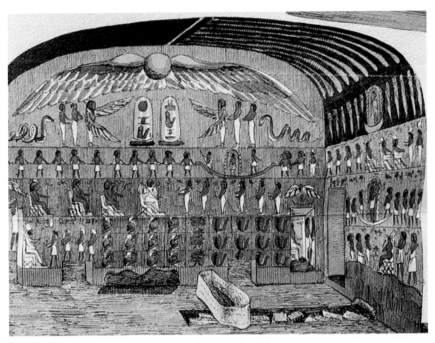

Color Plate 1. The Italian adventurer Giovanni Belzoni discovered the tomb of King Seti I, with its spectacular alabaster sarcophagus still in place.

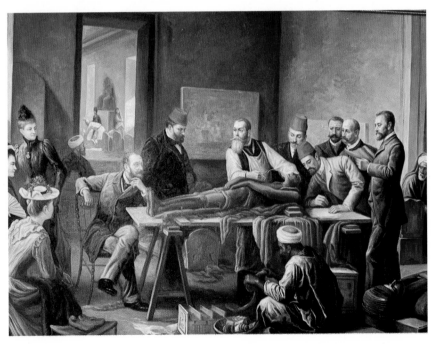

Color Plate 2. The unwrapping of the royal mummies was more a social event than scientific research, and little was learned. (Painting by Paul Philippoteaux.)

Color Plate 3. Young Carter began his career copying paintings of birds at the tombs at Beni Hasan.

THOTHMES I.

Color Plate 4. Young Howard Carter worked at Deir el Bahri for several seasons and refined his copying techniques there.

Color Plate 5. Carter not only excavated the tomb of Queen Hatshepsut for Theodore Davis, but also supplied illustrations for Davis's lavish publication. Here Hatshepsut wears the false beard of the pharaoh.

Color Plate 6. Before Carter and Carnarvon entered the tomb, newspapers speculated what it might look like. (From *Le Pèlerin*, January 24, 1923.)

Color Plate 7. The backrest of the gold throne shows the young couple in an intimate pose—unusual for Egyptian royal art. (Photo by Pat Remler.)

Color Plate 8. The gold throne still bears Tutankhamun's original name, Tutankhaten. (Photo by Pat Remler.)

Color Plate 9. When the king is hunting, Ankhesenamun holds his next arrow. (Photo by George B. Johnson.)

Color Plate 10. On the small gold shrine, Tutankhamun and Ankhesenamun are always touching. (Photo by George B. Johnson.)

Color Plate 11. After lifting the sarcophagus lid, the excavators had their first glimpse of the first of three nested coffins. (Photo by George B. Johnson.)

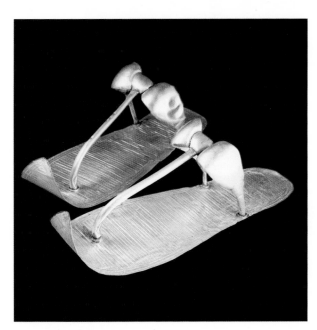

Color Plate 12. Tutankhamun's gold funerary sandals. (Photo by George B. Johnson.)

Color Plate 13. Traditionally, the lid of one of the four canopic jars containing the mummy's internal organs was in the shape of the jackal god Duamutef. (Photo by Pat Remler.)

Color Plate 14. The outside of the outermost shrine is decorated with knots of Isis and *djd* pillars—magical proactive amulets. (Photo Griffith Institute.)

Color Plate 15. Fifteen years before Carter discovered Tutankhamun's chariots, he did this painting of the chariot found in the tomb of Yuya and Tuya, Tutankhamun's great-grandparents.

He didn't unwrap the larger one, and the fetuses remained unexamined for years. In 1932 Carter sent both to Kasr el Einy Hospital in Cairo to be examined by Professor Douglas Derry in the Anatomy Department. Derry determined that the unwrapped smaller fetus was female, with an intra-uterine age of about five months. He couldn't tell if it had been mummi-fied. He unwrapped the second, larger mummy, revealing a second female fetus, which he estimated to be about seven months. Four inches longer than her sister, this child was developed enough to have been embalmed. Across the left side of the abdomen ran an embalmer's incision less than an inch long. The abdominal cavity was stuffed with linen, but Derry says nothing about the internal organs, which were probably still inside. Had they been removed, tiny canopic jars would have been provided.

Derry could see that despite the fetus's small size, the embalmers had removed the brain and forced linen into the cranium. Never one to worry about preserving a mummy, Derry broke through the cranium to remove the linen and found there a wire used to force the fabric into the skull. This is the only embalmer's tool ever found inside a mummy. Derry threw it away. He never returned the fetuses to Carter, nor did he turn them over to the Egyptian Museum in Cairo. For decades the location of the fetuses was unknown.

Derry said of the smaller fetus that "there is no abdominal incision and no indication of how it was preserved." Why would one be mummified and not the other? I contacted Dr. Fawzi Gabella, head of Kasr el Einy Hospital's Anatomy Department, to see if he could locate the mummies. Without hesitation, Gabella told me he had the mummies and I was invited to come to the hospital to examine them.

Gabella's wife, Zaizafon H. Badawy, also an anatomist teaching at the hospital, greeted me. Both she and her husband were eager to see what we could learn about the fetuses. They ushered me into a storage room piled high with small wooden boxes with intriguing labels: "Middle Kingdom Princess?" "Old Kingdom Head Only." Gabella located two small wood boxes, slightly larger than shoe boxes. When the lids were removed, we were face-to-face with Tutankhamun and Ankhesenamun's children.

I had brought Harry Burton's photographs of the fetuses, taken when they were first discovered. In the seventy years since the photographs, the fetuses had deteriorated somewhat, but because of this deterioration, I was able to answer my question about mummification of the smaller fetus. The cranial bones of the smaller fetus were now disarticulated, allowing us to see that, just as with the larger fetus, linen had been packed in the skull. Also, the skin on the abdomen was cracked, revealing a bit of linen protruding from the abdominal cavity. The smaller mummy had indeed been embalmed. Remembering how much Derry had damaged the mummy of Tutankhamun, I didn't even want to touch the extremely fragile fetuses; I just looked. It is undeniable that Derry's handling of the three mummies in Tutankhamun's tomb was irresponsible, causing irreparable damage, and that a great deal of valuable information was lost. But Derry was working in an era when the field of mummy studies was in its infancy and he shared the attitude of most of his predecessors, who believed that mummies in themselves were of little value.

The Deir el Bahri cache of royal mummies found in 1881 had the potential of providing considerable data on royal mummification techniques, yet the mummies were ravaged by notable Egyptologists who did not know what to look for, nor did they take the time to make careful notes when they performed an unwrapping. Gaston Maspero, director of the Antiquities Service, was in France when the mummies were transported from Luxor to Cairo, so it was Émile Brugsch, his assistant, who began their unwrapping. Chastising him in the official report, Maspero wrote, "Within the first few weeks of their arrival at Boulaq, Mr. Émile Brugsch could not resist the desire to see for the first time one of their faces, and opened, without permission, and during my absence, the mummy of Tuthmosis III." Occupied with translating the coffin's inscriptions and the labels on the mummies, Maspero waited several years before unwrapping the mummies. But when he began, he was in a frenzy, tearing through one mummy after another. By order of the khedive of Egypt, on June 1, 1886, the mummy of Ramses II was unwrapped. Attending were the khedive, his entire council of ministers, various doctors, archaeologists, artists, and others.

In his report, Maspero attempts to create the impression that everything was done scientifically and with caution. He explains that every measurement was taken by two of those present, then verified by two other attendants.[5] In truth, the proceedings were shoddy. Maspero unwrapped *three* mummies that day, two kings and a queen. This was bad Egyptology. The next week, in a single day, Maspero unwrapped the mummies of Seti I, Seqenenre Tao II, and Ahmose I. In less than a month, between June 9 and July 1, twenty-one mummies of the Deir el Bahri cache were stripped of their wrappings. One can only wonder what Maspero's hurry was. This was how royal mummies were treated, and Derry's treatment of the mummies in Tutankhamun's tomb followed this tradition. The fetuses were the last big surprise in the Treasury, which took two years to clear. When that was done, Carter and Lucas moved on to the Annex.

The Annex

The Annex was quite different from the Treasury. The Treasury was relatively well organized. Almost everything had to do with the burial and life after death, and despite the break-in by ancient thieves, it was in relatively good order. The Annex, however, was a mess. Things were randomly piled on top of one another. Carter felt that the room had been plundered twice, but the officials who were responsible for restoring order were lax in their duties. Jars that clearly had originally been in the Annex were found by Carter in the Antechamber, where the thieves had dropped them three thousand years ago. But it wasn't just the inefficiency of the officials that caused the mess. There had been two robberies, and the robbers were looking for quite different things in each. In the first case, the robbers were looking for the obvious—gold. The second break-in involved the dozens of jars that were stored in the Annex.

Tutankhamun's Wine Cellar

The jars fell into two distinct categories. There were thirty-four clay wine jars shaped something like traditional amphorae. For the most part, these were left untouched by the robbers. Modern wine bottles have printed labels; Tutankhamun's wine cellar had the information handwritten on the jars. It told the year, the vineyard, and even the vintner's name. Tut's wine came primarily from two vineyards: the Estate of Aton and the Estate of Tutankhamun. The wine-growing area in ancient Egypt was the Delta, in the north. Sometimes the jars were labeled "wine of good quality." Of all the jars, only four were labeled "sweet." Tutankhamun liked his wine dry.[6] Some of the jars seem to have been family heirlooms. One was dated to year 31 of the reign of Amenhotep III, Tutankhamun's grandfather, which would make the wine about thirty-five years old when put in the boy-king's tomb. These wine jars were not touched by the thieves. The other jars were.

The Great Unguent Heist

Unlike the simple clay wine jars in the Annex, there were elaborately carved alabaster vessels in the Treasury; all had been emptied of the contents they once held. By analyzing the residue in the bottom of the jars, Lucas was able to determine that they had once held oils and unguents. Carter had found some empty alabaster jars on the floor of the Antechamber when he first cleared it several years earlier. With all these clues, Carter put together a scenario describing what had happened in Tutankhamun's tomb three thousand years ago.

Soon after the burial, thieves entered the tomb and searched the Antechamber, the Treasury, and the Annex looking for gold and other portable valuables. This is when they dropped the five gold rings tied in a piece of linen that Carter found in the Antechamber. When the necropolis officials discovered the tomb had been robbed, they put things back in order as best they could and resealed the tomb. Some time later, but not much later, the second robbery took place, perhaps even by the same thieves. Like the first robbery, they had to tunnel through the rubble covering the steps to the tomb and through the rubble that filled the passageway, and then break through the resealed wall that led to the Antechamber. Their loot was not gold; they knew that was gone already. Rather, they were intending to steal the oils in the alabaster jars. This robbery revealed to Carter and other Egyptologists just how valuable oils must have been in ancient Egypt, as the thieves were willing to risk their lives to steal them.

This second robbery had to have been carefully planned. The heavy alabaster jars when filled with oils would have been too heavy and clumsy to carry through the tunnel they had made in the rubble. So the robbers brought bags made out of skins, like wineskins, to empty the oils into and bring them to the surface of the Valley of the Kings.[7] When Carter cleared the rubble, he found one of these skins that the thieves had left behind. Because the Annex was a relatively small room, some of the alabaster jars had to be brought into the Antechamber by the thieves for emptying and were left there.

To get to the alabaster jars, which were up against the walls, the thieves had to move other objects out of the Treasury, so they dumped them helter-skelter in the Antechamber, which explained the disorder Carter found, with objects piled on top of each other. Did the oil thieves get away with it? Were they caught and executed? How did they sell the oils, and to whom? Perhaps one day a papyrus chronicling the trial of the thieves will be found. More likely, we will never know.

Tutankhamun's Magic Trick

In the 1970s, when I used to take my students on study tours of Egypt, we would visit the Egyptian Museum in Cairo, where the Tutankhamun objects were kept on the second floor. Off to the side, rarely visited, was an alabaster vase. I would show it to the students and explain that the elaborate handles were of the god Heh, who holds two palm fronds. Heh is presenting Tutankhamun with "millions of years." A million was the largest number the Egyptians could write, and the hieroglyph is great fun. It shows a man with his hands in the air in amazement, like "Wow, a million!" 𓁨 Once I had explained all this to my students, I would ask them to look inside the vase and then look at the outside, so they could see that both surfaces were undecorated. Then I would walk over to an unmarked light switch on the wall and flip it. Presto! A scene of Ankhesenamun and Tutankhamun, both seated, appears *inside* the alabaster (Figure 6.7).

An ancient artist had devised a trick to delight his young king and queen. The secret is that there is a second carved alabaster liner that fits perfectly inside the vase. The scene is painted on the outside of this inner liner, and when the vase is illuminated, the scene appears.

I did this for years, but sometime in the 1990s, either the switch went or the bulb in the vase burned out; the magic was gone. The lamp was recently moved to the new Grand Egyptian Museum, and I hope they give it a place of honor where all can enjoy King Tut's magic trick.

Agreement at Last

While Carter and Lucas were emptying the Annex, Carter was also working out a final settlement for Lady Carnarvon with the Antiquities Service.

Figure 6.7. Tutankhamun's elaborate lamp was really a magic trick. (Griffith Institute p0659B.)

Recall that the original concession agreement between Carnarvon and the Antiquities Service had stated that if the tomb had been plundered, a division of the finds could be expected. Thus, Carter and Carnarvon could reasonably expect to receive something. When the political situation changed and Carter was locked out, Lady Carnarvon, who now had the concession, gave up all legal rights to objects from the tomb. Still, Carter was assured that the Antiquities Service would be generous to Lady Carnarvon, giving her duplicate objects that it was not necessary for Egypt to keep for scientific purposes. However, by 1930 the government had changed once again and it was clear that no Tutankhamen objects would leave Egypt. Nevertheless, the concession still required that Lady Carnarvon be compensated for expenses incurred during the excavation. Lawyers were involved in the negotiations, and in the end Lady Carnarvon received £35,867, a considerable amount for the time and one that almost everyone involved felt was fair. Lady Carnarvon gave nearly one-quarter of that to Carter for the exceptional services he had rendered both to her and to her husband. Throughout the years, Carter had demonstrated his loyalty to Lady Carnarvon and the deep responsibility he felt to protect her interests.

So now it was finally decided: no Tutankhamun objects would leave Egypt. As we will see later, however, this is not exactly what happened.

Done at Last

When Carter and Lucas completed emptying the Annex, they still had another important task to complete. One of the most difficult parts of the entire excavation had been dismantling the giant nested shrines that surrounded the sarcophagus in the Burial Chamber. The panels forming those shrines had remained in the tomb for all the years of excavation, leaning against the walls. They were originally made of sturdy wood that was carved with hieroglyphs and figures of the gods, inlaid with faience amulets., and finally covered with gold leaf. Over the centuries the wood had dried and shrunk, pulling away from the inlays and gold foil, which was barely clinging to its surface. In 1928 Lucas, working inside the tomb, had brushed nearly a thousand pounds of paraffin wax on the surfaces of the shrines to stabilize them and keep the gold from flaking off.[8] This was a conservation technique that required a great deal of skill, but Lucas had worked out how much wax and how much heat. The virtue was that it was nondestructive and reversible: later the wax could be removed with the application of a bit of heat. Even with the panels stabilized, they waited several more years before removing them from the tomb.

In spite of all their efforts, the panels were still quite fragile and had to be crated in the tomb before they could be moved. This, in turn, would require enlarging the breach in the wall they had made when the tomb was first opened, and they wanted to wait for the very end to do this. As usual for Carter and Lucas, their careful techniques and patience meant that opening the wall and removing the panels went off without a hitch.

Millions of visitors to the Egyptian Museum in Cairo have wondered at the massive and beautiful shrines. They have Carter and Lucas to thank.

The great founder of scientific Egyptology, Sir Finders Petrie, summed it up in a letter to Percy Newberry when Carter and Lucas first began work on the tomb: "We can only say how lucky it is all in the hands of Carter and Lucas."[9] How right he was.

The Long Decline

At the end of the 1931–1932 season, work on the tomb was completed and Carter brought out the third and final volume of *The Tomb of Tut. Ankh.Amen.* It contained two appendixes. The first was Derry's report of his examination of the two fetuses. It was three pages long. The second was by Lucas, the chemist who had faithfully worked with Carter for ten years excavating the tomb. It is simply called "The Chemistry of the Tomb."

The three-volume set was never intended as the final word on Carter's work on the tomb and its treasures. The set was a popular work, intended to inform the general public about the excavation. Carter planned a six-volume scientific publication of all aspects of the discovery that was to have Sir Alan Gardiner's translations of the texts on the shrines and coffins, detailed chemical analyses of the materials used in the mummification, essays on ancient Egyptian religion as revealed by the objects in the tomb, and other features. But after the work in the tomb was completed, Carter seems to have lost interest in the project. Indeed, he seems to have lost interest in Tutankhamun. He could have done another lecture tour, but none was ever planned. He could have written popular articles for magazines, but he didn't.

For his remaining years, he was surprisingly alone. He still spent winters in Luxor at his house, Castle Carter, but seldom had visitors. Often he would go to the Winter Palace Hotel for a drink, where visiting tourists would recognize him and strike up a conversation. The Metropolitan Museum of Art excavation team was still working on the west bank, but he wasn't a regular guest for dinner with the team, nor did he seem to have any close friends there. Over the years his favorite niece, Phyllis Walker, came to visit for part of the season, but she seems to be the only one to have stayed for any length of time.

In London, where he kept his flat, it was pretty much the same thing. He had plenty of invitations to dinner parties, but as far as one can tell, he had no close friends. Among his Egyptological colleagues, Percy Newberry was the only one with whom he remained in close contact. The money Carter earned during his American lecture tour, combined with Lady Carnarvon's generosity, made Carter relatively comfortable in his retirement, able to dine out when he chose and travel where he liked. But as mentioned before, he seems to have lost interest in Tutankhamun. He never even attempted to bring out the definitive six-volume set on the excavation that he had planned. Now he had plenty of time to work on it, but no desire. Indeed, he seems to have lost all interest in Egyptology in general. There were lectures at the Egypt Exploration Society in London, but he didn't attend them. It is as if he were experiencing postpartum depression following the closing of the excavation.

In his last years, he suffered from cancer (Hodgkin's lymphoma) and was cared for by his niece Phyllis. Howard Carter died at home on March 2, 1939. He was sixty-five years old. As far as we can tell, no Egyptologist attended his funeral at Putney Vale cemetery in London. Carter had made out his will in 1931 and named Harry Burton, his photographer, as one of the two executors of his estate. The other executor, Bruce Ingram, also had a connection with the tomb. Ingram was the editor of the *Illustrated London News*. Carter had had many business dealings with Ingram when he supplied drawings and information about Tutankhamun to the periodical. Ingram wasn't a close friend, but obviously Carter trusted him.

The will tells us something about Carter. He remembered his faithful native supervisor of the excavation, Abd-el Ahmed, and left him 150 Egyptian pounds, which was equivalent to several hundred dollars, a significant amount for the time. His house at the entrance to the Valley of the Kings he left to the Metropolitan Museum of Art, whose staff had been crucial throughout the clearing of the tomb. And to his niece Phyllis he left the remainder of his estate, saying, "And I strongly recommend to her that she consult my executors as to the selling of any Egyptian or other antiquities included in the bequest."[10] This is where Burton's Egyptological background was crucial. Carter's small collection of Egyptian antiquities included several pieces with Tutankhamun's name on them that could be traced to the tomb. Burton knew to advise Phyllis not to sell these, as it would damage Carter's reputation. But what should be done with the objects? Phyllis and the executors agreed they should be discreetly given back to the Antiquities Service, perhaps in a diplomatic pouch. But Rex

Engelbach, head of the Egyptian Museum in Cairo, had never been on good terms with Carter and was not cooperating. Carter had been a difficult man, and many wanted it known he had taken objects from the tomb. Then World War II broke out, and it would be nearly seven years before the objects were returned to Egypt.

Finally, after the war, a solution was reached. Egypt's King Farouk offered to help. The objects were turned over to the Egyptian embassy in London, flown to Egypt, and given to the king to present to the museum. No one dared question His Majesty about their origin.

By discreetly returning the Tutankhamun artifacts to the Egyptian Museum, Burton, Phyllis Walker, and others involved were trying to protect Carter's legacy. But, unknowingly, they may also have been protecting Lord Carnarvon's reputation. When Carter was asked by Lady Carnarvon to sell her recently deceased husband's collection of Egyptian antiquities, Carter held back the pieces inscribed with Tutankhamun's name, knowing the lord would be accused of stealing objects from the tomb. These may have been the pieces in Carter's collection that King Farouk helped repatriate.

Carter's reputation has held up quite well over the one hundred years since his discovery of the tomb. Among Egyptologists, it is generally agreed that Carter did a masterly job of putting together a team and clearing the tomb. Still, when everything was done, Carter remarked again that in the end he thought Tutankhamun had eluded him. I get a similar feeling about Carter. He was a complex man who chose not to reveal himself willingly, and we will never fully understand him. But he and Tutankhamun have left us a legacy that we are still trying to figure out today.

PART II

Tutankhamun Revealed

We are getting to know ... what he had, but of what he was ...
we are still sadly to seek.

—Howard Carter

7

Translating Tutankhamun

When Howard Carter finally completed clearing Tutankhamun's tomb, he was disappointed for two reasons. The first is one we have mentioned already: he felt that he really hadn't gotten to know Tutankhamun ("In the end Tutankhamun eluded me"). He learned what Tutankhamun had, but not who he was. The second disappointment was that there were no papyri in the tomb. He may have been hoping for written records that might reveal who Tutankhamun's parents were, but there was nothing. Or perhaps Carter was hoping for a Book of the Dead, a long, beautifully illustrated papyrus roll intended to help Tutankhamun on his long and dangerous journey to the next world. Tut didn't have one of these either. But he did have something to take the place of a Book of the Dead; it was just in a form that nobody expected.

Guidebooks to the Next World

The Book of the Dead had its origins in the Old Kingdom (2686–2181 BC), a thousand years before Tutankhamun, during the golden age of pyramid building. After the large pyramids on the Giza Plateau were built, Unas, last king of the Fifth Dynasty, built a small pyramid at Saqqara. From the outside it doesn't look like anything special, but inside was an innovation that would revolutionize Egyptian religion for thousands of years. Covering the walls inside Unas's pyramid are beautiful hieroglyphs, magical spells to help him ascend to the heavens.

The hieroglyphs are colored blue, so they stand out clearly against the white limestone walls (Figure 7.1). Long vertical columns, from ceiling to floor, separate each magical spell, called "an utterance" by the ancient

Figure 7.1. The magical spells in the pyramid of King Unas were intended to help him make the journey to the next world. They are the first large body of writing in the world. (Photo by Pat Remler.)

Egyptians. These inscriptions are the Pyramid Texts, magical spells to assist the king through his three stages of resurrection: (1) Unas's awakening in the pyramid, (2) his ascension through the sky to the netherworld, and (3) his admittance into the company of the gods. The magical principle behind all the spells is the same: the word is the deed (that is, saying something, or inscribing it on a wall, makes it so). This notion of magic was so important that one of the first spells you encounter in the pyramid, carved at the entrance to the Antechamber, is "Unas does not give you his magical power."[1] Later spells tell how Unas will get to the heavens: "The Opener of the Ways lets Unas fly towards heaven, amongst his brothers, the gods."

This innovation in Unas's pyramid was copied by the pharaohs who came after him. Who wouldn't want a guidebook to the next world? These texts were purely the prerogative of the king and his family. Even the nobles didn't have anything like this in their tombs. Seemingly, the magical spells were a carefully guarded secret. These Pyramid Texts are the precursor to the New Kingdom Book of the Dead, but not a direct one.

The next step in the evolution toward a proper Book of the Dead came in the Middle Kingdom (2040–1782 BC). When the Old Kingdom collapsed (we don't know why), a period of lawlessness called the First Intermediate Period (2181–2040 BC) followed and the pyramids were broken into by robbers. For the first time, commoners saw the Pyramid Texts, and everyone wanted them. The First Intermediate Period lasted more than fifty years, and when stability returned in the Middle Kingdom, there was a new innovation—the nobility began inscribing these magical spells on their coffins, creating what became known as the Coffin Texts. But coffins are much smaller than the inside of a pyramid, so all the texts couldn't fit. The solution appeared in the New Kingdom (1570–1070 BC): the Book of the Dead.

By writing the magical spells on a papyrus roll, you could have every spell you wanted; no need to leave any out. You could add illustrations, paintings of the gods, even pictures of yourself successfully making the journey to the next world. You could have lists of all the passwords you would need to get through gates guarded by demons; you could have it all. The Book of the Dead was born. Now you really did have a guidebook to the next world. Producing these "books" became a major industry in ancient Egypt, with scribes producing Books of the Dead for eager customers who wanted the scrolls next to them in their coffins, to guide them when they began their journeys to the next world. Some of these papyrus rolls were one hundred feet long with beautiful illustrations. Others were brief and had no illustrations. It all depended upon what you could afford. Frequently the books were prepared before there was an intended customer, with spaces for the deceased's name left blank; after the purchase, the buyer's name would be filled in by the scribe. These are the first "document forms" in history.

Books of the Dead were primarily for the nobles, the only ones who could afford them. The pharaohs didn't need them. They had hundreds of feet of walls in their tombs where artists, using vivid colors, could paint the kings' Books of the Dead. This is what tourists visiting the Valley of the

Kings see on the walls. All those mysterious gods, celestial boats, evil ones with their heads cut off, night skies—all are sections of the Book of the Dead. The great kings of the New Kingdom—Tuthmosis III, Seti I, Ramses the Great—all had their Books of the Dead inscribed on their tomb walls. But not Tutankhamun.

Unlike other pharaohs, Tutankhamun didn't have a huge tomb with lots of wall space for religious texts, because he died unexpectedly and didn't have years to prepare his tomb. Egyptian religion required that the body be placed in the tomb seventy days after death, so the tomb couldn't be constructed after he died. Tutankhamun had to make do with a small tomb that had already been prepared in the Valley for someone else. Still, he had to have spells to help him journey to the next world. Tutankhamun's Book of the Dead is written on the four gold shrines that surrounded his sarcophagus and coffins—the same shrines that Carter had so much difficulty dismantling.

The texts on these shrines are an important source and tell us how ancient Egyptian religion worked. The only thing resembling Tutankhamun's shrines were the badly damaged fragments of Queen Tiye's shrines, discovered by Theodore Davis in KV-55, and hardly anything could be read on them. With Tutankhamun's shrines we have line upon line of well-preserved texts and illustrations. They went untranslated for decades. Why?

Part of the reason is that everyone was preoccupied with the gold, glitter, and beauty of the "treasures," so the unglamorous texts were forgotten. But there is more to the story than that. When Carter first opened the tomb, he thought he would find papyri and figured he would need a translator. He had two main candidates. First was Sir Alan Gardiner, the great philologist. Gardiner was probably the most capable translator alive and was willing to help. The second candidate, James Henry Breasted, was less willing to help. He had never liked Carter, but kept in contact because he hoped Carter's newfound fame might help him raise money for the excavation compound the University of Chicago was planning on building on the east bank of the Nile at Luxor. Breasted had translated historical texts, but he was certainly capable of working on religious texts as well. So, with two excellent scholars at hand, why weren't these new religious texts translated? The answer is Carter's personality. By the time the shrines had been removed from the tomb, Carter had alienated both men.

As we have seen, when Breasted asked Carter for a few of Burton's photographs to use in a book he was preparing, Carter charged him for them. Breasted was incensed, and that was the end of his offer to help. With Sir Alan Gardiner, it was even worse. Gardiner was eager to translate any material found in the tomb. He had encouraged Carter to publish the planned comprehensive six-volume work on the tomb, and probably figured his translations would be part of that, but it was not to be.

In the 1930s Carter gave Gardiner an amulet but didn't tell him that it came from Tutankhamun's tomb. When Gardiner showed it to Rex Engelbach, director of the Egyptian Museum, Engelbach immediately recognized it as coming from the tomb. We will discuss this incident later in the book, but for now let's just say that Gardiner was furious about being given stolen property and wrote to Carter saying so. Now Carter had lost both his translators, and no one else seemed interested in translating the shrines, so they simply sat on the second floor of the Egyptian Museum, looked at by tourists who never understood their significance. Then things changed.

The Translator and the Ballerina

Alexandre Piankoff, a Russian Egyptologist who specialized in translating religious texts, had spent years in the Valley of the Kings copying and translating the texts in the tombs of the kings. The tomb of Seti I contains a text known as the Book of the Cow. Piankoff remembered that on Tutankhamun's shrines was the same text, only in better condition and the earliest known example. So at the end of World War II, he asked the director of the Antiquities Service, Étienne Drioton, for permission to translate and publish the texts on the shrines. Piankoff had already translated and published the texts in the tomb of Ramses VI and was perfect for the job.[2] Finally, Tutankhamun's guidebook to the next world would be translated.

Piankoff worked with Natacha Rambova, who edited his translations and later saw his last publication through the press after he died. It might seem natural that a Russian Egyptologist would have a Russian colleague as editor, but sometimes things are not what they appear. Rambova is one of the more colorful characters in Egyptology, and that says a lot. Natacha Rambova was born Winifred Shaughnessy into a prominent Mormon family in Salt Lake City, Utah, in 1897. As a teenager, she became a ballerina with the New York–based Imperial Russian Ballet, directed by the Russian choreographer Theodore Kosloff. There she took the stage name Natacha Rambova. Soon the teenager became Kosloff's lover, and when he was hired by Cecil B. DeMille to choreograph dances for DeMille's films, the two settled in Los Angeles. Not long after their move to California, Natacha left Kosloff, because she had been designing the costumes for the productions but Kosloff was taking the credit. She quickly established herself as an outstanding Hollywood designer, and a few years later she met and married the silent-film idol Rudolph Valentino. The marriage lasted only two years, but her career as an Egyptologist began when in 1932 she traveled to Egypt with Valentino and became fascinated by ancient Egyptian religion; she studied Egyptology for the rest of her life.

The inscriptions on the shrines published by Piankoff and Rambova give us insight into ancient Egyptian religious beliefs. There was order, structure; it wasn't just the jumble of gods and goddesses that tourists experience when they walk through the pharaohs' tombs in the Valley of the Kings. Tutankhamun's shrines provided a clear path for the young king's resurrection. You just have to know a bit about Egyptian mythology to see it.

The Myth of Isis and Osiris

Central to the Egyptian belief in life after death is a myth that is alluded to over and over again on the shrines. It is the story of Isis and Osiris. According to the myth, Isis and Osiris are husband and wife, brother and sister. They have two other siblings, another couple, Nephthys and Set. Osiris brought civilization to Egypt, introducing farming and cattle-raising, thus freeing the early inhabitants of the Nile Valley from misery. It worked so well that he left Egypt to bring civilization to the rest of the world, leaving Isis, the powerful goddess of magic, to keep their evil brother, Set, in check.

Upon Osiris's return, Set obtained his brother's exact bodily measurements by trickery, and constructed a beautiful wood chest to fit him precisely. During a banquet, Set offered the magnificent chest as a prize to whoever could fit into it, but guest after guest tried and failed. Then Osiris tried, and it fit perfectly—not unlike Cinderella's slipper. However, as soon as Osiris was inside the chest, Set sealed the chest, poured molten lead over it, and threw the chest into the Nile. A violent storm carried the chest to Byblos in Lebanon, where it washed up into the branches of a tree. In time, the tree grew to extraordinary size, its trunk enveloping the chest with Osiris inside. When the king of Byblos was building his palace, he had the tree cut down to be used as one of the pillars.

When Isis learned what had happened to her husband, she set out to recover his body. She figured out where he was and took a job as the handmaiden to the queen of Byblos. Eventually Isis explained that her husband was in a chest in a pillar in the palace. The queen was sympathetic, the pillar was cut open, and Isis recovered the body of her dead husband and brought it back to Egypt for proper burial. Set, ever evil, found the body of Osiris, hacked it into fourteen pieces, and scattered them throughout Egypt. Isis, assisted by her sister, Nephthys, searched for the body parts of the dismembered Osiris and found all but one, the phallus, which had been thrown into the Nile and devoured by fish. Isis reassembled her deceased husband and fashioned an artificial phallus for him. Then, transforming herself into a bird, Isis hovered over Osiris, recited magical words, and brought him back to life. Osiris, the first ever to resurrect, became the god of the netherworld, the Lord of the West.

Almost all the beliefs of the ancient Egyptian funerary cult can be parsed from the myth of Isis and Osiris. The importance of a proper burial on Egyptian soil was emphasized by Isis's journey to recover the body and bring it back to Egypt. The chest that exactly fit Osiris was the precursor of the anthropoid coffin, shaped like the deceased and intended to protect his body. We also see from this myth just how important it was to have an intact body for resurrection. Isis searched throughout Egypt to find all the pieces, and when she couldn't find the phallus, she shaped an artificial one to replace the missing one. Finally, and equally important, she spoke the proper words and Osiris resurrected. He retained after death the same body he had inhabited while alive. Mummification thus became essential to immortality; in order to have an afterlife, the body must be preserved.

The four shrines of Tutankhamun are covered with references to Isis, Osiris, and Nephthys, but not Set. To say his name would give him power. But the shrines are inscribed with far more than just references to the myth of Isis and Osiris. They mention dozens of other gods and goddesses, who also provide their magical words to ensure Tutankhamun's resurrection in the next world. It might be possible to teach an entire course on ancient

Egyptian religion with only the shrines of Tutankhamun as the textbook—there is so much there.

To this day, Egyptologists use Piankoff's numbering system for the shrines. The outermost shrine is I and the innermost is IV—the order in which Carter took them apart. The shrines are not all exactly the same shape. From the earliest times in Egypt's long history, there was a Palace of the North and a Palace of the South, affirming that the pharaoh was king of both Upper and Lower Egypt. These symbolic structures were first constructed in the era before Egypt built in stone, so they were made out of perishable materials and none have survived, but we do have early drawings of them. The back and roof of Shrine IV, the innermost, are in the shape of the Palace of the North, indicating Tutankhamun's rule over Lower Egypt. ⏏ (The reason Lower Egypt is in the north is that the direction the Nile flows. It is the only major river that flows south to north. So when you go "up the Nile" you go south, and Upper Egypt is south.) The backs of the middle two shrines are in the shape of the Palace of the South 🏠. So the shapes of the innermost three shrines establish that Tutankhamun is Lord of Upper and Lower Egypt.

The outermost shrine is in the shape of the *heb-sed* pavilion, and is perhaps the most important of all the shrines. The *heb-sed* was a ritual the pharaoh periodically performed so that he would be magically rejuvenated. In ancient times, rulers were not only the political heads of their countries, they were also the military leaders. In Egypt, it was expected that the pharaoh would lead the army in battle. If the pharaoh became too old to lead, then the country could become weak. This situation may have led to the *heb-sed* festival. Periodically (traditionally every thirty years, but many pharaohs held it at shorter intervals), pharaohs would demonstrate their vigor by running a course, wrestling with younger opponents, accurately shooting arrows, and so on. The festival was not so much a demonstration of physical prowess as a magical rejuvenation. The younger opponents would permit the king to win, the arrows would never miss, et cetera. The back of Tutankhamun's fourth shrine is in the shape of the tent used for the *heb-sed* festival (archaic representations suggest it was more of a tent than a building). 🏛 Just as the king is rejuvenated in the *heb-sed*, Tutankhamun will be resurrected in the next world; it is the ultimate *heb-sed*.

The shapes of the shrines tell us the order in which the priests intended us to read the texts—from the inside out—and this makes sense. The shapes of the innermost three shrines indicate that they are concerned with the king's existence on earth, as Lord of Upper and Lower Egypt. When we get to the outermost shrine, we are dealing with the pharaoh's resurrection in the next world. What the shrines' shapes tell us is reinforced by the texts on their walls. The innermost shrine, the one closest to the mummy of Tutankhamun, protects the mummy. Isis and Nephthys are on the doors of the shrine, their outstretched wings protecting the deceased Tutankhamun, just as they assisted in the resurrection of Osiris (Figure 7.2). You can tell who is who by looking on their heads. Each has her name on top. Isis is the one with the throne, because she is the seat of power. In ancient Egyptian

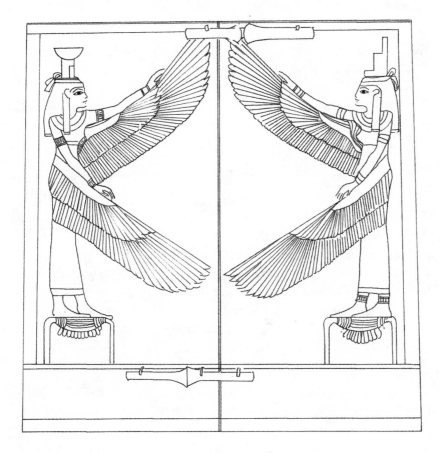

Figure 7.2. The door to the innermost shrine is protected by Isis and her sister, Nephthys. (Drawing by Mary Jordan.)

the word for throne was *ist*. When the Greeks entered Egypt, they added their Greek ending, and she became Isis. Nephthys has on her head two hieroglyphs that translate to "Mistress of the Temple." Isis and Nephthys are goddesses of this earthly realm. They do not appear in the west, which would have characterized them as goddesses of the dead. They protect the mummy here on earth.

On the outside of the innermost shrine we have magical words spoken by both Isis and Nephthys:

> *Words spoken by Isis the Great:* I have come to the protection of my brother Osiris, King Tutankhamun. . . . Thou makest all the transformation thou likest.
> *Words spoken by Nephthys:* I am behind thee, my brother Osiris, King Tutankhamun. . . . Thou shalt be justified in heaven, powerful on earth! Thou makest all the transformations thou likest.[3]

Tutankhamun is called "my brother" because by saying so, he becomes Osiris, the brother of both Isis and Nephthys, and like Osiris, he too will resurrect.

On the back panel of the smallest shrine are more magical spells that make it very clear that the purpose of this shrine is to protect the mummy of Tutankhamun.

> *Words spoken by Nephthys:* Thou livest, thou shalt not decay, thy body shall not perish![4]

To resurrect you needed your body, and the purpose of the innermost shrine is to make sure the body is protected and preserved.

The next shrine, working outward (Shrine III), is a transitional shrine. We are still concerned with preserving and protecting the mummy, but we also have spells for the journey to the next world. On the doors of this shrine, we again have Isis and Nephthys, protecting Tutankhamun's mummy. Inside the shrine we get other gods joining in to preserve the body. Qebesenuf, one of the four sons of Horus, who normally protects the internal organs of the mummy, says:

> *Words spoken by Qebesnuf:* I have come to be thy protection. Thy bones have been gathered together, thy members reassembled. I have brought thee thy heart.[5]

This declaration is interesting for two reasons. First is the indirect but the clear reference to Osiris, whose body parts were gathered together and reassembled by Isis. By means of this spell, if anything happened to Tutankhamun's mummy, it would be reassembled. This spell was Tutankhamun's plan B. Given what Douglas Derry did to his mummy, he needed it.

The second point to note is that the heart is singled out for mention. This is not an accident. The ancient Egyptians believed that you thought with your heart, so it was the most important organ in the body. The idea of thinking with your heart is not an unreasonable deduction. When you get excited, you feel your heart beat quickly; you don't feel your brain. This is why we say things like "Be still my foolish heart," and on Valentine's Day we send chocolate hearts, even though we should be sending little chocolate brains. The ancient Egyptians didn't understand the function of the brain; we don't find brains in the canopic jars because the brains were destroyed when they were removed through the nasal passages at the time of mummification. The heart, however, is the only organ left inside the body after mummification. You were going to need it to think, so that you could say the magical spells to resurrect. The importance of the heart is highlighted in Chapter 125 of the Book of the Dead, where the heart of the deceased is weighed against the feather of truth to determine if the deceased is worthy of joining the other westerners.

The Egyptians were so concerned about the heart that they created a special amulet to be placed on the mummy, the heart scarab. The amulet was in the shape of a scarab. As we saw in Chapter 2, the ancient Egyptian word *kheper* meant both "beetle" and "exist." So if you had an amulet in the shape of a beetle, you would exist forever. But the heart scarab wasn't intended to protect the heart of the deceased. It was to keep your heart silent while you were being judged by the gods. You were going to have to convince the gods that you had done no wrong; in other words, you had to lie. Spell 30b of the Book of the Dead was carved on the flat bottom of the scarab amulet, imploring the deceased's heart to shut up while the deceased was busy lying to the gods: "O heart of my mother, heart of my mother, stand not up against me in the tribunal."

So the heart was crucial to the ancient Egyptians, and that's why Qebesenuf specifically says that he is bringing Tutankhamun's heart. The problem is that Tutankhamun's heart is missing, and we don't know why. In Chapter 9 we will discuss the first X-rays taken of Tutankhamun's mummy, in 1968. It was discovered then that the heart is not inside his body. The boy-king certainly had a top-of-the-line mummification. All indications are that no expense was spared. So why is the heart missing? We just don't know. We can only hope that the magical spells made up for the physical absence.

In addition to protecting the mummy, Shrine III also helped Tutankhamun's journey to the next world, a journey that would be made by boat. The only way an ancient Egyptian could travel a great distance was by water. (The ancient Egyptians didn't have camels; those came with the Romans.) So they imagined that the deceased journeyed through the sky in boats. Inside the shrine we see Tutankhamun in his celestial barge, accompanied by the gods (Figure 7.3). The caption reads: "All the gods who accompany Tutankhamun." The last in line is Tutankhamun, whose cartouche is on his head.

On the outside of the shrine, Tutankhamun is approaching his goal, the west, and the gods encourage him: "Come then in thy beautiful forms, come to the gods of the west, be one of them." The next world was in the west because that is where the sun dies every day; the west was the territory of the dead.

On the next shrine (Shrine II), we see Tutankhamun being welcomed by Osiris. He is now a westerner and can take his place with the gods. So if Tutankhamun has reached his goal, what is the purpose of the last and largest shrine? It's Tut's victory lap. He's proclaiming that he has made it.

Words spoken by Tutankhamun, true of voice: I am the god on the side of the barge. I have fought for thee! I am one of those gods. . . . I belong to thy subjects, O Osiris. I am one of the gods.

Figure 7.3. Tutankhamun in his celestial boat journeys across the sky accompanied by the gods. (Drawing by Mary Jordan.)

Words spoken by the gods: Come thee, be with us. Thy members do not differ from those of a god.

To confirm Tutankhamun's rightful place next to the gods, there is a text on the left inside panel that says:

Words spoken by all the gods of the silent region: Let the king, Lord of the Two Lands, Neb-Kheperu-Re, son of the sun, beloved by him, Tutankhamun, ruler of Heliopolis of the south, be One of the Council, by the side of Osiris.

Tutankhamun's long journey is over.

Many of the texts are from what has been called the Book of the Divine Cow. An image of this cow is on the back panel inside the last shrine (Figure 7.4). Her name is Mehetweret, which means "The Great Flood." She is the goddess responsible for the annual inundation by the Nile. According to one myth, the deceased ascends to the heavens on the back of the Divine Cow. On the shrine, she is supported by Shu, the god of air, indicating

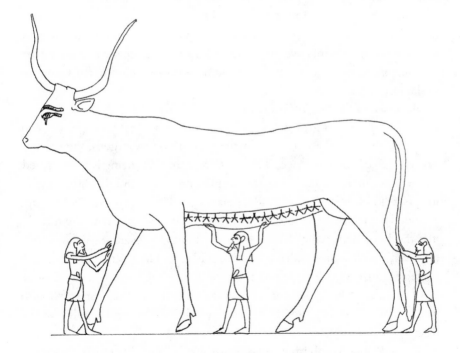

Figure 7.4. The Divine Cow, Mehetweret, is supported by Shu, the God of Air, indicating she is part of the sky. (Drawing by Mary Jordan.)

that she is also part of the sky. This is why she has stars on her belly; she is celestial.

Mehetweret makes another appearance in Tutankhamun's tomb, but not where you might expect her. When the antechamber was first opened, one of the most striking groups of objects consisted of three funerary couches standing against the back wall (see Figure 3.2). Each couch had the heads of two identical animals in the front: one had lions, one had hippos, and one had cows—Mehetweret, the Divine Cow. The "couches" were extremely high—four and a half feet—so they certainly were not for sitting. Perhaps the mummy lay on the different couches during different parts of a ritual and the height made it easier for the officiant, whom he wouldn't have to bend over. I believe that Tutankhamun's mummy rested on these couches, and when it was on the Mehetweret couch, it symbolized the Divine Cow taking him to the next world.

There are inscriptions on the front crossbars of the couches. Surprisingly, on the lion couch is an inscription for Mehetweret.[6] The couches are each made of four pieces of gilded wood; they must have been brought into the tomb in pieces, and when the workmen assembled them, they didn't (or couldn't) read the inscriptions and so put them together incorrectly. Remember, the shrines weren't oriented according to instructions either, and the resurrected Tutankhamun would have walked out into the east rather than the west.

Mehetweret features prominently on the inside of the outer shrine because she has done a great service to the king in bringing him to the next world. With Tutankhamun now in the west among the gods, the shrines' stories and functions are over. The outside of this last shrine is uninscribed. There is no more to say. What we are presented with are dazzling pairs of inlays of "knots of Isis" and "Osiris pillars" (see Color Plate 14). We are not absolutely sure what the knot of Isis is supposed to represent. Some think it is the knot with which Isis ties the garment she wears 𓎬. We do know, however, that it is an amulet associated with life. The Osiris pillar is much more certain. Called in Egyptian the *djd* pillar, 𓊽 it represents the backbone of Osiris, and indeed the hieroglyph for this looks like vertebrae; it is also the word for "stability." So Tutankhamun will have life and stability in the next world.

When Piankoff published his translations of Tutankhamun's shrines, it was the first substantial research on the tomb's treasures in twenty years. It didn't cause much of a stir among the general public, but Egyptologists took notice. They saw possibilities for future research. The great thaw had begun.

8

X-raying Tutankhamun

Before Alexander Piankoff published his translations of Tutankhamun's shrines, Egyptologists never realized the academic gold mine that Tutankhamun objects could provide. There were articles to be published, studies to be conducted, all kinds of possibilities. But no one sprang into action. Why not? What happened is what Dr. Kara Cooney once called in an interview "fetishizing." She makes the point that because Tut's treasures were in the Egyptian Museum in Cairo in glass vitrines, they were for seeing, not touching; they had become objects of veneration, fetishes, and scholars were hesitant to approach them.

When the first major Tutankhamun exhibition toured the world in the 1970s, an image of the Gold Mask of Tutankhamun was used on the posters and other materials advertising the exhibition. This was the first time the mask had received worldwide publicity, and it was exhibited at the British Museum. Harry James, keeper of Egyptian antiquities at the time, told me about his encounter with the famous Gold Mask.

All of the mounts and Plexiglas cases for the Tut exhibit were in place at the British Museum when the wood crates arrived from Cairo. When the crate with the Gold Mask was opened, there was a communal gasp among the curators. There it was, the famous Gold Mask, not on the second floor of the Egyptian Museum in Cairo, but right in front of them in London. After they'd stared at it for a while, it dawned on everyone that it had to be taken out of the crate and installed in its vitrine. But no one wanted to touch it. As Harry tells it, he put on his white gloves, lifted the mask out of the crate (it weighs twenty-two pounds), and walked with it through the galleries, preceded by two colleagues who opened the doors for him. Finally he placed it in the vitrine where it would be viewed by millions.

Because researchers were hesitant to approach the treasures of Tutankhamun, it was a while before the next big Tutankhamun research project. When it finally came, the project wasn't on a gold object; it was on something most people had forgotten about, one that many didn't care about—the mummy of Tutankhamun. The mummy wasn't in a glass case in a museum; Tutankhamun was still in his tomb, waiting.

In the first section of this book, we discussed the initial examination and rough handling that Tutankhamun's mummy received at the hands of Douglas Derry. Part of the problem was that there was a long tradition of perceiving mummies as expendable, not as precious artifacts that had to be preserved. Almost exactly a hundred years before Derry hurriedly unwrapped Tutankhamun, another anatomist was doing pretty much the same to every mummy he could get his hands on.

King of the Mummy Unwrappers

In the eighteenth century adventurous travelers began going to Egypt and bringing back mummies. Curious about what lay beneath the bandages, many of the mummies were unwrapped, often by physicians. The king of all the mummy unwrappers was Dr. Thomas Pettigrew, the son of a naval surgeon, who became a prominent physician (he vaccinated Queen Victoria).[1] In 1820 the Italian adventurer Giovanni Belzoni asked Pettigrew to examine some of the mummies he had brought back from Egypt. Intrigued by these mummies, Pettigrew soon after purchased a mummy of his own that had been brought to England in 1741 by another physician, Charles Perry. Pettigrew leisurely unwrapped the mummy in the privacy of his home.

Ten years passed before Pettigrew had a chance to unroll another mummy. He purchased a mummy for £23 at the 1833 auction of Henry Salt's collection of antiquities. His friend Thomas Saunders purchased another at the same sale for £36 15s. Both mummies were unrolled on April 6, 1833, to a packed audience in the lecture hall of Charing Cross Hospital, where Pettigrew was professor of anatomy.[2] Little was learned, but the combination of England's fascination with mummies and Pettigrew's social connections made his public demonstrations a huge success, and soon his mummy unrollings became a vogue.

A few weeks after the Charing Cross demonstration, Dr. John Lee asked Pettigrew to unwrap another mummy from the Salt sale, so on June 24, 1833, Pettigrew gave another performance. He began with some remarks on Egyptian religion and the purpose and technique of mummification, and provided running patter throughout the unrolling. John Davidson, who attended this unwrapping, was so enthralled by the event that he asked Pettigrew to help him unwrap a mummy he owned. The "mummy of the month" was unwrapped on July 13, 1833, in front of a standing-room-only audience at the lecture hall of the Royal Institute. Pettigrew was enjoying his fame as a mummy unroller so much that he began searching out mummies to unwrap.

He knew that Davidson's mummy had come over to England along with a second mummy that had been given to the Royal College of Surgeons, so he asked if he could unwrap that one. Permission was granted, and there was such a demand for invitations to the event that plans had to be made to accommodate those who could not get in. The diary of William Clift, conservator at the Royal College of Surgeons Museum, notes:

Prepared large Notices against the Meeting tomorrow, to obviate as much may be the effects of disappointment to those who will not be able to gain admission: *Gentlemen who may be disappointed in witnessing the unrolling of the Mummy this day, will have an opportunity of viewing it in the Museum every Monday, Wednesday, and Friday from 12 till 4 o'clock, Jan 16, 1834.*[3]

By the time of the unwrapping, the auditorium was so crowded that even the archbishop of Canterbury and the bishop of London had to leave because of lack of space. At one o'clock a procession led by the mace-bearer, president, and council of the Royal College of Surgeons filed into the theater, leading Pettigrew and his two assistants. It was a smashing success, and Pettigrew unrolled two additional mummies before the end of 1833, providing wonderful publicity for his upcoming book, *History of Egyptian Mummies.*[4] Many of the book's purchasers were those who attended Pettigrew's lectures. The illustrations were drawn by George Cruikshank, who was later to become Charles Dickens's illustrator. The book provided the first comprehensive history of mummification and remained a standard reference for nearly a century.

Pettigrew went on to create a series of six public lectures on ancient Egyptian funerary customs that always culminated with "Recapitulation— Unrolling an Egyptian Mummy." Tickets were one guinea for mummy-side seats and half a guinea for seats in the rear. Ladies were admitted. Pettigrew would continue unwrapping mummies for decades. His extensive experience made him uniquely qualified for his last and greatest performance: the mummification of the Duke of Hamilton.

Thirty years before his death, the Duke had purchased a black basalt sarcophagus for his eventual burial. On the grounds of Hamilton Palace, he erected a mausoleum that the *Times* of September 7, 1852, described as "the most costly and magnificent temple for the reception of the dead in the world—always excepting the Pyramids." Following the Duke's instructions, Pettigrew not only mummified His Grace, but also officiated as high priest at his burial.[5]

Pettigrew's unrolling of mummies was the tradition that Douglas Derry was following when he unwrapped Tutankhamun. There was little concern for the preservation of the mummy, and much of the focus was on the amulets found within the wrappings. No scientific tests were done in Pettigrew's day; everything was based on visual observation. To a great extent this was Derry's technique also. Fortunately, research on Tutankhamun's mummy did not stop with Derry, but before we look at the subsequent research, one point should be made about Derry's participation in the excavation of Tutankhamun's tomb.

As we have seen before, Carter had no great interest in mummies, and when he selected Derry as his mummy expert, he may not have made the best choice. Pettigrew, a hundred years earlier, had at least been interested in the history of mummification; he had studied it and had written a book about it. He even took the time to learn the basics of hieroglyphs. Not so for Derry. He was not a scholar and was not used to publishing research. He never published a full report about his unwrapping of Tutankhamun. A better choice to examine Tutankhamun might have been Sir Grafton Elliot Smith, another anatomist, but one who had extensive experience with mummies and had already published the definitive work on the royal mummies.[6] Derry just didn't have enough experience and didn't seem to be aware of possibilities other than visual inspection. For example, X-raying Tutankhamun's head would have helped reveal how he had been mummified, but this would not happen for another sixty years. Further, there were techniques available for studying soft tissues that might have revealed the presence of disease, but Derry didn't seem interested. True, it is difficult to work with the soft tissue of mummies, but it could have been done.

When a body is mummified it is dehydrated, and over the centuries it becomes brittle and with rough handling can break. It was a problem waiting to be solved. Sir Armand Ruffer, a physician intrigued by mummies, came up with the solution. Ruffer, the son of a French baron, had studied at Oxford and later with the great Louis Pasteur, so he was a real scientist. While researching a serum for diphtheria, he contracted the disease, and like so many wealthy Europeans of his day, he went to Egypt to recuperate. He fell in love with the country and stayed, eventually becoming president of the Sanitary Council of Egypt.

When Ruffer attempted to slice mummy tissue thinly enough to put under a microscope, it was so brittle it crumbled. So he developed a method to soften the tissues by soaking them in a solution of alcohol and 5 percent carbonate of soda. This softened the tissue enough for sectioning and microscopic investigation. The solution, still known today as "Ruffer's solution," opened a new field of study, paleopathology—the study of diseases in the ancient world.[7]

This technique for studying soft tissue was available to Derry but as far as we know, he didn't try it. In a letter to Carter he said:

> I have received the boxes containing the two foetuses & viscera, but have not had time to open them yet. When I do & have made another very careful examination I will write to you. Both Prof. Urquhart and Dr. Aziz Girgis have made several attempts to get something definite from the viscera they have been examining, but all cellular tissue has gone with the exception of some muscular fibres in what is almost certainly stomach or intestines. Apparently the organs had undergone extensive decomposition before mummification. Even eight hours in hot weather is enough to spoil tissues for microscopic work and it would seem therefore that in the 21st Dyn. they had much more perfect methods, as we got plenty of good stuff from mummies of that date.[8]

It is not clear which viscera the two doctors were working on. Derry wrote he hadn't had time to open the boxes Carter sent, so it probably wasn't Tutankhamun's. It would be helpful to know what they tried, what worked and what didn't. Did they try Ruffer's solution? No one ever published anything on Tutankhamun's viscera. As mentioned before, the fetuses went missing for decades because Derry never returned them. Same with Tutankhamun's viscera. Now, a recently discovered letter suggests they might be in storage at Derry's hospital. It would be good to know which organs were placed in the four miniature coffins. If the stomach is there, its contents might tell us if Tutankhamun suffered a long, lingering death. The liver could tell us about possible diseases. Are the kidneys there? It doesn't seem as if everything could fit in those small coffins. There is a great deal to be learned once we find the organs.

How could the fetuses and viscera disappear for decades, unrecorded? The answer is simple: no one cared. Carter never asked Derry to return the fetuses or viscera. Rex Engelbach, director of the Egyptian Museum at the time, never asked where they were. These were human remains, so no one wanted to deal with them. It was a similar story with Tutankhamun's mummy; it didn't disappear, it was still in the tomb, but no one wanted to deal with it. After he was reassembled on the sand tray and placed in his sarcophagus, the mummy was forgotten for decades. Few visitors to the tomb realized he was still inside his sarcophagus. Carter and Derry probably wanted it that way. No one knew what ravages the mummy of the boy-king had suffered. Better to leave him undisturbed in the sarcophagus.

This was the situation in 1968 when Dr. R. G. Harrison, professor of anatomy at the University of Liverpool, requested permission to X-ray Tutankhamun. His main goal was to investigate the similarities between Tutankhamun and the mummy in KV-55 that Theodore Davis had found. When Tutankhamun was unwrapped, everyone was impressed by the similarities between the two skulls. Could they have been brothers? Father and son? Harrison was granted permission to examine Tutankhamun's mummy, but the logistics were extremely difficult. The research team was not permitted to remove Tutankhamun from the tomb for the X-raying, so Harrison and his team had to bring a portable X-ray unit to Luxor, across the Nile to the Valley of the Kings, and finally into Tutankhamun's tomb. They found an old 1930s Siemens portable machine that held up and produced good results.[9]

When they lifted the lid to the coffin to begin work, everyone was shocked by what they saw. For the first time they realized what poor condition the mummy was in, but this was not the only shock. Something else was very wrong: part of Tutankhamun's sternum and some ribs were gone. In Harry Burton's photos of Tutankhamun on the sand tray, just before he was put in the sarcophagus, he looks complete (see Figure 5.3). Further, Derry never said anything about missing ribs. He may have been careless with preserving the mummy, but he was a good anatomist, and he would have noticed. But even more was missing.

When Tutankhamun was placed in the sarcophagus, he had a bead pectoral on his chest. Now that was gone. So too was the beaded cap on his head (Figure 8.1; see also Figure 5.2). Both the pectoral and the cap were embedded in the resins that had been poured on Tutankhamun at the time of burial and Carter couldn't remove them without further damaging the mummy, so he left them. There had also been a gold band that went around the young pharaoh's head. Where was that?

Harrison hadn't even X-rayed Tutankhamun yet, but even so, his exhumation spawned theories about Tutankhamun's death. Dr. Ben Harer, a physician with a deep interest in ancient Egypt, believed that the missing ribs were the cause of Tutankhamun's death. His theory was that the damage done to the body is consistent with being kicked by a horse, and that this is how Tutankhamun died.[10] He later refined his theory and suggested that it was more likely a hippopotamus that killed Tutankhamun.[11] In a subsequent article he discusses how embalmers would have dealt with such a damaged mummy.[12]

Most Egyptologists, however, believe that the damage is postmortem. There are too many changes between 1926, when the body was replaced

Figure 8.1. The beaded cap on Tutankhamun's head mysteriously disappeared sometime between 1931 and 1968. (Griffith Institute p0813.)

in the sarcophagus, and 1968, when Harrison examined it. Something happened to Tutankhamun's body during this period. When Derry reassembled Tutankhamun on the sand tray the arms were crossed at the abdomen. When Harrison found him, they were at Tutankhamun's side. So again, what happened?

One researcher presented the theory that Carter himself removed the ribs.[13] This is unlikely. Carter was not comfortable with mummies and generally left work on them to others. I just don't see him sawing away at Tutankhamun's ribs. Besides, when would he have had time for such a clandestine operation after the mummy was on the sand tray?

Far more likely is a theory suggested by T. G. H. James, the author of a masterly biography of Carter. He believed that during World War II, when security in the Valley was lax, there was a break-in and souvenir hunters took the pectoral, cap, and gold band, further damaging the mummy in the process. James never published his theory; he was a very cautious scholar, and this was speculation. However, a plausible recounting of his theory has been published by others.[14]

With the shock of Tutankhamun's poor condition behind them, Harrison's team began X-raying. They had to work quickly, as the team had permission to work for only two days, but at least the disarticulated state of the mummy made their task a bit easier. The pharaoh could be X-rayed in pieces. The head, because it was detached, could be X-rayed by itself, as could the arms, hands, and so on. On the first day they made a set of test exposures, which they developed that same evening in the bathroom of their hotel. Fortunately, they were staying at the Winter Palace, a grand old hotel in Luxor with commodious bathrooms. They developed their X-rays in one sink, fixed them in another, and then washed them in the bathtub. The images came out fine.[15] The only real difficulty they had was getting a good set of dental X-rays. With living patients, the film is placed inside the mouth. This couldn't be done with Tutankhamun, because his mouth was closed, and the team had to improvise.

CSI on the Nile

I first heard about Harrison's findings on an old BBC television documentary. There was Harrison on my TV screen, looking at the X-ray of Tutankhamun's skull (Figure 8.2). He pointed to a density on the X-ray at

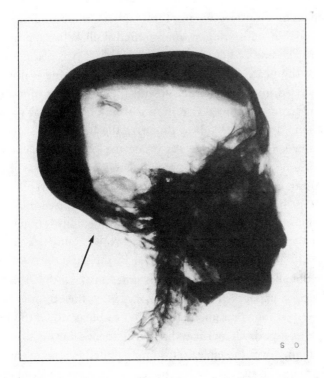

Figure 8.2. Dr. Harrison's X-ray of Tutankhamun's skull led to a murder theory. (Courtesy Department of Human Anatomy and Cell Biology, University of Liverpool.)

the base of the skull and said, "This is within normal limits, but in fact it could have been caused by a hemorrhage under the membranes overlying the brain in this region. And this could have been caused by a blow to the back of the head and this in turn could have been responsible for death."[16] Harrison was correct to be cautious—saying "*could* have been caused," "*could* have been responsible"—because the cause of death was not clear. In a book presenting a theory that Tutankhamun might have been murdered, I used this X-ray to present the possibility that the boy-king might have died from a blow to the back of the head. A later, more detailed CAT scan of the mummy showed conclusively that there was no blow to the back of the head. (See Chapter 9.)

Still, the X-ray of the skull is fascinating, and Harrison's collaborator Dr. R. C. Connolly kindly sent me a copy. Harrison's X-ray allows us to look back thirty-three hundred years and reconstruct the mummification of Tutankhamun. However, we must remember we are dealing not with a normal X-ray but with one of a mummified skull. What appears to be an abnormal thickening of the interior of the skull in two places—at the top and back of the head—is misleading. What we are seeing is not bone but resin, introduced into the cranium during Tutankhamun's mummification. After Tutankhamun's brain was removed through the nasal passages, hot resin was poured into the skull to cauterize the interior, in case any brain tissue remained. Once the resin was inside the skull, it hardened and became radiopaque, like bone. What Tutankhamun's skull shows is two fluid levels of the resin as it was poured in and then hardened. This means that the resin must have been introduced into the skull at two different times, with the mummy in a different position each time. This is how we can reconstruct what happened in the embalmer's shop.

Imagine the body of Tutankhamun flat on its back on the embalmer's table. A flexible hook is inserted into his nose, breaking the ethmoid bone, behind the nasal passages. (Harrison's X-rays show the ethmoid is broken.) The hook enters the cranium and is rotated to break down the brain so it becomes semi-liquid. Then Tutankhamun is turned on his stomach, with his head hanging over the table, so his brain, pulled by gravity, runs out the nose. The cranium is now ready for the resin. The resin is placed in a special ceramic bowl with two tubular spouts. The body is put on its back once again, and the tubes are placed in the nostrils and the bowl tilted so the resin runs through the nose and into the cranium. Gravity controls where it goes. Since Tutankhamun is positioned on his back, the resin forms a pool at the back of the skull. This resin burns out any bits of brain tissue that might have remained and caused putrefaction. When it cools, it creates the first of the two liquid levels. Next, the body of Tutankhamun is repositioned on the table so the head hangs over the end, with his chin pointing to the sky. Once again, resin is poured in and forms a pool at the lowest point, this time in the top of the head. The resin burns out any remaining bits of brain in the front of the skull and creates the second fluid level on the X-ray. Thus, the X-ray lets us reconstruct a specific event that took place in the distant past.

We can see something else on the X-ray that is often misunderstood because we never got Harrison's full explanation of it. A bone fragment is clearly visible inside Tutankhamun's skull. Many believed that it could be the result of the "possible" blow to the back of the head—that it was dislodged by the blow. Actually, the little piece of bone is a red herring in the case. It has nothing to do with the possible blow. As a matter of fact, Harrison first suggested it was a fragment of the ethmoid bone, broken off when the embalmers forced the hooked instrument into the cranium to remove the brain. But this explanation can't be right. The word *ethmoid* means "sieve" in Greek, because the bone is porous—it has a honeycomb texture, and splinters when broken. The bone inside the cranium is substantial, not a splinter, so it can't be a piece of the ethmoid. Indeed, it looks like part of a vertebra. It must have been broken off after mummification, otherwise it would have been stuck in the resin.

For the sake of argument, let's say it was broken off by a blow to the back of the head while Tutankhamun was alive and he died as a result of the blow. Now imagine the embalming process once again. The brain is removed, but the fragment remains loose in the skull. It is time to pour resin into the skull while Tutankhamun is lying on his back on the table. The bone fragment would now have fallen to the lowest point inside the skull—the back of the head. When the resin cools, the fragment would be embedded in the resin. If by some chance the bone was adhering to another part of the skull and the resin missed it, then the second application of resin to the top of the skull—when Tutankhamun's head hung over the embalmer's table—would almost certainly have enveloped the bone fragment within the resin. The bone fragment must have been loosened not only after death but also after the introduction of resin into the skull. The most likely time for the fragment to have broken off is when Derry and Carter were using heated knives to get the head out of the Gold Mask.

Harrison's examination accomplished several things. He was able to confirm Derry's estimation of Tutankhamun's age at death as around nineteen. He also confirmed that the cranial features of Tutankhamun were remarkably similar to those of the mummy in KV-55. His report mentioned that there would be a more detailed report to come, but that was not to be; Harrison died before he could publish a full report. Clearly, something more would have to be done about research on Tutankhamun's mummy.[17]

Searching for the Fetuses

Many researchers were disappointed by the lack of a full publication of Harrison's results. Dr. F. Filce Leek, a dentist who had been with Harrison's team in 1968, tried to pull together the unpublished material relating to

the three humans in Tutankhamun's tomb, and to a great extent he succeeded. He tracked down Derry's detailed notes on his examination of
Tutankhamun, and published them in full in his book, *The Human Remains
from the Tomb of Tut'ankhamun*.[18] It is full of important details, and we all
owe Leek a debt of gratitude. Further, in the same volume Leek gathered
together all references to the work on the mummy that Howard Carter
entered in his diary. This is how we learn that Carter coated the bead cap
on Tutankhamun's head with paraffin wax and left it in place, and other
important details.

Although Leek was successful in bringing to light previously unpublished material relating to the mummies in Tutankhamun's tomb, he was
not so successful when it came to his own attempt at research. His description of the search for the two fetuses reveals how maddening it could be to
conduct research in Egypt in the 1970s:

> The Egyptian Department of Antiquities kindly gave permission for an ana-
> tomical and x-ray examination of the two bodies, but when, in January 1971,
> the time came to make the examination the whereabouts of the remains
> could not be established. The glass case in the Tut'ankhamun gallery in the
> Cairo Museum was opened, and the small anthropoid coffins were found to
> be empty. With the help of Dr. Riad a search was made of other likely con-
> tainers, but without success, and neither were the fetuses to be found in the
> Museum's two magazines.
>
> In the index of the Museum's Temporary Journal, the coffins were seen
> to have been recorded under three different headings, but there was no
> mention of the foetuses. Nor was there any reference to them in the Journal
> d'entrée.
>
> As hope of finding them in the Museum receded, it was thought that they
> might have been retained in Derry's collection of specimens held in the Kasr
> El-Ainy Hospital. Examination of that portion of the collection retained in
> the Anatomy School, and partial examination of the remainder now housed
> in the basement of the hospital, proved equally unsuccessful.[19]

Leek was very close to finding the fetuses when he searched in Kasr
El-Ainy's basement.

If there is a "curse of Tutankhamun," it seems to have fallen on those
who attempt to do research on his mummy. Derry never published his
findings, Harrison died before he could publish his work, James Harris,
the dentist who had been given permission to examine Tutankhamun,
never published his dental findings, and when Leek finally got permission

to examine the fetuses, he couldn't find them. It would seem as if Tutankhamun didn't like being examined. It would be decades before permission would be granted to examine Tutankhamun's mummy one more time. When that examination happened, it would utilize space-age technologies.

9

Scanning Tutankhamun

Much of the research on Tutankhamun's mummy has been disappointing. Some of it was carried out by people who didn't have the right background or attitude toward mummies, and some didn't publish their results. Because things are much more public now—there's the internet and popular magazines about Egyptology—you couldn't study Tutankhamun's mummy and not publish a proper report. More important, mummy studies has become a discipline of its own. There is a Paleopathology Association that studies mummies to learn about diseases in the ancient world. There is a Mummy Congress—a meeting of researchers who are specialists in mummies, where the latest research is presented.[1] Throughout the 1980s and 1990s the number of mummy specialists was growing, forming a community of scholars interested in similar research. And as the number of mummy specialists has grown, so has the number of scientific techniques available to them.

In the 1980s and 1990s X-ray was the best method for nondestructive examination of mummies, but it was only good for examining high-density material such as bone. It doesn't work for soft tissues. Today the medical profession has two different techniques that study soft tissues, MRI and CAT scans. The two techniques are totally different.

MRI (magnetic resonance imaging) is used extensively in medicine for diagnosing soft tissue problems. If you have a broken leg, you need an X-ray. If you have a torn muscle or a diseased organ, you need an MRI. The problem with MRIs for mummy studies is that it works off the hydrogen in the water (H_2O) of soft tissues. Dehydrated mummies no longer contain water, so if you put a mummy in an MRI you won't get an image. So, as useful as they are for living patients, MRIs do not work for mummies. CAT scans are another story; they are revolutionizing mummy studies.

CAT (computerized axial tomography) scans are good for both bone and soft tissue and can take hundreds of X-ray images at one time, each a thin slice of part of the body. Later, a computer assembles these images to give a three-dimensional picture of the body. Another great advantage to CAT scans is that you don't have to reposition the body for different images, as you do with standard X-rays. With such a high-powered tool available, it was inevitable that it would be applied to the study of mummies.

The Egyptian Mummy Project was born at the beginning of the twenty-first century. The idea was to obtain CAT scans of all the royal mummies and publish a definitive work presenting the results.[2] The two co-authors each brought different skills to the project. One was Dr. Zahi Hawass, the former director of the Antiquities Service. He's probably the most famous archaeologist in the world. He also knows Egyptian archaeology better than anyone alive. For years he was responsible for protecting and overseeing all of Egypt's monuments. He knows the tombs and temples intimately, and more important, he knows where the mummies are and can get easy access to them. The Egyptian Mummy Project was under his direction. Hawass's co-author, Dr. Sahar Saleem, an MD specializing in radiology, is always looking for the newest development in scanning. Their skills complement each other perfectly. Hawass knows what questions to ask about the mummies: Could this mummy really be of someone who died at the age of forty? Is there any evidence of Fröhlich's syndrome in this mummy? Could this pharaoh have been murdered? Once Saleem knows what to look for, she figures out what images are needed and goes after them. Later she and Hawass analyze the images together. The two also have a support team with all the skills needed for an in-depth study of mummies. The first mummy to be scanned would be Tutankhamun.

Just as Harrison had to bring his 1930s X-ray machine to Tutankhamun, two members of the Egyptian Mummy Project had to drive a portable scanner on a trailer from Cairo all the way to the Valley of the Kings and park it outside Tutankhamun's tomb. The scanning took place on the evening of January 5, 2005. Like all research involving Tutankhamun's mummy, it would not be easy. First, there was a sudden driving rainstorm that swept through the Valley. Then the scanner wouldn't work—sand had gotten into the cooling system and had to be cleaned out, something that took over an hour. Finally the boy-king was ready to become the first pharaoh ever scanned. Within half an hour, more than seventeen hundred images were taken, a complete record of the mummy of Tutankhamun.

The team met on March 4–5, 2005, to discuss the results. Some things were as expected. From Harrison's 1968 examination, they were alerted to the fact that the mummy was in poor condition, so that was not a surprise. Also, the CAT scans indicated that Tutankhamun's age at the time of death was approximately nineteen years, confirming Derry's and Harrison's estimates. No surprises there either. However, Harrison had suggested there might be indications of a blow to the back of the head. The superior imaging capability of the CAT scanner showed clearly that there was no blow to the back of the head.

One surprise was that Tutankhamun may have had a clubfoot (per Web 11). We had no reason to expect this finding; how had everyone missed it before? Derry, a skilled anatomist, had examined Tutankhamun's feet carefully. He had removed the gold toe covers (called toe stalls) and gold funerary sandals and didn't notice anything unusual. Then when Harrison did his X-raying of Tutankhamun, he never mentioned any deformity. We must remember, however, that he never published a detailed analysis of the X-rays. Still, when the Egyptian Mummy Project team examined the scans in March 2005, they didn't notice anything either. It was only during a 2009 reexamination of the scans that the deformity was noticed: "The CT image also revealed a left club foot deformity. . . . With such a deformity in his left foot, the king would have walked on his ankle or on the side of his foot."[3]

If his clubfoot was so severe, wouldn't there be an asymmetry in the bones of the legs? Even the pelvis might be asymmetrical. Soft tissue influences bone, but Tutankhamun's legs appear to be symmetrical. In a letter to the *Journal of the American Medical Association*, Dr. James Gamble, an orthopedic surgeon at Stanford, also didn't see the clubfoot. So I asked the team's radiologist, Dr. Sahar Saleem, what she thought. She believed that the deformity was mild, not severe enough to cause the long bones to deform, nor to cause Tutankhamun to walk on his ankle. The confusion about the severity of the possible deformity arose because a large team was trying to present a consensus. Some probably saw it, and some didn't, and they were trying to present a single understandable conclusion.

One deformity of Tutankhamun's left foot seems undeniable. Tutankhamun was born missing a bone (the middle phalanx) in the second toe on his left foot. This wouldn't have caused any great problem walking, but some team members also thought that this was evidence of Kohler's disease, a condition where there is bone necrosis in the foot. If this is correct, then Tutankhamun might have limped. Some support for this view is provided by objects found in the tomb. First, there were 130 walking sticks in the tomb, and Tutankhamun is shown leaning on a walking stick. But we must be careful here. The use of a walking stick is not proof of infirmity. Officials are often depicted with a walking stick, as it was a sign of authority. So we can't conclude the boy-king limped.

As mentioned in Chapter 8, Harrison thought a blow to the back of the head might have caused Tutankhamun's death. Nearly twenty-five years ago, I used this as a bit of evidence for my theory that Tutankhamun was murdered.[4] Now the CAT scans of Tutankhamun showed that there was no blow to the back of the head. Tutankhamun may have been murdered, but it wasn't the way I thought.

Recent research has suggested all kinds of deaths for the boy-king. The strongest evidence for foul play was a frantic letter written by Tutankhamun's widow, Ankhesenamun. We learn about this letter because the Hittites were great record-keepers. Excavations in Turkey have yielded thousands of clay tablets from their archives, recording everything from land deeds to military exploits. At the beginning of the century a dig at the ancient capital of Bogazkoy found archives from the reign of King Suppiluliuma's son, Mursilis II (1321–1295 BC). Today they are known as "The Deeds of Suppiluliuma as Told by His Son Mursilis II." Ankhesenamun's letter is the seventh of these tablets. She says:

> My husband died. A son I have not. But to thee, they say, thy sons are many. If thou wouldst give me one son of thine, he would become my husband. Never shall I pick out a servant of mine and make him my husband. . . . I am afraid![5]

The letter is extraordinary: the queen of Egypt writes to the king of Egypt's traditional enemy, the Hittites, saying she is afraid and wants to marry a Hittite prince and make him king of Egypt. Why is the queen of Egypt afraid? And why does she think she is being coerced to marry a servant? What is going on?

These events were transpiring more than three thousand years ago and we will probably never know for sure what happened, but we do know that the letter was so strange that the Hittite king did not believe it.

> When my father heard this, he called forth the Great Ones for council [saying]:
> "Such a thing has never happened to me in my whole life!" So it happened
> that my father sent forth to Egypt Hattusa-ziti, the chamberlain, [with this
> order]: "Go and bring thou the true word back to me! Maybe they deceive
> me! Maybe [in fact] they do have a son of their lord! Bring thou the true word
> back to me!"[6]

When Hattusa-ziti returned he was not alone. Lord Hani, the queen's rep-
resentative, came with him. We have the Hittite account of Hani's speech
to the king:

> Oh my lord! This [is . . .] our country's shame! If we had [a son of the king]
> at all, would we have come to a foreign country and kept asking for a lord for
> ourselves? Nib-hururiya, who was our lord, died; a son he has not.[7] Our lord's
> wife is solitary. We are seeking a son of our lord for the kingship of Egypt, and
> for our lady, we seek him as her husband! Furthermore, we went to no other
> country, only here did we come! Now, oh our lord, give us a son of thine![8]

From the archives, we know what happened next. A prince was sent, he
was killed on the border of Egypt, and the Hittites went to war with Egypt.
There is much more to this story, but the question that haunts me is, what
happened to Ankhesenamun?

Her frantic letter is the last we hear from her. From the north wall in
Tutankhamun's tomb we know that Aye, Tutankhamun's advisor, succeed
him as pharaoh. We see him as king performing the Opening of the Mouth
Ceremony on the mummy of Tutankhamun. How did Aye, a commoner,
become king of Egypt? By marrying Ankhesenamun. We have a finger ring
that has the cartouches of Aye and Ankhesenamun together, indicating they
were married. Was Aye the "servant" Ankhesenamun was so desperately
avoiding? It seems likely. We hear nothing more of Ankhesenamun; she dis-
appears from history. Her tomb has never been found. She does not appear
on the walls of Tutankhamun's tomb, nor does she appear as queen on the
walls of Aye's tomb. She has vanished without a trace.

What do the CAT scans suggest about how Tutankhamen died? One
theory is that he died of a broken leg. This was news to me; I had never heard
this. It seems the CAT-scan revealed that Tutankhamun's femur, the largest
bone in the body, was broken. Dr. Michael Gillam, a well-known emer-
gency room physician who was also director of the Healthcare Innovation
Lab at Microsoft, argues against that theory. According to Dr. Gillam, the
CAT-scan showed that Tutankhamun had an open fracture of the leg (that

is, a fracture in which the broken ends of the bones protrude through the flesh), and that the fracture was comminuted (the bone was broken into more than two pieces). However, Dr. Gillam pointed out that the edges of the bone were dull, which is something modern physicians almost never see with a fracture of that type. Nowadays this type of injury is classified as a 33C3 fracture, and in young people with normal bone density the only time you see such injuries is with a particular type of high-velocity impact, either from a gunshot wound or from an automobile crash. Neither cause is likely for Tutankhamun, of course.[9] So I went back to the publication to see exactly what was being said. As in the case with the clubfoot, there was clearly disagreement among team members:

> [Some] team members maintain that the king may have suffered an accident that badly broke his leg and left an open wound. The fracture would not have been fatal, but could have triggered lethal cascades, such as bleeding, pulmonary or fat embolism, or infection. However they also indicated that this fracture could have been caused by the embalmers, though this was less likely. . . . At the outset, part of the team believed that the above scenario was absolutely incorrect. . . . However, in the final analysis, this interpretation was rejected and the traumatic fracture was seen as the correct diagnosis.[10]

Again, we see that there was an attempt to present a single conclusion. But this may be misleading. I think it is fair to say that it has not been demonstrated that Tutankhamun "died from a broken leg." In a brief two-page article on the cause of Tutankhamun's death, Dr. Angelique Corthals presents the theory that he may have died from a chariot accident "comparable to a car accident."[11] But the problem is that the two are not comparable. You can't get enough velocity from a chariot for that kind of injury.

Once again, we seem to have encountered the curse of Tutankhamun's mummy. We don't have this kind of problem interpreting the physical findings with the mummies of other pharaohs that the team scanned.

A few years after the Egyptian Mummy Project CAT-scanned Tutankhamun, they made use of another technology that Carter and Carnarvon could never have imagined: DNA.

IO

Tutankhamun's Family Tree

Of all the scientific advances in the last fifty years, DNA research may be the most significant discovery for mankind. The structure of the DNA molecule, which determines our heredity, was discovered in the 1960s by James Watson and Francis Crick, assisted by Rosalind Franklin.[1] It is two sugar-phosphate strands twisted around each other forming a double helix, looking a lot like a twisted ladder. The strands are connected to each other by a series of base pairs (the "rungs" of the ladder), each pair incorporating two different bases: either guanine (G) and cytosine (C), or adenine (A) and thymine (T). This is why when a sequence of DNA is transcribed, it is written as a sequence of G's, A's, T's, and C's. The order of these four letters (bases) is the genetic code—what makes an individual that individual. Soon after the discovery of this structure, it was realized that there is a similar molecule, RNA, that is crucial to the process of replicating DNA, and modern genetics was born. Progress in studying DNA was slow, but in the 1980s a group of Berkeley scientists began to wonder if it was possible to detect DNA from extinct animals; there was even talk about the possibility of bringing back extinct animals. First, though, you had to get some old DNA. A grad student, Russell Higuchi, was interested in a type of zebra called the quagga, which became extinct less than two hundred years ago. He knew there were quagga skins in museums in Germany and got permission to take a sample of a skin with a small fragment of muscle tissue attached to it. His idea was to dissect out the muscle tissue, where the DNA might have survived, and mix this with DNA from a modern zebra, in the hope that they would be similar enough to bind.[2] It worked; it was possible to extract DNA from an extinct animal.

Around the same time a Swedish molecular biologist, Svante Pääbo, was looking for DNA from much older samples. He had studied Egyptology before getting his PhD in biology and was quite familiar with mummies. Here were preserved tissues more than two thousand years old. He attempted to extract DNA from cells from a mummy's ear and succeeded in sequencing five hundred base pairs.[3] There was no useful information in Pääbo's five hundred base pairs, but he saw the possibilities. He went on to become the father of molecular archaeology, and is still active in the field, with one of the most respected laboratories in the world. But before real progress could be made, there had to be exponential progress in replicating DNA.

It was known at this time that there was an enzyme called polymerase that helped in replication and could even repair DNA. Could it be possible to speed up this process of replication and repair outside the body, and replicate and repair snippets of DNA much faster than before? It was, but again, it wasn't easy. The process involved heating the double strands so they separated, then adding what are called "primers" (short strands) and then cooling the DNA so it reattaches, but to the primers. Now you had four strands of DNA where before you had two. This is a bit of an oversimplification, but it doesn't misrepresent the process. The system, called PCR (polymerase chain reaction), was so sensitive that if an eyelash from the researcher fell in the mix, the DNA from that would be replicated too. And, problematically, things like that were happening in labs across the world. People thought they were getting ancient DNA, but they weren't. In one famous case, Scott Woodward, a molecular biologist at Brigham Young University, published the first study of what was claimed to be dinosaur DNA. It turned out to be *human* DNA that the PCR had replicated.[4]

Contamination was the problem, and elaborate precautions had to be taken to keep the labs sterile.[5] The results of one lab had to be confirmed by a second, independent lab. It would take decades before it would be possible to trace ancestry quickly and easily and detect disease markers in DNA. The man most responsible for the quantum leap that made this possible, Craig Ventnor, had no interest in archaeology or mummies; he just wanted to sequence the entire living human genome.

Around the beginning of the twenty-first century the Human Genome Project was born—a multi-institution program intended to improve PCR so much that an entire human genome could be sequenced. Ventnor believed that the process being used was unnecessarily slow, so with private funding behind him he embarked on his own maverick genome project using what was then called "shotgun sequencing," a technique most molecular biologists thought was too inaccurate to work. In 2001 Ventnor announced he had succeeded—years before his colleagues had any hope of completing their approach to the project.[6] Ventnor's work was the big step forward that allowed police to solve long-cold cases through DNA, and it was what made Ancestry.com possible. And with the new PCR techniques, extracting DNA from ancient Egyptian mummies was at hand.

Tutankhamun's DNA

The Egyptian Mummy Project, which started out scanning the pharaohs, had molecular biologists on their team who were eager to see what they could find out about the royal mummies. They knew it was a risky project. In 2010 the application of PCR to mummies was still cutting-edge science. There were two DNA laboratories in Cairo, but they had only been used for modern DNA studies, so they had to be entirely rebuilt to work with ancient DNA. It was a bold project, and Tutankhamun was going to be their first subject. One of the reasons for this choice was that there were so many questions about his family. Now DNA might finally provide answers.

There was general agreement about who Tutankhamun's father was—most believed it was Akhenaten—but even this wasn't certain. As soon as Derry and Carter had unwrapped Tutankhamun, they noted the similarities between his skull and that of the mummy Theodore Davis discovered in KV-55. Visual inspection suggested to many that they might be related. Could the KV-55 mummy be Akhenaten? If so, was he really Tutankhamun's father? Then there was the question of Akhenaten's deformity. Perhaps they could find genetic markers for one of the various diseases that had been attributed to the royal family of the Amarna period. Had they really suffered from these maladies? Hopefully some of these questions might be answered by studying the DNA of the mummies involved.

In principle it was even possible to go back further in Tutankhamun's ancestry than just his father. We have the mummy of Amenhotep III, which was found by Victor Loret in the second mummy cache. Was Amenhotep III really Tutankhamun's grandfather? He should be; he was the father of Akhenaten. Then there were the mummies of Yuya and Tuya, discovered by Theodore Davis in the Valley of the Kings. They were the parents of Queen Tiye, Amenhotep III's wife. That would make Yuya and Tuya the great-grandparents of Tutankhamun. There were so many possibilities, but this was pioneering work with lots of hurdles to overcome. The big one was contamination.

The mummy of Tutankhamun had been handled by lots of people over the previous ninety years, so if you took a skin sample to sequence, there's a chance you would end up with Howard Carter's or Douglas Derry's DNA. Over the years, a consensus has formed that the best place to look for ancient DNA is in teeth. The hard dentine on the outside protects the inner tissues from contamination. Drilling into teeth had become standard practice, but this wasn't possible for Tutankhamun because his mouth was shut.

The second-best source is bone. Again, a hard outside surface protects what's inside from contamination. So by drilling into the bones, samples were obtained from Tutankhamun and eleven of his possible family members. Of the eleven, the identities of only three were known for certain: Amenhotep III and his in-laws, Yuya and Tuya. Two to four samples were extracted from each mummy in the study and sequenced. Part of the study looked specifically at Y-chromosomal DNA, the part that reveals the male parental lineage. In addition to sequencing the mummies' DNA, the DNA of the male researchers working in the laboratory was sequenced, to make sure it differed from that of the mummy DNA—another precaution against contamination. Still one more precaution was taken. Duplicate sets of the samples were sequenced by a second Cairo DNA lab, to confirm the findings of the first lab. All the precautions were in place; now they just had to get DNA.

They were successful for six of the mummies, and the results were reported in the prestigious *Journal of the American Medical Association*.[7] If their findings are correct as reported, they did indeed settle questions about Tutankhamun's family tree. The mummy in KV-55 is indeed Tutankhamun's father. Further, by comparing KV-55's DNA with Amenhotep III's DNA, it was possible to establish that they are father and son, so almost certainly the mummy is Akhenaten, the heretic king. This is pretty much what most Egyptologists had expected based on historical records, but it was still very important to have DNA confirm these beliefs.

How Old Is the Mummy in KV-55?

While the Egyptian Mummy Project's DNA results fit Egyptological theory, they don't perfectly align with earlier anatomical studies of the KV-55 mummy. According to the historical record, Akhenaten must have lived into at least his late thirties. We know he ruled for seventeen years and we also know that near the beginning of his reign he started changing the religion and with his followers moved out of the capital and into the desert to found his new city. He couldn't have been a child when he did this. Also, statues at the beginning of his reign show him as an adult. So if we assign to him an age of twenty when he starts making all these momentous changes, and add to this his seventeen years of rule, we get a minimum age of around thirty-seven at the time of death.

Grafton Elliot Smith, who studied the royal mummies and wrote a book about them, said that the bones found in KV-55 indicated an age of around thirty—too young to be Akhenaten, but almost in the ballpark. Smith was aware that the physical data clashed with the Egyptological evidence, but was still willing to say the mummy was Akhenaten. In fact, he does this several times in his published account.[8] It is almost as if he just wants to believe it is Akhenaten. R. G. Harrison did a later analysis of the bones and also noted that Smith seemed determined to confirm that the mummy was Akhenaten regardless of the physical evidence.[9] Harrison's careful and detailed examination of the remains led him to conclude that the mummy could not have been older than twenty-five and was possibly closer to twenty at the time of death. Thus, he could not have been Akhenaten. A still more recent analysis of the bones by an expert from the British Museum places the age at death in the early twenties.[10] So while the bones suggest the mummy was in his early twenties at the time of his death, the DNA suggests we have Akhenaten, the father of Tutankhamun. Which do we accept?

The Egyptian Mummy Project was focusing on DNA of Tutankhamun's family, but they were also the ones who CAT-scanned the royal mummies. What did their scans say about the age of the mummy in KV-55? In the section of their book on the mummy in KV-55, they don't go into details about how they determined the age. They merely say, "The CT study of the skeleton of the KV-55 mummy indicates an adult man, 35–45 years old."[11] They don't say which bones indicated what, what sutures they used to determine age, and so on. Not enough detail to decide who is right about the age.

Tutankhamun's Relatives

The DNA results also confirmed that Tuya and Yuya were the great-grandparents of Tutankhamun, which fits with the Egyptological record. The mummies were found in their tombs with plenty of written records identifying them as Yuya and Tuya, so we know for sure that they were the parents of Queen Tiye, Tutankhamun's grandmother. One more finding that fit the Egyptological record was the DNA obtained from the two fetuses. Tutankhamun was probably the father.

One bonus is that the team may also have identified Queen Tiye, whose mummy had been missing. When Pierre Lacau discovered KV-35 in the Valley of the Kings, he found it contained the second cache of royal mummies. Along with those mummies that were labeled, there were two badly damaged, unidentified female mummies. Ever since their discovery they have been called the Elder Lady and the Younger Lady. There had been considerable speculation about their identities. There was a tentative identification of the Elder Lady based on a locket of Tiye's hair found in Tutankhamun's tomb that matched the hair of the Elder Lady.[12] So the team decided to run the DNA of both mummies. The Elder Lady turned out to be Tutankhamun's grandmother. Queen Tiye had been found. This was another finding that fit in nicely with existing research.

One finding that was a big surprise and doesn't quite fit into the Egyptological record involves the Younger Lady. Her DNA indicates she is Tutankhamun's mother, but who is she? As we know, there is no clear record of Tut's mother. Some believed she must be Kiya, the only known minor wife of Akhenaten. Others thought his mother might be Nefertiti. Kings could have any number of wives, but only one was the Great Wife, and Nefertiti was Akhenaten's. But the younger lady was neither Nefertiti nor Kiya. The DNA also showed that she was Akhenaten's sister. Tutankhamun's parents had been brother and sister. Marriage within the family was not unusual for the royals. It was a way of consolidating power. So Tutankhamun's mother may have been located, but she has been identified only as a sister of Akhenaten; their father, Amenhotep III, had many daughters, and we are not sure which one Tut's mother was. Still, these are amazing findings, most of which matched the Egyptological record, tracing Tutankhamun's lineage for five generations.

How did Tutankhamun Die?

There has been quite a bit of speculation about the cause of Tutankhamun's premature death. Some favor a violent cause of death; others prefer a portrait of a pharaoh weakened by disease. Most of the speculations have been brought together in a survey article that attempts to show the wide variety of such theories.[13] The authors, Frank Rühli and Salima Ikram, don't draw many conclusions, but they do mention a bewildering number of possibilities. Could DNA research help settle some of the issues? With DNA analyses it is possible to find genetic markers for diseases. Because Akhenaten depicted himself as deformed, it has been suggested that he may have suffered from Marfan's syndrome (a genetic disorder that causes diverse physical problems) or some other illness that could have caused him to look that way. The researchers didn't find any evidence for such ailments, but that doesn't mean he didn't have them; the evidence just wasn't found. But they did discover that he had contracted malaria several times. Yet another new discovery.

At the end of their groundbreaking article in the *Journal of the American Medical Association*, Hawass and the Egyptian Mummy Project team permitted themselves a bit of speculation about what Tutankhamun's life might have been like. They present Tutankhamun as a frail young man, weakened by multiple bouts with malaria, limping along with a clubbed foot, needing walking sticks to support himself.[14] The team suggests that with a weakened immune system, Tutankhamun died of multiple causes. The team was well aware that this was speculation, but how probable is the scenario they present? We have already seen that not everyone is convinced about the clubbed foot. What about the weakened-from-malaria theory?

There are four basic kinds of malaria, and Tutankhamun had the worst kind of malaria: falciparum. Sometimes this can cause death, especially in young children, but it is far from a death sentence. In a population with a high incidence of malaria, often the adults build up immunity and function normally, so we can't conclude Tutankhamun was weakened by malaria

and that it contributed to his death. In a brief article on the malaria question, Bernard Lalanne says, "There is no evidence that malaria alone took
the young king to the Beautiful West."[15] Still, the team can be permitted to
indulge in a bit of speculation. They had achieved something remarkable.
They had gotten more DNA out of Egyptian mummies than any other
study, determined the lineage of Tutankhamun for five generations, and
identified two previously unidentified royal mummies. It was more than
anyone could have expected.

The results were so good that some researchers didn't believe them.
Soon after publication, researchers were writing letters to the *Journal of the
American Medical Association* expressing doubts. Two highly respected molecular biologists wrote, "We question the reliability of the genetic data presented in this study and therefore the validity of the authors' conclusions."[16]
They just didn't believe the results. They discuss the possibility of contamination and the difficulty of getting DNA from Egyptian mummies. Perhaps
the reason for the doubts is that no one else had ever gotten so much
DNA from Egyptian mummies. And who were these newcomers? Their
laboratory didn't have a track record of working with ancient DNA—it
was brand-new. And the study's lead molecular biologist had no previous
experience with ancient DNA; he had never even published an article on
mummy DNA. Others also questioned the team's results. In his assessment
of the DNA work, Marc Gabolde questioned the data from a different
angle, pointing out that sometimes it is a matter of interpretation, not fact.
For example, if two individuals share 50 percent of their genetic markers,
we may have a parent/child relationship, but won't know who is the parent
and who is the child.[17] Thus even with modern DNA techniques, the results are often open to interpretation.

Others wrote in to question the death-by-malaria theory, making the
same point I suggested above. One letter-writer said, "In endemic areas,
malaria is a life-threatening disease commonly affecting children until the
age of 6 to 9 years, not semi-immune adults of 18 to 19 years, the age
that Tutankhamun apparently reached."[18] Other criticisms piled on. Svante
Pääbo, perhaps the most respected voice in the field of ancient DNA, said
the study was not well done, and others agreed.

So how can the Egyptian team convince the world their results are legitimate? Share their data. The best solution would be to give samples of
the mummies to a highly respected, well-established laboratory outside of

Egypt. But the Egyptian authorities have a stated policy of not permitting any samples of the royal mummies out of Egypt. Still, I am optimistic the situation will soon be resolved.

In the decade since the Egyptian Mummy Project began, there have been tremendous advances in how we study ancient DNA. Next-generation sequencing goes far beyond what PCR was capable of in 2010. Now we can extract fifty-thousand-year-old Neanderthal DNA from the soil in a cave where these early humans lived. There are new, powerful tools to filter out contaminants. If the Egyptians, working with an outside team, rerun their tests with current techniques, we will know the truth. Or, if they decide to share their samples with outside labs, I am sure we will finally know for sure who Tutankhamun's parents were and if the mummy in KV-55 really is Akhenaten. Perhaps the curse of Tutankhamun will finally be broken.

11

Tutankhamun's Chariots

As we have seen, research on the human remains in Tutankhamun's tomb seems cursed with ambiguity, poor research techniques, indifference, and a host of other problems. These difficulties fade away when one moves to research concerning the inanimate objects found in the tomb—no speculative murder theories, no fantasies about death by horse or hippo, just cold facts. When it comes to Tutankhamun's treasures we are almost always on firm ground. One group of objects that desperately needed research were Tutankhamun's chariots.

The chariot was central to Egypt's economy; they were the high-tech military vehicle that enabled Egypt's army to conquer foreign lands and bring back the spoils of war. Egypt must have built thousands of them. When you visit any of the great temples of the New Kingdom—Luxor, Karnak, Medinet Habu, and so on—you always see images of the pharaoh in his chariot, leading the army in battle. These battle scenes were so numerous that when Napoleon's savants first saw the temples of Egypt, they called them "palaces" because they couldn't imagine a temple, a place of worship, celebrating war. War was so ingrained in the Egyptian mentality that when in the twenty-first year of his reign (1259 BC), Ramses the Great signed a peace treaty (the first recorded in history), it was such a remarkable event that he carved it on the walls of Karnak Temple.[1] Ramses records that the Egyptian army sat down with the Hittite army to have a meal, "no one fighting."

Both the Egyptian and Hittite armies used the chariot in battle, but there were differences. The Hittite chariot was sturdier and carried three soldiers: a driver, an archer, and a spear thrower. Neither the Egyptians nor the Hittites introduced the chariot to warfare; that distinction seems to belong to the Hyksos, a Semitic people who invaded Egypt approximately four centuries before Ramses signed his treaty.

The chariot gave the Hyksos a tremendous military advantage, and they remained in Egypt for slightly more than a hundred years.[2] When the pharaoh Kamose finally attempted to expel the Hyksos, he mentions the Hyksos chariots, adding credence to the idea that the Hyksos introduced the chariot into Egypt.[3] Realizing the utility of the chariot, the Egyptians quickly incorporated it into their army. From the numerous carvings on temple walls, it appears that the chariots were what is called the "pole and yoke" design. A long pole fixed by struts to the body of the chariot extends out and ends in a two-pronged yoke to which the two horses are hitched, each controlled by two reins (Figure 11.1). This much was clear from the carvings, but there were many questions still to be answered about these chariots.

The battle scenes on temple walls always show the pharaoh larger than everyone else and alone in his chariot (Figure 11.2). He shoots arrows at the enemy while controlling his two horses by the reins tied around his waist—an impossibility in the heat of a battle. Almost certainly the pharaoh had a charioteer. Scenes of Ramses the Great at the Battle of Kadesh show him alone in the chariot, but the hieroglyphs describing the scenes mention his charioteer, Menna. As a matter of fact, the account is so detailed

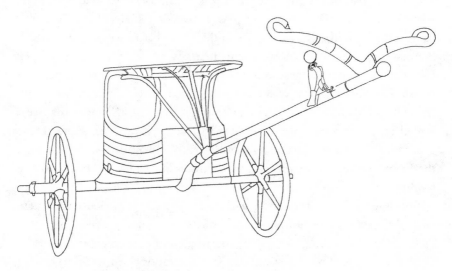

Figure 11.1. A long pole connected the chariot body to the yoke which, in turn, was attached to the two horses. (Drawing by Mary Jordan.)

Figure 11.2. The pharaoh was often shown in battle, alone in his chariot, controlling the horses with the reins tied around his waist—an impossibility. Note the solar disk behind the horses' necks. (Photo by Dr. Clark Haskins.)

that we even know the names of the horses who pulled Ramses's chariot: Victory in Thebes and Mut Is Content.[4] The walls at Luxor Temple show Ramses's army bivouacked, with military carpenters repairing broken chariots (Figure 11.3).

This scene of repairing chariots provides the answer to a question frequently asked: if Egypt produced thousands of chariots, where are they? Until the nineteenth century, no chariot had ever been found in Egypt. Part of the explanation is that chariots were fragile and broke easily. Wood was rare and valuable in Egypt, so if a chariot had outlived its usefulness, the wood would have been recycled. There were no old chariots in Egypt. Another reason we don't find chariots is that after the New Kingdom (1570–1070 BC) the chariot went out of favor.[5] No longer do we see great battle scenes on temple walls; Egypt's military dominance had come and gone. Now there was more than a thousand years of recycling the wood from chariots.

The first chariot found in Egypt was in 1829 by a Franco-Tuscan expedition, but Ippolito Rosellini, the leader of the Tuscan group, brought it back to Florence, where it is today.[6] Then, for more than a century, no chariot

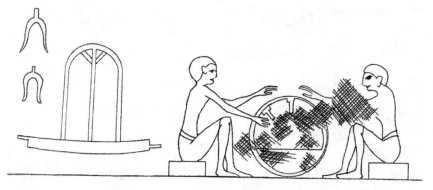

Figure 11.3. Chariots were fragile vehicles and are often shown on tomb and temple walls being repaired. (Drawing by Mary Jordan.)

was found in Egypt. So when Theodore Davis, excavating in the Valley of the Kings, found a chariot in the tomb of Yuya and Tuya—Tutankhamun's great-grandparents—it caused quite a stir. The chariot Davis found was in near perfect condition, and Percy Newberry, the Egyptologist who wrote most of the book for Davis, conjectured: "It is doubtful whether it was ever used except for the funeral procession, for the leather tyres are hardly scratched."[7] Davis published the finds in his sumptuous book, and Howard Carter, then down on his luck, did a painting of the chariot that served as the book's frontispiece (see Color Plate 15).[8] Because it wasn't a military chariot, many of the questions Egyptologists had about chariots shown in battle scenes remined unanswered. So when Carter saw there were complete chariots in Tutankhamun's tomb, he knew this was an important discovery. Before Tutankhamun's tomb was found, there were only two Egyptian chariots in the world; now Carter had several.

Carter's first encounter with the chariots were the four dismantled ones in the Antechamber. The narrow passageway leading down into the tomb had been too small for a complete chariot to be carried in, so the workers sawed off the ends of the axles, removed the wheels, and brought in the chariots in pieces. Nothing like them had ever been seen. Carter was ecstatic:

> In the re-assembling and restoration of these chariots we have a prodigious task ahead of us, but the results will be gorgeous enough to justify any amount of time that is bestowed upon them. From top to bottom they are covered with gold, every inch of which is decorated, either with embossed patterns and scenes upon the gold itself, or with inlaid designs in coloured glass and stone.[9]

Carter made his notes and drawings on cards, creating a permanent record of the entire excavation. More than one hundred of those cards are devoted to the four chariots in the Antechamber. The chariots were singled out for special treatment by Harry Burton, whom we encountered earlier and who was on loan to Carter for the duration of the excavation. Burton's photos were mostly black and white, but a few objects were photographed in color, not an easy process in those days. The chariots appeared in glorious color in British and French newspapers (see Color Plate 16).

With all the excitement created by the chariots, it remains surprising that it would be more than fifty years before the chariots were studied in detail. Perhaps neglect is the true curse of Tutankhamun; research on Tutankhamun has always gone in spurts. After the tomb was fully cleared and the objects were put on display in the Egyptian Museum, very little was done till Piankoff's translations of the shrines. Then there was silence once again. Many Egyptologists realized that there was a vast amount of material to be studied and published; it just wasn't being done. It was a frozen world.

Then, in the 1960s, when the Aswan Dam was being raised to provide hydroelectric power to Egypt's growing population, the Egyptological world thawed and sprang into action. The increase in the height of the dam was going to create Lake Nasser, the largest human-made body of water in the world. Many of Egypt's monuments were going to disappear beneath these waters if something was not done, and an international rescue effort was organized by UNESCO.

To call attention to the plight of Egypt's threatened monuments, and to help raise funds, a small traveling Tutankhamun exhibition was sent to several countries. Along with creating renewed interest in Tutankhamun, the exhibition helped raise millions of dollars for the relief effort, with many great individual successes. The most famous was the moving of Abu Simbel to higher ground by a Swedish team, but there were many more wonderful triumphs, including moving Philae Temple to a higher island nearby and moving many smaller temples inland, away from the rising waters.

Just as interest in Tutankhamun research was increasing, the focus of this research became centered at Oxford University's Griffith Institute. When Howard Carter died, he left his archive of drawings, notes, and photographs of the Tutankhamun excavation to his niece, Phyllis Walker. Soon after World War II ended, she gave all these materials to the Griffith Institute. Not much was done immediately with the material, but with the increased interest in Tut in the 1960s, the Griffith began the first step forward. They initiated their Tutankhamun's Tomb series in 1963 when they published Howard Carter's records of the excavation.[10] The slim volume wasn't anything you might want to read; it was a reference work where you could look to see if Carter had created a card on Tutankhamun's sandals, or if he had copied the inscription on Tutankhamun's sarcophagus. In his introduction to the volume, R. W. Hamilton said, "It is hoped that the present work will serve not only for convenient reference by scholars drawn to Tut'ankhamun's tomb as a source of first-hand material, but also as a preliminary step towards an eventual systematic publication of the treasure itself."[11] Over the next few decades, the Griffith Institute published a dozen works on Tutankhamun's treasures, each written by a specialist on a certain group of objects.[12] When the chariots finally received their due, it was as part of the Griffith Institute's series.[13]

The book dealing with the chariots is a skillful pulling together of everything related to the chariots; as intended by the series, the authors make extensive use of Carter's note cards to describe the chariots and the restoration process. The chariots were stabilized in the tomb so that they could be moved to the conservation laboratory that had been set up in the vacant tomb of Seti II. From Carter's cards, it seems as if the process of conservation was repeated over and over again for each element of these artifacts: "washed with warm water and ammonia, waxed." The chariots and their trappings were not in pristine condition because periodically humidity had entered the tomb in ancient times, perhaps from the occasional rainstorms that plagued the Valley of the Kings. This humidity was very bad for the leather trappings, which had disintegrated to the consistency of glue and run onto various parts of the chariot. Also, some of the parts had been lashed together by rawhide, and when this disintegrated, it freed some of the wood that had been held in shape, permitting the pieces to deform. Still, no one was complaining. It was a fantastic find.

The chariots were made of at least two kinds of wood, elm and birch, both imported. Elm is a straight-grained wood and can be bent by steaming, and it was used to make the six-spoked wheels, probably the most vulnerable part of the chariot.[14] Chariots were driven hundreds of miles on uneven roads to battle sites in foreign countries, and wheels constantly had to be repaired. When we see depictions of chariot wheels on temple walls, it is natural to think that the spokes are made of six straight pieces of wood, but it is more complicated than that. To give the wheels additional strength, the spokes were formed out of three steam-bent, V-shaped pieces of wood that fit together inside the wheel rim and were then wrapped in leather for additional strength (Figure 11.4).

Although there were no real shock absorbers for the wheels, there was a clever substitute for the passengers. Chariots were manned by a driver and an archer. The chariot floor where they stood was woven of leather strips forming a mesh, thus absorbing a considerable amount of the shock that would otherwise be transmitted to the legs of the men.

It was remarkable having four actual chariots from the tomb, but the decoration on Tutankhamun's chariots made them doubly special. The designs were often outlined on sheet gold and then affixed to the chariot body by a thin layer of gesso, a kind of plaster. For geometric designs, colored inlays of faience and glass were inserted directly into the gesso. The four chariots in the Antechamber were labeled A1, A2, A3, and A4 and the decoration for each is unique. As might be expected with military chariots, many of the designs are war-related. For example, the body of A2 depicts captive foreigners bound in very uncomfortable positions. These are the "nine bows"

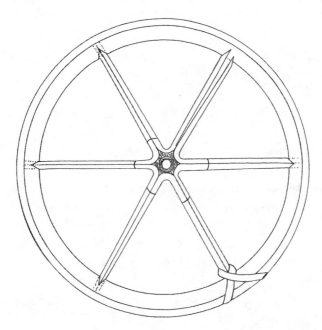

Figure 11.4. Spokes were steam-bent into V-shapes for greater strength. (Drawing by Mary Jordan.)

that were under the pharaoh's feet. One of the hieroglyphic inscriptions on the chariot says, "All lands and all foreign countries [are] beneath the feet of the Radiant God," while another describes Tutankhamun as "the Dual King, ruler of the Nine Bows."[15] Even the yokes of this chariot terminated in captives.

Another military element that appears on the chariots is the god Bes. Depicted as a bearded, bandy-legged dwarf with a lion's face, Bes may have been a foreign import, but he became a fixture in Egyptian culture. He is a guardian both at childbirth and during war, perhaps because both involve pain and possible loss of life. He was often painted on the walls of bedrooms and nurseries, but in his military aspect he brandishes a sword. He too makes his appearance on Tutankhamun's war chariot.

Indeed, the "military chariots" are so heavily decorated that Carter repeatedly refers to them as "the State Chariots."[16] He thought they were used not for battle but for state events, and waxes poetic:

> Their effect when in motion under Egyptian skies must have been one of dazzling splendour, with the jewelled trappings flashing back the light, the horses' plumes waving, in a pageant of brightness, colour, gleam and richness, probably rarely surpassed at any other period, or by any other splendor-loving race.[17]

Carter is of course right in questioning how they were used. Some of their decoration is so fragile that it is clear it couldn't have sustained heavy use. A delicate frieze of prisoners is remarkable for its artistry but totally impractical for a battle machine. The reason we call them "military chariots" is because they have the design of what we see in the battle scenes, but they probably never saw action. However, two replica chariots have been constructed, and when tested they showed that Tutankhamun's chariots could have been used.[18]

Although these "military chariots" may never have been used in action, they do solve a mystery that art historians had wondered about for years. In many of the chariot battle scenes, a disk is shown behind the necks of the horses pulling the pharaoh's chariot (see Figure 11.2). What exactly is it? Is it a metal solar disk attached to the horses' reins? M. A. Littauer and J. H. Crouwel have the definitive answer. Along with the four chariots in the Antechamber, Carter discovered three gilded wood statues of Horus, the falcon god, with a solar disk on his head (see Color Plate 17). On the solar disk was Tutankhamun's name. A groove runs through the bottoms of the statues, so that they could fit on top of the chariots' main poles. The statues had drilled holes through which leather straps passed to affix the statue to the pole. It was something like the elaborate hood ornaments on cars of the 1930s. It was especially appropriate that the pharaoh should have a Horus hood ornament on his war chariot. Every pharaoh had five names, and two associated the king with Horus. The pharaoh went into battle with his insignia before him for protection. Ancient Egyptian artists always showed chariots in profile, so in order to render the disk so it could be seen in the composition, it was shown frontally. There were four chariots in the antechamber but only three falcon statues. Littauer and Crouwel believe the three were for the highly decorated chariots A1, A2, and A3, and that because A4 was a much simpler affair, it didn't warrant one.[19]

The horses' extensively decorated trappings include a spectacular set of blinkers decorated with Eye of Horus symbols. Made of thin wood, curved to the shape of the horse's face, the wood was coated with gesso, overlaid with sheet gold, and inlaid with faience and stone. Harry Burton took a color photograph of the blinkers that appeared in newspapers around the world. The blinkers' main purpose was to keep the horses focused on what was ahead so they weren't distracted by what was next to them. Blinkers are still used today by carriage and race horses.

As the clearing of the tomb continued, two other chariots were discovered in the Treasury and were removed and conserved during the fifth excavation season (1926–1927). At this point in the excavation, Carter seems to have lost interest in chariots; he refers to them as "hunting chariots" and hardly mentions them again.[20] When he discovered the four in the Antechamber, he devoted more than a hundred of his notecards to describing and drawing them, but for the two in the Treasury, just three cards sufficed. At this point in the excavation, Carter seems to have become jaded. When he first cleared the Antechamber and studied the first four chariots, it was all new. Now, at this stage, he has already seen four others, opened the Burial Chamber, and seen the gold mask, solid gold coffin, all the jewelry, and other treasures. Two more chariots were nothing new. Still, Carter could have been right that the last two chariots were hunting chariots. We have representations of Tutankhamun hunting from a chariot on the famous "painted box," which was the first object Carter removed from the Antechamber. The large chest was filled with articles of clothing and was decorated with scenes of Tutankhamun in chariots. The lid shows him hunting desert animals with bow and arrow (Figure 11.5).

Littauer and Crouwel were quite impressed with Tutankhamun's chariots. At the end of their study they say, "This is the great period of chariot warfare, and, in the vehicles of Tut'ankhamun, we may well have examples of the most sophisticated chariots ever made—not just from the point of view of decoration, but also in construction."[21] The Tutankhamun chariots are unique. Since their discovery, no other Egyptian chariots have been unearthed. We have many illustrations of later pharaohs such as Ramses the Great and Ramses III fighting bravely in their chariots, but their tombs were plundered and it is unlikely we will find any more complete chariots. At the time they were writing, in 1985, Littauer and Crouwel mentioned that of the six Tutankhamun chariots, five had been restored, and they pointed out that it was good to have the sixth chariot still dismantled, as they were better able to study construction techniques. Leaving the sixth chariot dismantled was a thoughtful decision by Rex Engelbach, the director of the Egyptian Museum. In a letter to Carter he wrote:

> With the exception of the chariots, practically all the exhibitable objects from the tomb are now on view. . . . [H]owever far I manage to restore them, I shall leave one (the worst) unassembled, since the details of jointing are, to me, of the greatest interest, and should in due course be studied before being covered up.[22]

III. THE DESERT-HUNT

Figure 11.5. Tutankhamun's painted chest showed him hunting desert animals in his chariot. Again, note the solar disk behind the horses' necks. (Photo by Anthony Marks.)

Some years after the Oxford book on the chariots was published, a young conservator, Nadia Lokma, restored that chariot as part of her master's thesis. That chariot was put on display in the 1990s in the Military Museum in the Citadel in Cairo, and Lokma went on to become the Senior wood conservator at the Egyptian Museum.

A great deal was learned from studying the actual chariots, but still more was learned from actually constructing one. In 2015 a professor of engineering mechanics who is also an expert on chariots, Bela Sandor, joined forces with an expert in training horses and horses' trappings, Kathy Hanson, to attempt to reconstruct a chariot in the ancient Egyptian manner.[23] They weren't reconstructing one of Tutankhamun's chariots but constructing a generic ancient Egyptian war chariot. The idea was to learn how they were built, but also to see what they could do. They had a great deal of difficulty steam-shaping the large main pole, and also the steamed V-shaped spokes for the wheels, but after several failed attempts they eventually succeeded. When they assembled the chariot, there was an aha moment: the joint where the chariot's main pole fit into the axel beneath the chariot body was intentionally loose, to absorb some of the bumps.

With the chariot successfully assembled, the next step was to see if it could function in a battle as shown on the temple walls. Could an archer actually shoot arrows accurately from a rapidly moving chariot? First, they tested the top speed: 24 mph, quite fast. With the chariot going at near top speed, a military historian skilled in archery shot arrows at targets, hitting them with remarkable accuracy. He also noted that the cut-out parts of the chariot body had a function other than lightening the chariot: it gave him a place to brace his knee when he was shooting arrows, thus increasing accuracy. These chariots were well designed for their purpose.

In recent times, still more thought has been given to Tutankhamun's six chariots. There is general agreement that four of the chariots are "military"—they are constructed in the military style and *could* have been used in battle. The remaining two have been called "state chariots"—vehicles that could have been used on ceremonial occasions. In a recent article by Edwin Brock, he suggested that one of the state chariots originally had a canopy.[24] There was, indeed, a four-posted canopy found in the tomb near the chariots, but for decades the canopy was considered to be a separate entity, something independent of the chariots. When Brock suggested that perhaps it was attached to one of the chariots, he had real doubts about his own hypothesis. On one of the chariots there seemed to be four places where the poles would fit, but they didn't seem substantial enough to support the canopy.[25] It was impossible to settle the issue because the chariot was not available for either close inspection or precise measurements to see if the canopy was a good fit. That's where the situation remained for several years.

However, quite recently the chariot and canopy were moved to the new Grand Egyptian Museum and both were available for study, leading to an important collaboration. The Japanese Conservation Agency had been helping the Supreme Council of Antiquities set up their new conservation program at the museum, and the organizations teamed up to determine if the canopy and the chariot went together. Nozomu Kawai and his team conserved the chariot and canopy and took exact measurements of both. It was a perfect fit. They went even further, doing a computer-generated virtual reconstruction of the canopy on the chariot and demonstrating that the canopy did indeed belong to the chariot.[26]

12

Tutankhamun as Warrior

The belated research on Tutankhamun's chariots revealed quite a bit about their construction and functions. Clearly not all chariots were equal. There were military chariots and chariots for state occasions, some with canopies. Tutankhamun had both. The fact that he was buried with several military-style chariots indicates that he wanted to be viewed as a warrior, but did he ever really go into battle? Other objects found in the tomb nudge the needle toward yes.

Tutankhamun's Armor

During the first season of excavation, Carter discovered damaged leather armor. Like several other objects from Tutankhamun's tomb, it was unique; no complete armor had ever been found before. From battle scenes on temple walls, we had some idea of what armor looked like, but no one had ever found the real thing, except for some small isolated fragments. Because leather is prone to degrade and is very difficult to restore, practically nothing was done with it till 2018, when it was moved from storage in the Egyptian Museum in Cairo to the new museum's conservation center. This was a once-in-a-lifetime chance for a highly skilled team of specialists, including leather and armor experts, to study King Tut's armor.

The armor, called a cuirass by military historians, fit over Tutankhamun's chest and back like a sleeveless tunic and was originally formed of approximately four thousand small shield-shaped pieces of rawhide overlapped to form a fish-scale pattern. Now only an estimated quarter of the cuirass remains.[1]

The cuirass was in poor condition, with most of the rawhide scales deteriorated to a greater or lesser extent and many scales loose, their lacings long gone (Figure 12.1). Only a very small portion of the scales were still in reasonable condition, so extensive conservation and reconstruction were necessary in order to exhibit it in 2023 at the Grand Egyptian Museum's opening. Harry Burton's photo of the cuirass in its original find spot was extremely helpful because of the armor's current compromised state. Each scale had several holes in the same places for lacing it into the backing. In addition, each scale had a groove and ridge in almost the same place that prevented the scales from sliding apart when hit by an arrow. Tests done with arrows shot at dummies wearing similar armor showed the protection to be quite effective.[2] The scales seem to have been mass-produced by pressing them into molds to create the ridges and grooves.

The garment was made of several layers, with the scales laced onto a thin layer of leather backed by up to six layers of linen. The linen would have absorbed sweat in the heat of battle and made it more comfortable to wear, and the thin layer of leather would have been light but flexible, adding strength. This was a very sensible and well-made piece of military gear, but

Figure 12.1. Most of the scales of the armor had deteriorated and were loose. (Photo courtesy Dr. André Veldmeijer.)

it was also a bit of a fashion statement. The cuirass was composed of scales dyed in two different colors, red and green, probably with different rows of each color.

Much was learned from just visual inspection of the cuirass, but some things required more than just looking. The team wondered: had the leather been treated, or was it rawhide? Rawhide is just what it sounds like. It is simply the hide of the animal with the flesh scraped off it. The virtue of rawhide is that it is flexible; treated leather is harder and stiffer. Because the leather was now thirty-three hundred years old, they couldn't tell just by looking at it if it was treated or untreated. They decided to answer the question by experimenting, so they made scales with both treated and untreated leather. They began by tracing the shape of the scales onto the two types of leather and cutting them out. The moment of truth came when they pounded the two kinds of leather scales into the mold to give them the ridges and grooves. The treated leather shattered; it was too brittle. Tutankhamun's armor was rawhide.[3]

The armor research came about when a forgotten object was moved from storage in Cairo to the new museum. The move coincided with the availability of a new research tool that led to yet another discovery about the armor. Reflectance transformation imaging (RTI) showers the surface of any object with light from any direction desired so that when a photograph is taken, details of the surface are revealed that the naked eye would have missed. RTI revealed wear patterns on the edges of the scales suggesting not only that this was a carefully crafted piece of armor but also that it had been worn. Perhaps in battle by Tutankhamun?

Tutankhamun's Bows

One of the earliest books in the Griffith Institute's Tutankhamun's Tomb series was a study of the composite bows found in the tomb.[4] In ancient Egypt, the bow was the weapon of choice. Every chariot carried an archer, and in naval battles, the ships' decks were used as platforms from which bowmen could shoot arrows. While the Nubians were one of the traditional enemies of Egypt, they were also admired for their prowess as bowmen and were sometimes hired as mercenaries by the Egyptians. The ancient Egyptian term for Nubia was Ta-sety, "Land of the Bow."

Egyptian archers used two kinds of bows, simple and composite. The composite was the one to have and was introduced into Egypt from Asia during the Second Intermediate Period (1782–1570 BC), the era when the Hyksos invaded Egypt. By gluing together three different materials in layers, fabricators could considerably increase the strength and durability of the bow. An ancient Egyptian composite bow could shoot an arrow more than two hundred meters, and pharaohs often depicted themselves shooting arrows that pierced copper ingots.

It took considerable skill to create a compound bow. Usually the center layer was wood (ash), the back of the bow was a layer of sinew, and a layer of horn was on the front. All this was then often covered with a layer of bark. Composite bows were a luxury item, owned only by royalty and the nobility. Before the discovery of thirty-two of these bows in Tutankhamun's tomb, fewer than a dozen composite bows had been discovered in Egypt, and these were mostly fragmentary. Carter's first encounter with Tutankhamun's bows involved the thirteen in the Antechamber. Years later he would clear another sixteen from the Annex, and then found three more in a box in the Treasury, nearly tripling the number of composite bows found in Egypt. Carter was clearly impressed by the bows he found in the Antechamber:

> Resting on the northernmost of the couches [were] a quiver of arrows, and a number of compound bows. One of these last was cased with gold and decorated with bands of inscriptions and animal motifs in granulated work of almost inconceivable fineness—a masterpiece of jeweller's craft.[5]

Carter didn't know it, but he had singled out for praise the most interesting bow in the tomb. As Carter says, the gold decoration is spectacular and led to this bow being called the Bow of Honor, as it was unlikely that a bow so extensively decorated in gold was ever used. Another point of interest is that only this bow had been wrapped in linen, like a mummy, before being placed in the tomb. Further, the two inscriptions on the bow give us more insight into the burial of Tutankhamun. They are traditional inscriptions: "King of Upper and Lower Egypt, Lord of the Two Lands, Possessed of Might, Neb-Kheperu-Re." and "Son of Re, of his body, his beloved, Neb-Kheperu-Re." What makes them interesting is that they have replaced an earlier inscription.

Wallace McLeod, an expert on bows in the ancient world, asked Geoffrey Martin to examine the inscription closely. Martin agreed with other experts: the cartouches of Tutankhamun seem to have replaced the cartouches of Akhenaten's co-regent, King Ankhkheperu Neferneferuaten.[6] We have seen such replacements before. The miniature coffinettes that once held Tutankhamun's internal organs had been reinscribed for Smenkare, and Tutankhamun's unfinished sarcophagus may also have been taken from Smenkare's tomb. Again, we have a picture of the frantic pace with which officials were trying to assemble Tutankhamun's burial. My impression is that someone really must have cared. Why take a bow and reinscribe it when you already have twenty-eight other highly decorated bows? The answer is that this bow is the finest of the finest, and someone wanted Tutankhamun to have it.

There were other interesting aspects to the inscriptions on the bows. Four of the bows bore the name Tutankhaten, the name Tut was born with and which he changed during his first year as king. So these four bows must have been given to the boy-king when he was nine or ten years old, perhaps to be used for hunting, as he was not yet old enough for battle.

The compound bows were the Lamborghinis of archery, but Tutankhamun also has a supply of self-bows—the kind we all think of when we think "bow and arrow." The self-bow was a single staff of wood, notched at both ends to hold the string. Tutankhamun was buried with fourteen of these, most of them in an unexpected place: the burial chamber, where they were found between the shrines, some standing upright in a corner, most lying flat on the floor. Why were they placed there? Did they have special significance to the boy-king, and a loyal servant placed them near his master?

Most of the self-bows are simple undecorated affairs, but there was a highly decorated bow case similar to Tutankhamun's famous painted chest. Here, too, Tutankhamun is shown in his chariot defeating Nubians and Asiatics (a term used by the Egyptians for Syrians and their neighbors), but also with his saluki hounds, hunting in the desert. Along with the bows and bow case, Tutankhamun was buried with more than four hundred arrows. As McLeod commented, "He was interred with a veritable armory of archery tackle."[7]

The feeling one gets from all this archery equipment is that it meant something to Tutankhamun. I would bet he enjoyed hunting. There's no glory in shooting ducks on a pond, so why show yourself in that activity if you didn't do it? Going into battle is another matter. However, some recent research nudges the needle toward Tutankhamun as warrior. Again, it's one of those projects that come out of Tutankhamun's treasures being moved to the new Grand Egyptian Museum.

King Tut's Hunting Fan

There was one other object in the tomb that suggests Tutankhamun may have been a warrior: a fan. In a warm country with relentless sunshine, fans are important. Some fans, called sunshades, were the prerogative of royalty. They were made of wood, often gilded, and consisted of a long pole with a round-topped board at the top. Ostrich feathers were frequently inserted into small holes drilled into the round top. Such a fan would have been carried by a servant and positioned appropriately as the sun moved.

One of these fans is shown in the famous scene in Akhenaten's tomb at Amarna, where we see the birth of Tutankhaten. He is shown as a baby in a nurse's arms. Behind them is a servant with the sunshade, so we can be sure we are looking at a royal baby.

One of the fans (no. 242) found in Tutankhamun's tomb commemorates a specific event in the boy-king's life. The round-topped board at the top is covered with a thick gold foil that on one side is embossed with scenes of Tutankhamun hunting ostriches. The other side shows the triumphant return home, with Tutankhamun bringing ostrich feathers he obtained "while out hunting in the desert east of Heliopolis."[8]

It is clear that the fan commemorates an actual hunting party in which the young king participated. If we know he enjoyed hunting, that makes it all the more possible that he actually stepped onto a battlefield. So when we pull everything together it seems more plausible to view the young pharaoh as being as healthy as other young men in ancient Egypt, enjoying hunting in the desert, and perhaps even leading them into battle.

The Boy-King Leads the Army

As we've seen, when the tomb was cleared, Carter said he had learned what Tutankhamun had, but not who he was. Carter couldn't have imagined what scholars seventy or eighty years later would discover about the boy-king. Some research was carefully planned, but sometimes it arose from unexpected places. One of these opportunities came about because Dr. Ray Johnson just happened to be in the right place at the right time and possessed the right skills to recognize what was happening.

Pharaohs often didn't respect the sanctity of their predecessors' temples. Sometimes they might take down a temple just to obtain inexpensive building material for their own monuments. It is cheaper to reuse blocks already quarried than to quarry your own. But there are other reasons for taking down a monument. Sometimes the goal was to erase a pharaoh's name from the records, as happened with Akhenaten, Tutankhamun's father. Because he was viewed as a heretic, soon after he died Akhenaten's monuments were taken down and recycled. The temple Akhenaten built at Karnak in the early years of his reign was taken down and thousands of carved blocks from this temple were reused as filler inside the pharaoh Horemheb's massive gateways at Karnak. The city that Akhenaten built in the desert, the Horizon of the Aten, was mostly abandoned within five years of his death and the monuments were systematically taken down by Seti I and Ramses II.

We know that Tutankhamun's first major building project in Thebes was to complete a monument begun by his grandfather, Amenhotep III. His grandfather had built a 150-foot-long colonnaded hall at Luxor Temple, but Amenhotep died before it was decorated. When Akhenaten became king, he banished the gods of Egypt and moved to Amarna, so the Luxor columns and walls stood bare for more than a decade. When Tutankhamun succeeded his father, the boy-king returned to Thebes and was advised to complete the decoration of the hall, in order to show that Tutankhamun was like his grandfather, not his father, and would give the people back their religion.

Tutankhamun decorated the Colonnade Hall with scenes of the most glorious of Thebes's festivals—the Opet Festival. Opet was the ancient name for Karnak, home to the traditional Theban trinity of Amun (the father), Mut (the mother), and Khonsu (their son). At the opening of the festival the statues of Amun, Mut, and Khonsu were taken from their shrines in Karnak Temple, placed in divine barques, and sailed one and a half miles along the Nile to Luxor Temple (southern Opet), where they remained for a week of celebrations. Tutankhamun's decorations show marvelous details of the joyous procession from Karnak as it traveled south to Luxor Temple and then returned to Karnak at the end of the festival. Tutankhamun is prominently featured in the reliefs on the west wall of the colonnade, where he makes offerings to Amun, Mut, and Khonsu. Unfortunately, he doesn't get credit for his devotions; his name has been erased and replaced by Pharaoh Horemheb's (Figure 12.2). This is well known; these reliefs have been studied many times, especially by the University of Chicago's Epigraphic Survey of the Oriental Institute (based at Chicago House in Luxor), which for more than thirty years has been recording the scenes on

Figure 12.2. At Luxor Temple, Tutankhamun's youthful portrait remains, but his name has been erased and replaced by King Horemheb's. (Photo by Dennis Forbes.)

the walls of Luxor Temple. This work recording Tutankhamun's hall is what led to a surprising discovery.

For many years the Antiquities Service (now the Supreme Council of Antiquities) had planned to uncover an ancient pathway of sphinxes that led from Karnak Temple to Luxor Temple, but the avenue was covered by later buildings that would have to be removed. Over the years, buildings were taken down, some from Luxor's medieval period. During the removal, it was discovered that the foundations of these medieval structures contained inscribed blocks from the ancient temples in the area. The Antiquities Service collected these reused blocks and stored them for future study. As the blocks accumulated, the Chicago House Egyptologists decided to examine them to see if any were from the Tutankhamun colonnade. The top few feet of the colonnade walls were missing, so it was reasonable to assume some of those blocks might have been taken in the Middle Ages. They were right. More than fifteen hundred missing blocks were found and were later included in the Oriental Institute's two publications on the Tutankhamun colonnade.[9] So, thanks to good detective work, they were able to fill in missing scenes at the tops of the walls. But this isn't the research that comes from an unexpected place. That's the second part of this story.

One of the people looking at the blocks was a young graduate student, Ray Johnson, who would later become the director of the Epigraphic Survey and continue working at Luxor for more than thirty years. He noticed that there were some two hundred additional reused Tutankhamun blocks that didn't belong to the Luxor colonnade. They had Tutankhamun's cartouches, so they were his, but the scale of the carving and the style were different from those seen in the Luxor blocks. They came from another monument referred to on the blocks as "the Mansion of Nebkheperure at Thebes." They were from Tutankhamun's mortuary temple, a previously unknown monument started by Tutankhamun and finished by Aye as a memorial to the young king after his untimely death. This was big news. A new source of information about Tutankhamun had been uncovered.

During the New Kingdom, every pharaoh built a mortuary temple where priests would make offerings for the soul of the deceased king. These temples were built on the west bank of the Nile, not far from the Valley of the Kings, the realm of the dead. These mortuary temples are some of Egypt's most famous monuments. Deir el Bahri is Hatshepsut's, the Ramesseum is Ramses the Great's, and Medinet Habu is Ramses III's. On the walls of these temples the pharaohs carved the deeds of which they were most proud. As we saw in Chapter 2, Hatshepsut's recorded the expedition she sent to the land of Punt, in the south, to bring frankincense and myrrh trees back to Egypt. On the walls of the Ramesseum we can see and read about Ramses the Great's heroic efforts at the Battle of Kadesh. And at Medinet Habu we see Ramses III repelling the attack of the Sea People, a group of immigrants from the Mediterranean area. The mortuary temples are important historical documents, providing information about the reigns of the pharaohs who built them. They are primary sources that enable us to reconstruct the lives of the rulers of ancient Egypt. What might Tutankhamun's mortuary temple tell us about his life that had eluded Carter? Ray Johnson wondered about this too.

But there were only a couple of hundred blocks from the mortuary temple. Was that enough to reconstruct anything about Tutankhamun's shadowy life? The answer was yes, but only because of the unchanging nature of Egyptian art. Ancient Egyptian artists were often told to copy what previous generations did. If you look at the Ramesseum, Medinet Habu, or the mortuary temple of Seti I, you will see the pharaoh alone in his chariot, horses' reins tied around his waist, shooting arrows at the enemy. On one wall it might be the Nubians who have the arrows in them, on another it is the Asiatics, but it is basically the same scene. It is practically boilerplate art, and because the artists used grids to plan the wall scenes, even the proportions are the same. So if you have only a few blocks but know what the rest of the scene should be, you can pretty much fill in what is missing. For example, if you have a block that shows reins tied to a waist, you know it is the pharaoh's waist and that there will be a pharaoh shooting a bow above the waist, a chariot beneath the waist, a pair of horses to the left, and so on. And if you have one block with a Nubian with an arrow in him, you know there will be lots more Nubians with arrows in them. The static nature of Egyptian art permits such a reconstruction.

Reconstructing the scenes on Tutankhamun's mortuary temple took Ray Johnson the better part of ten years and became his doctoral dissertation.[10] It is a brilliant piece of work requiring numerous skills. Almost all the members of the Oriental Institute's team at Luxor possess these skills. Many have doctorates in Egyptology; they can translate the hieroglyphs on the walls they are studying. It's not just pictures to them. They are also all artists, capable of making very accurate copies of what is on the wall and also capable of drawing what is missing. They are a remarkable group of people. These are the skills that Ray Johnson brought to the task of reconstructing Tutankhamun's mortuary temple on paper.

From the newly discovered blocks, it became clear to him that there were two battle scenes, one in which Tutankhamun and a division of charioteers were attacking a Syrian fort and one showing the young pharaoh defeating the Nubians, Egypt's enemies to the south.

Aside from emphasizing Tutankhamun's skill as warrior, the reconstruction is important for understanding the development of the standard battle scene. Prior to the reconstruction, battle scenes were generally believed to be a development of the Nineteenth Dynasty, the dynasty that followed Tutankhamun's, starting with Seti I's mortuary temple. Johnson's reconstruction shows that Tutankhamun's reign played a significant part in the development of this type of scene. Because Tut came after the Amarna period, when there was a new freedom of artistic expression, it should not be surprising that Tutankhamun's artists retained a bit of this spirit. Ray Johnson says:

> The carving style of Tutankhamen's reign is easy to recognize, since it combines Amarna-period naturalism with the traditional carving style of his Tutmosid predecessors. As a result Tutankhamun's scenes exhibit a liveliness and energy that sets them apart from temple decoration before and after the late Eighteenth Dynasty.[11]

Tutankhamun's artists were almost certainly contributing to the development of the battle scene genre, but there are also some unique details that had never been seen before. In the traditional battle scenes of later pharaohs, there is usually a scene showing the counting of the enemy dead at the end of the battle. This was done by cutting off the hands of the dead and piling them up in one place, where military accountants record the number (Figure 12.3). In Tutankhamun's Syrian battle scene we have something unusual: the soldiers are shown with several skewered hands on their spears (Figure 12.4). Another unique detail in Tutankhamun's war scene involves the voyage home after the victory. On one block we can see a bound Syrian prisoner suspended in a cage as a trophy of war (Figure 12.5).

This reconstruction is important for several reasons. First, it gives us a new perspective on Tutankhamun. He wanted to be viewed as a warrior. His warrior image is reinforced on the famous painted chest found in the

Figure 12.3. At the end of battles, the hands of the enemy killed were cut off and placed in a pile for counting. (Photo by Pat Remler.)

Antechamber of his tomb. Here too he is shown defeating Nubian and Asiatic foes (see Color Plate 18). Of course, just because he wanted to be shown in battle, it doesn't mean he was actually there, but it is possible. All this new information came from an unexpected source: the foundations of medieval buildings at Luxor. Ray Johnson was able to trace the blocks back to Karnak Temple's second pylon, where Horemheb reused the dismantled Tutankhamun mortuary temple blocks as fill; some are still visible in the pylon. This pylon, in turn, was partly quarried in the Middle Ages for building material and the blocks transported to medieval Luxor. A French

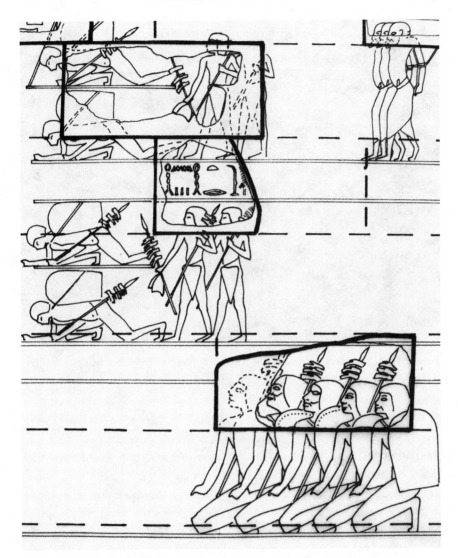

Figure 12.4. In Tutankhamun's battle scene, the hands of the enemy are shown skewered. (Drawing by Dr. Ray Johnson.)

scholar working at Karnak, Marc Gabolde, had analyzed some of the blocks still at Karnak, and he and Johnson realized that they were studying different blocks from the same monument. They are now collaborating on a final publication. It is possible, almost probable, that in the future a similar find will fill in more details.

Figure 12.5. A Syrian being bought back to Egypt in a cage as a trophy of war. (Photo by Dr. Ray Johnson.)

When pharaohs recorded battles on their mortuary temples, they almost always recorded the year in which the battle took place, such as "year 5 of the reign of Ramses." When we have a year, this is a pretty good indication that a battle really did take place. The king may not have been as heroic as he claims, but something happened. Do Tutankhamun's battle scenes have dates? We don't know, for too many blocks are missing. However, as future building projects in the city of Luxor progress, undoubtedly more blocks will be found from Tutankhamun's mortuary temple. It will be interesting to see if either the Syrian or Nubian campaign is dated. Tutankhamun ascended to the throne when he was about nine years old and ruled only for ten years. So for the first four or five years of his reign, it is a good bet that he never went into battle. If, however, we discover a battle scene dated to year 9 or so of his reign, he probably actually participated. If the two battle scenes are undated, they are generic and most likely the boy-king stayed home.

If we put all the recent research together, we get a portrait of Tutankhamun quite different from what is frequently presented in popular media, and even in scientific publications. Our survey of the X-ray and CAT-scan research has shown that we should not be so quick to draw a portrait of Tutankhamun as the frail monarch who walked on his ankle and suffered from a variety of disorders. Even the study of his footwear, as we will see in Chapter 13, moves the discussion away from Tutankhamun as disabled. And the staffs he was buried with were signs of authority, as is testified by tomb paintings throughout ancient Egypt. Similarly, because Tutankhamun is shown on the little golden shrine hunting ducks while sitting down, some have argued that this was necessary because he was frail. Nonsense. As Marianne Eaton-Kraus has shown, hunting while sitting is a common motif in ancient Egyptian art.[12] There has even been a recent article by someone who has bought into the frail-pharaoh version of Tutankhamun but still correctly points out that holding a staff and hunting while seated are not signs of disability.[13] Indeed, there may even be a scene of Tutankhamun's father, Akhenaten, hunting while seated.[14] Again, was Tutankhamun a warrior? The needle is moving toward yes.

13

Tutankhamun's Shoe Closet

Objects found in tombs fall into two categories: funerary objects (coffins, canopic jars, ushabti figures, etc.) and daily life objects (everything else). Because the Egyptians believed that the next life would be pretty much a continuation of this one, they tried to take everything with them—clothes, toys, linens, even mummified pets. This is one of the reasons we know so much about daily life in ancient Egypt. Tutankhamun was no exception, and his daily life objects are just now getting the attention they deserve. Some have been in display cases on the second floor of the Egyptian Museum in Cairo for decades, but many have been in storage. As we have seen, this is now changing.

The new Grand Egyptian Museum (GEM) was under construction for more than a decade, but its Conservation Center was up and running for years before the GEM's opening. During this time, there was a continual flow of objects from the old Egyptian Museum in Cairo to the GEM's Conservation Center. Many of Tutankhamun's possessions had been in storage for decades, unseen by scholars. Now these daily life objects are accessible, and researchers are jumping at the chance to study and photograph them as they are being conserved. One collection that has recently been studied is Tutankhamun's sandals.

The boy-king was buried with approximately thirty-five pairs and more than a dozen singletons of footwear, in a variety of styles for different purposes. Some were for daily use, some were for ceremonial use, and a pair of gold sandals was created specifically for his journey to the next world. The everyday footwear in ancient Egypt was the sandal, and this is reflected in the contents of Tutankhamun's tomb. He had several styles of sandals, some of leather, some of a combination of materials, but most are what André Veldmeijer, an expert on ancient Egyptian footwear and leather, calls "sewn sandals."[1] These sandals are made of a combination of halfa grass, doum palm leaf, and papyrus, all materials that were available to Egyptians of any social status.

To create a sandal, a transverse bundle of halfa grass was wrapped with palm leaf that was used simultaneously to sew it to the previous bundle. This was repeated, forming the approximate shape of the sole. When complete, the sole shape was cut to the desired size and finished along the edges with a comparable set of halfa grass bundles (up to three) wrapped and sewn together (Figure 13.1). The strap, in Tutankhamun's sandals made of papyrus (*Cyperus papyrus*), was then secured to the sole. Tutankhamun had dozens of this kind of sandal. One of Veldmeijer's tasks was to assess the condition of the sandals and then determine the best method of preservation by the scientists of the GEM's Conservation Center.

When the sandals were first discovered, Carter reported that many were quite fragile. Over the centuries in a hot dry tomb, they had dehydrated, which preserved them (bacteria will not act on material if there is no moisture present) but also made them fragile. The leather sandals and shoes were in a far worse state of deterioration because in some parts of the tomb there were relatively high humidity levels. To preserve the sandals when they were first discovered, Lucas and Mace gave them a coating of wax, which stabilized them. This was an approved technique in those days, but over the next hundred years, the wax darkened and changed the color of the sandals, and it also attracted dust and grime. Tutankhamun's sandals had a layer of modern dirt on them. It was clear that the wax would have to be removed.

First came a mechanical cleaning, in which fine picks were used to remove the top layer of dirt and wax from the surface of the sandals. The conservators then tested different chemicals to see what would be best to remove the remainder of the wax. A mixture of white spirit and ethyl alcohol proved best, and with Q-tips dipped in the mixture, they removed most of the remaining wax by gently rolling the Q-tips over the surface of the sandals.[2] The last stage of cleaning was with an ultrasonic steam cleaner scalpel. Think of how rugs are cleaned—but on a microscopic level, and very gently. This last cleaning had two purposes. The first was to remove the last layer of wax by heating and dissolving it. The second purpose was to gently introduce a small bit of humidity back into the fibers, making them less brittle and more flexible. This careful, thoughtful sequence of

(a)   (b)

Figure 13.1. Tutankhamun's sewn sandals. (Courtesy Dr. André Veldmeijer.)

procedures is the kind of treatment many of the Tutankhamun objects are now receiving, which will enable them to be handled and studied.

Many of the sewn sandals showed signs of wear, and it is important to note that when the researchers examined them, no one observed that there was extreme wear to one side more than the other. This argues against the idea that Tutankhamun had a severe clubfoot and walked on his ankle.[3] The leather sandals and shoes were in such poor condition that such features could not be seen anymore.

Tutankhamun's sewn sandals had a parallel with the ones he was wearing in his gold coffin. When the mummy was unwrapped, Carter discovered that he was wearing a pair of solid gold sandals (Color Plate 12) that closely imitate a pair of the sewn sandals. Engraved on the soles are representations of bundles of halfa grass wrapped and sewn together with palm leaves. Similarly, the strap also mimics in gold the papyrus strap of the normal sandals. Obviously, the gold sandals were never worn in life. They were funerary, intended to protect the boy-king's feet till he resurrected in the next world. Toward this end, his toes were also encased in gold covers, called stalls.

For the Egyptians, gold was the stuff of immortality because it never tarnishes or decays. Gold was prized by most ancient civilizations, but for Egyptians, gold was necessary for the next world. Because it never changed, anything it covered might also never change. Tutankhamun's inner coffin was solid gold, to protect the mummy in an imperishable container. There were once significant deposits of gold in Egypt, but by Tutankhamun's time they had been depleted. Nubia, her neighbor to the south (modern Sudan), had plenty of gold. Egypt's rulers made sure to keep the Nubians under their control to ensure a steady stream of gold.

We mentioned before that many representations of Tutankhamun were destroyed because of his association with the Amarna Heresy. One of the few that have survived is in the tomb of Huy, Tutankhamun's viceroy to Nubia. The painting on one wall shows Tutankhamun in a tented pavilion presenting Huy with his symbol of authority before he departs for Nubia. On another wall we see Nubians bringing tribute in the form of gold rings. Tutankhamun's funerary sandals may well have been made from gold sent back to Egypt by Huy.

The most complex of all of Tutankhamun's sandals were the ones that made the biggest political statement. Tutankhamun had a pair of sandals that permitted him to literally tread on his enemies wherever he went (Figure 13.2). On the soles of each sandal are representations of two of Egypt's traditional enemies, one an Asiatic and one a Nubian. Wherever Tutankhamun walked, he was stepping on his enemies.

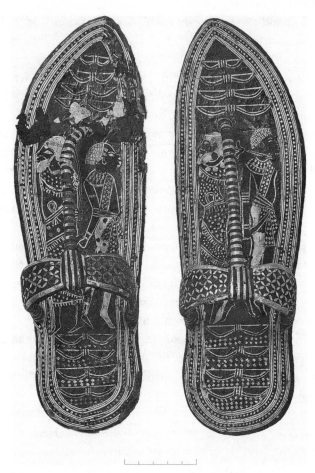

Figure 13.2. Mosaic sandals designed so Tut could walk on his enemies. (Courtesy Dr. André Veldmeijer.)

As we've seen, Egypt had nine traditional enemies, often called the Nine Bows. Statues of pharaohs frequently show them standing on the Nine Bows carved on the pedestal. Sometimes only eight bows decorate smaller objects, and that is what we have with the sandals. Veldmeijer follows Carter in calling these sandals "marquetry veneer sandals," and they are quite complex. The sole of the sandal is wood, covered with a thin layer of gesso, and that is topped by a piece of leather. The figures of the eight bound captives and the decorative borders around them are created with white birch bark, red bark, gold foil, and green leather, all inlaid into the leather top like a mosaic.

The two sandals are not artistically identical. For example, on the left sandal the Nubian is tied at the elbows, but on the right he is tied at both his neck and elbows. There are other differences in the details, suggesting that the two sandals may have been made by two different craftsmen.

At the end of his book on Tutankhamun's footwear, Veldmeijer makes an interesting observation about what was not in the collection of Tutankhamun's footwear. Where are his baby shoes?[4] There are no sandals of a size for a child under the age of ten. Why not? We have his "baby throne," the one he had as a child (see Chapter 3). Veldmeijer makes some suggestions, and they seem reasonable. Tutankhamun became king at about ten years of age. Perhaps no one was expecting him to become king, and thus his childhood clothes and footwear were not saved. He had six sisters who might have been expected to produce heirs. No need to keep the baby sandals.

One section of the book has the heading "Not Kept Objects."[5] This raises a troubling issue. There was a careful catalogue made of all the objects in the tomb—as a matter of fact, several. When Harry Burton photographed the tomb contents, he placed a number card next to each object. That was the first record. Then, when each item was removed from the tomb, Howard Carter recorded it on his index cards, and these cards still exist today at Oxford's Griffith Institute. Then when the objects were transferred from the Valley of the Kings to the Egyptian Museum in Cairo, the museum gave them another number in its *journal d'entrée* (a large ledger book; remember, the French were running the Antiquities Service at the time, so everything was in French). So all objects (or almost all) were carefully recorded. It seems that there were sandals photographed by Burton and recorded on cards by Carter that then disappear from history. Veldmeijer mentions one such item: "Carter's entry 085c is a sole of a left sandal, made of leather (Card No. 085c; figure 1.4, table 9). As mentioned, the sandal was in poor condition and not kept."[6]

It is difficult to imagine today that a Tutankhamun object was just thrown out because it was in poor condition, but there are other examples of royal sandals that didn't make the cut as well. Were they given away as souvenirs, as were the seals on the tomb's doorway? Were they merely discarded? We will probably never know. Some might have been left in Thebes and stored there, like most of the baskets.

Tutankhamun's Staves

The research on Tutankhamun's footwear led Veldmeijer with his colleague Salima Ikram to a crossover study of Tutankhamun's walking sticks.[7] Both footwear and walking sticks involve locomotion, but more importantly, some of the staffs were created using the same marquetry craftmanship as the sandals. In all, Tutankhamun had 130 staves in his tomb, and some are unique.

Staffs and walking sticks played a significant role in ancient Egyptian society. They could be a symbol of authority, a political statement, or just an aid in walking. (Sometimes a stick is just a stick.) An indication of just how central staffs were to ancient Egyptian society is in the standard textbook for teaching Middle Egyptian, the language used in Tutankhamun's time.[8] At the back of the book is a dictionary where you can look up words alphabetically, as in most dictionaries, but you must know the sound associated with each hieroglyph. If you don't know the sound of a particular hieroglyph, you can look it up in the signs list, which is arranged according to subject. So all the animal hieroglyphs are grouped together, all the hieroglyphs of trees are together, and several staff hieroglyphs are grouped together. There were enough of them, and they were important enough that they are a category. One was pronounced *heqa* and meant "ruler." | Pharaohs held in their crossed hands a *heqa* scepter and a flail, signifying their power. It is probably just an extension of a shepherd's crook, by which the pharaoh controls his flock.

The *was* scepter is another important symbol. *Was* meant "power." ⌐ There is the head of an animal on top (some think it is a ram) and a cloven hoof on the bottom. The capital of southern Egypt was called Wast in ancient times. The hieroglyphs forming the name of the city are: You can see the *was* scepter. The semi-circle is a loaf of bread and indicates that the noun is feminine. The circle with the lines in it depicts a crossroads. Wherever you have a crossroad, you have a city, so that hieroglyph tells you the word is the name of a city, Wast. The Greeks later called the city Thebes; still later the Arabs invaded and upon seeing the large ancient temples called it Luxor, Arabic for "palaces."

Not every staff was fancy. Often, in front of the tombs of the nobles, carved on the walls we see the deceased proudly striding forward with a staff of authority in his hand. These are usually just simple straight walking sticks. Even Tutankhamun was shown with a simple walking stick.

Some sticks share a similarity with the sandals, in that they were propaganda that pharaohs used to show that they had subjugated their enemies. Tutankhamun's sandals had foreigners on the soles so that he could step on them. He also had five canes featuring foreigners in the handle part, where he could crush them in the palm of his hand (Figure 13.3). The foreigner is arching backward, forming the handle of the cane, so he is firmly in Tutankhamun's grasp. These canes were almost certainly ceremonial. The tip of the cane is made of ceramic (faience) bearing Tutankhamun's name, and presumably Tut would not have wanted to grind his own name into the dirt as he walked.

Tutankhamun's staves, like the sandals, allow us to draw some conclusions about his health. Veldmeijer and Ikram point out that the staves show few signs of use, and they conclude, "It does not seem as if Tutankhamun leant

Figure 13.3. Tutankhamun's canes ensured he would always have the enemy in the palm of his hand. (Courtesy Dr. Andr Veldmeijer.)

heavily for support on the sticks that have been found in his tomb."[9] Some were never sturdy enough to support a person's weight. Thus, the large number of staves found in the tomb do not support the theory that he had so many because of his clubfoot. Another scholar, Emily Smith-Sangster, makes a similar point, but from an art historical point of view. Staves were symbols of authority, not disability. In a review article she shows that it was common for people of authority to be shown with walking sticks, and even leaning on them, so we can't conclude that depictions of Tutankhamun with staves indicate frailty.[10]

14

Tutankhamun's Sarcophagus

The daily life objects in Tutankhamun's tomb give us insights into who the boy-king was. Things like sandals, bows and arrows, chariots, and even a fan tell us he liked hunting, wanted to be viewed as a warrior, and probably didn't have a limp. Funerary objects, things prepared specifically for his burial, are different. Because they were prepared after his death by others, they will be less revealing of his likes and dislikes, but they can still yield information about ancient Egyptian belief in the afterworld, and also about the seventy-day period between the king's death and his burial.

There was, of course, a great number of funerary objects found in the tomb—ushabti statues, canopic shrines, amulets wrapped within the bandages encircling the mummy, coffins, the four shrines. When an expert examines such ritual objects, new information is almost always revealed. Sometimes there are surprising revelations. This is exactly what happened when, after seventy years of being ignored, Tutankhamun's sarcophagus was finally examined in detail.

The sarcophagus is one of the few objects that remained in the tomb after Carter completed the clearing. Seen by millions of tourists who visit the tomb, it was never carefully examined up close by an expert. Several surprises came out of the careful and thoughtful study by Marianne Eaton-Krauss, an expert on Tutankhamun. Almost certainly, all the pharaohs of Tutankhamun's era had sarcophagi to protect their mummies, but Tutankhamun's sarcophagus was the only one found unopened, so we know that three nested coffins protecting the mummy were placed inside his sarcophagus. For additional protection, Tutankhamun's sarcophagus has four goddesses carved at each corner. On their heads are symbols that tell us who they are: Isis, Nephthys, Neith, and Selket. They all have wings, and this is where the surprises begin. The wings were added later, as an afterthought, after the goddesses were carved. The goddesses are in what we call "high relief"—they really stand out. But the wings are in low relief (Figure 14.1). Also, the wings don't make any anatomical sense. They are not attached to the arms; they just fan out below them.

The next surprise involves the hieroglyphic text behind the wings. On all four sides of the sarcophagus are prayers spoken by the goddesses and other gods for Tutankhamun's well-being in the next world. Eaton-Krauss noticed that these prayers had been carved over an earlier set that was on the sarcophagus before the wings were added. The sequence of changes that the sarcophagus went through is something like this:

Figure 14.1. At the corners, four goddesses protect the boy-king's mummy. The wings were added later and aren't even attached to the arms. Note the knots of Isis and *djd* pillars at bottom are unfinished. (Griffith Institute po646h.)

1. The sarcophagus is completed with four wingless female figures and texts on the four sides of the sarcophagus.
2. It is decided to add wings, so the original texts have to be erased to accommodate the wings, which take up extra surface area.
3. Last, the new texts are added around the wings.

Eaton-Krauss wasn't the first to notice the changes. When Howard Carter copied some of the inscriptions, he noticed that there were traces of earlier hieroglyphs beneath the new texts. Why all the changes? There may be several reasons. First, the sarcophagus is the first one produced after the Amarna period, when the Aten was the only god permitted. Now we can have goddesses placed at the corners of the sarcophagus to protect the mummy, like in the good old days. We can contrast this with the sarcophagus made for Akhenaten, who was probably Tutankhamun's father. Fragments of his smashed sarcophagus were found in the royal tomb at Tel el Amarna. It too had four female figures at the corners, but they couldn't be goddesses because he was a monotheist. The female figures are Nefertiti, his wife. So one scenario we can easily imagine is that Tutankhamun dies suddenly and the royal carvers get to work on his sarcophagus. Trained at Amarna, they put female figures on the corners of the sarcophagus. Then it is decided they should be goddesses and wings can be added, so all the changes are put in motion: the original texts are cut back, wings are added to the goddesses, new texts are added.

That all makes sense and is quite possible, but another scenario is also possible: the sarcophagus may not have originally been Tutankhamun's. It may have been someone else's and was later appropriated and recarved for Tutankhamun. Why do this? Why can't the king of Egypt have his own sarcophagus? The problem is time. Most pharaohs could prepare their tombs over decades, with room upon room in their tombs to hold their treasures. Tutankhamun died prematurely at around the age of nineteen and didn't have time to prepare properly for the next world. Egyptian tradition dictated that the body be placed in the tomb approximately seventy days after death. That meant all of Tutankhamun's funerary equipment had to be prepared in a little over two months: the three nested coffins, the four shrines that surrounded them, the sarcophagus, the hundreds of servant statues, the gold mask, the canopic chest, and so on.

Every master craftsman in the country must have been called up to work frantically to prepare everything needed for the burial of their king. How long does it take for a sarcophagus? Can it be done in seventy days? Eaton-Krauss consulted Paul Hagedorn, a master stonemason skilled in working hard stone. Tutankhamun's sarcophagus was quartzite, which is softer than granite but still a hard stone. Hagedorn estimated that it would have taken approximately 840 man-hours at the quarry just to extract the rectangular block from which the sarcophagus would be fashioned. Four men could work simultaneously quarrying the rectangle, and if they worked an eight-hour day, it would take twenty-six days to free the rectangular quartzite block from the quarry bed. Then it had to be hollowed out. Because of the constricting space to be hollowed, only two men could work on it at the same time, which would take another 240 man-hours. So, this gives us another forty-one days of work. We are now at sixty-seven days and time is running out. We still have to transport the blank sarcophagus from the quarry to the Valley of the Kings, which will put us past our seventy-day limit, and we haven't begun to carve all the decorations and texts. In the end, Hagedorn estimated that it would take nearly a year to complete the sarcophagus from start to finish.[1]

This estimate is confirmed by ancient Egyptian records. Queen Hatshepsut erected four large granite obelisks at Karnak Temple. On the pedestal of the one still standing, she boasts that she quarried a pair of her obelisks in seven months.[2] This is more in line with Hagedorn's estimate of a year for the sarcophagus than it is with the seventy days we have for Tutankhamun's burial. Even with merely recarving someone else's sarcophagus, the workers seem to have run out of time. There are several signs that the sarcophagus was never completed. Of the four goddesses, only Isis and Nephthys have their jewelry fully carved. Neith has the jewelry on only one arm carved, with the jewelry on the other merely indicated by paint. Selket has all her jewelry just painted. The craftsmen ran out of time, and finished the decoration by painting rather than carving.

An indication of the frantic race to complete Tutankhamun's burial is the lid of the sarcophagus. It doesn't match the bottom of the sarcophagus, which is quartzite. The lid is granite. Clearly something happened to the original lid, but there wasn't time to quarry a new quartzite one. However, a block of granite was available, so a new lid was carved from that and the granite was painted to look like quartzite. But then disaster struck: the new granite lid cracked in half. No time to carve another one, so it was repaired and Tutankhamun was buried with a cracked, mismatched lid.

Another indication that the sarcophagus is unfinished is the frieze of alternating pairs of knots of Isis and Osiris (*djd*) pillars running along its base. These are standard funerary symbols, and we saw them on the outer shrine that enclosed the sarcophagus. We may not know for certain what the knot represents—perhaps the tie of Isis's gown—but we do know its power. According to Chapter 156 of the Book of the Dead, whoever wears a knot-of-Isis amulet will have the protection of Isis and her son, Horus, and will be welcomed into the next world.

> Thou hast [thy] blood Isis;
> Thou hast [thy] magic Isis.
> This amulet [is] the magical protection of the Weary-hearted One....
> Isis shall be his magical protection and Horus the son of Osiris
> Shall rejoice at seeing him.[3]

The Osiris pillar represents the god's backbone and is a guarantee of stability. So both the knot of Isis and the Osiris pillar are intended to help the deceased resurrect in the next world and are appropriate for a sarcophagus. But if we look at them closely, we will see more evidence that the sarcophagus was never completed. On one end of the sarcophagus they are clearly completed. On the other end they are unfinished (see Figure 14.1), much rougher than the surrounding carvings, still in need of polishing. This is yet another indication that time had run out for Tutankhamun's burial. But we still have to answer the question of where Tutankhamun got a sarcophagus to recarve, and whose it was.

We know that it wasn't his father's. Akhenaten's sarcophagus was found smashed to pieces in the royal tomb at Amarna. The best candidate is Smenkare, Tutankhamun's mysterious half-brother. Of all the royals at Amarna, he is the least documented and most controversial. His name appears on small objects of the Amarna period, such as finger rings, but not on monuments. There is some evidence he ruled for about a year after Akhenaten's death, just before Tutankhamun. Still, the evidence is so scant that some Egyptologists doubt that he ever existed. Dr. Geoffrey Martin, who excavated the royal tomb at Amarna, even suggested that Smenkare is really Nefertiti with a name change, and that she took over as Egypt's ruler after the death of her husband. Martin is not the only one who believes this.[4] Smenkare's tomb has never been found, so where did the sarcophagus come from? Perhaps from an as yet undiscovered tomb? It could be.

Another possibility is that it came from KV-55. As you will remember from our brief history of excavations in the Valley of the Kings (see Chapter 1), Theodore Davis discovered the tomb in 1907 and believed he had discovered the resting place of Queen Tiye, Tutankhamun's grandmother. This was because the tomb contained a badly damaged shrine carved with Tiye's name, and also because Davis was told that the mummy in the royal coffin was a female. It wasn't; by almost all accounts, it is the mummy of a young man. The tomb also contained magical bricks inscribed for Akhenaten, but the mummy can't be his; it is too young to be a king who ruled for seventeen years. But it could be Smenkare. What is important here is that there was no sarcophagus in KV-55, nor fragments of one, so Smenkare's sarcophagus is missing. Quite possibly it was commandeered and recarved for the recently deceased Tutankhamun. If the sarcophagus did indeed belong to Smenkare, it is not the only item of his in Tutankhamun's tomb. Both Carter and Nicholas Reeves the Tutankhamun expert, agree that at least one of the miniature coffinettes that contained the boy-kings internal organs was owned by Smenkare. Traces of his cartouche are beneath Tutankhamun's.[5]

There is one more bit of evidence that the sarcophagus in Tutankhamun's tomb was not originally carved for him. When Carter finally removed the three coffins nested inside the sarcophagus, he found gilded wood shavings at the bottom. He commented on this at length.

> These were at first puzzling, but their presence was accounted for upon further examination. The design of the gesso-gilt surface was identical with that on the edge of the first [outermost] coffin, from which pieces had been crudely hacked away by some sharp instrument like a carpenter's adze. The obvious explanation is that the foot-end of the coffin . . . was too high to allow the lid of the sarcophagus to be lowered in place, and it was therefore cut down by those whose duty it was to close the sarcophagus. This is evidence of want of forethought on the part of the workmen.[6]

One would think that if the sarcophagus were made specially to house the nested coffins, measurements would have been taken in advance to avoid such problems. A more likely explanation is that the sarcophagus was never intended to house Tutankhamun's three coffins. It had been made for someone else. Although the treasures in Tutankhamun's tomb were spectacular, and we all talk about how wonderful the craftsmanship was for many of these objects, it is clear that there was a frenzy going on behind the scenes to complete his burial in seventy days.

Color Plate 16. The discovery of the chariots caused a sensation. Burton's color plategraph of Tutankhamun's chariot first appeared in the French newspaper *L'Illustration*.

Color Plate 17. The falcon with the solar disk was fastened to the pole of the pharaoh's chariot—the world's first hood ornament. (*L'Illustration* photo.)

Color Plate 18. Tutankhamun's painted chest depicts him as a warrior defeating the Nubians.

Color Plate 19. Tutankhamun's successor, Aye, performs the Opening of the Mouth ceremony on Tutankhamun's mummy. (Photo by Pat Remler.)

Color Plate 20. Aye's cartouche has been repainted with faint traces of other hieroglyphs beneath. Why? (Photo by Pat Remler.)

Color Plate 21. Tutankhamun's *ka* figure wears a pleated kilt. When the tomb was first discovered the kilt had twenty-four pleats. A 1936 photo shows it with twenty-seven pleats. Who repainted it, and why? (Photo by Pat Remler.)

Color Plate 22. Winnifred Brunton's painting of young Tutankhamun holding the iron dagger made of meteoritic iron.

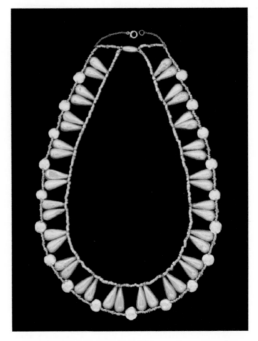

Color Plate 23. A necklace auctioned at Christie's in London seems to have been made from beads from Tutankhamun's tomb.

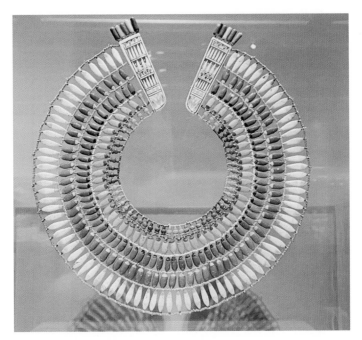

Color Plate 24. The Metropolitan Museum of Art's pectoral similar to one found in Tutankhamun's tomb

Color Plate 25. In Ahmed Souliman's Cairo shop, tourists could buy Touth-Ankh-Amen perfume. (Photo by Pat Remler.)

Color Plate 26. Back in England, you could buy a beautiful penknife featuring one of Tut's guardian statues. (Photo by Pat Remler.)

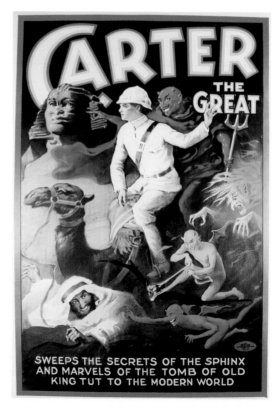

Color Plate 27. The magician Charles Carter capitalized on his surname to make an Egyptian connection for his act. (Photo by Pat Remler.)

Color Plate 28. New York's Metropolitan Museum of Art sold Selket replicas for more than $1,500. (Photo by Pat Remler.)

Color Plate 29. King Tut's Cologne was produced in Brooklyn, New York. (Photo by Pat Remler.)

Color Plate 30. King Tut Party Mix came in a pyramid box that featured a dancing pharaoh. (Photo by Pat Remler.)

15

Is Nefertiti in Tut's Tomb?

I often ask my students Egyptological trivia questions. They are straight-forward, with simple answers: Who was the oldest pharaoh? (Pepi II of the Old Kingdom. He lived into his nineties.) How many human mum-mies in Tutankhamun's tomb? (Three: Tut and two fetuses.) A remarkable new theory, put forth by the world's foremost authority on Tutankhamun, suggests that three may not be the correct answer. If Dr. Nicholas Reeves is right, the correct answer is four and the extra mummy is Nefertiti, wife of Akhenaten and Tutankhamun's stepmother.

Reeves, a tall handsome Englishman, is a recognized authority on Tutankhamun. He has spent his career studying the boy-king and writing some of the best books about him. His book *The Complete Tutankhamun* is used by all of us when we want to look up the dimensions of the burial chamber or how many servant statues accompanied Tutankhamun to the next world. His *Complete Valley of the Kings*, based on his Cambridge doc-toral dissertation and coauthored with Richard Wilkinson, is a standard work on the subject. Reeves even lived for years at Highclere Castle, helping the current Lord and Lady Carnarvon catalogue their collection of antiquities. He has all the credentials, so when he presents a new theory about Tutankhamun, everyone listens. Recently he has presented the most radical theory concerning Tutankhamun's tomb in the hundred years since the tomb was discovered.

Saving Tut's Tomb

It all started with an attempt to preserve Tutankhamun's tomb. It has been known for quite a while that the tombs in the Valley of the Kings have been deteriorating. With the tremendous increase in tourism in the last century, the rate of decay has been growing alarmingly. As tourists pack into the tombs, their breathing and perspiration change the humidity and temperature. With these changes the plastered walls expand and contract, the painted surfaces fracture, and the paint eventually flakes off and fall to the ground. The clearest solution is to close the tombs to tourism, leaving the tombs in darkness with the very low humidity they had enjoyed for centuries. But what about the tourist industry? The hope is that very accurate replica tombs could be built that would be just as good as the originals. This has been tried in France in the large prehistoric cave at Lascaux with great success. More than a quarter of a million people still visit Lascaux each year and leave pleased with their experience, even if they cannot view the original paintings.

In 2008 a Spanish company, Factum Arte, began a detailed high-tech laser scan of the walls in Tutankhamun's tomb in preparation for making a replica tomb. The scans were so accurate that not only did they record the paintings' colors and images, but they also mapped the irregularities of the wall surfaces. The idea was to take the information accumulated by the laser scans and print the images onto a rubberized thin skin that could be mounted on plasterboard or some other artificial surface to create a new replica tomb. The tomb would be placed near Howard Carter's house at the entrance to the Valley, so that when tourists visited Carter's house they could also see the tomb replica. The project has been quite a success. People who visit the replica tomb are happy with it. They don't have to wait in line, they can get closer to the walls than in the real tomb, they can take more time inside, and they are free to take photos. The question about the number of mummies in the tomb arose when Factum Arte released their data to the public—every scan of every inch of the tomb.[1]

A Radical New Theory

Looking over these detailed scans, Reeves saw on the north wall—the main wall with all the scenes of Tutankhamun undergoing rituals for the next world—what looked like two parallel vertical lines beneath the paintings, perhaps indicting a doorway behind the wall. In 2015 Reeves published a paper explaining what he had seen and suggested that Tutankhamun's tomb was originally intended for Nefertiti, whose burial has never been found, and that her burial was behind the north wall.[2] If true, it would be a sensational find, perhaps equal to Tutankhamun's treasures. The theory made news around the world. The *New York Times* ran the story with the headline "Scans of Tutankhamen's Tomb Hint at Grander Cache."[3] Egypt's director of antiquities, Mamduh Eldamaty, said it could be "the discovery of the century." The *Times* of London printed an extensive story with the headline "Is Nefertiti in King Tut's Tomb?"[4] This was a theory that had to be followed up.

In 2015 ground penetrating radar (GPR) scans were done by a Japanese radar expert, Hirokatsu Watanabe, who conducted the scans across the north wall at a single height. He said that his scans showed not only a void behind the north wall but also the presence of metal and organic material. But this was not clear to everyone who saw his data, and the report of his study has never been published.

A team at National Geographic Television, which was considering a TV special about the possibility of Nefertiti being behind the wall, decided to do their own scans. They used two machines and conducted scans of several walls at five heights, and concluded that these scans showed nothing there. It was like Al Capone's empty vault. They wrote a formal report for the Supreme Council of Antiquities, but it was never released to the public. The score was now 1–1, with one study indicating there was something behind the wall and one against. This was such an exciting idea, and so many people hoped and believed that Nefertiti might be behind the north wall, that the Supreme Council of Antiquities gave permission to a team from Turin University to conduct a third and deciding set of scans in 2018. The Turin scans were by far the most extensive of the GPR studies. They used three GPR systems set to different frequencies, each managed by a different, independent team. The three teams processed their data and drew their conclusions independently of each other. In the end, they came to the same conclusion: there were no hidden chambers in Tutankhamun's tomb. Their report was the only one published in a peer-reviewed journal.[5] Now it was 2–1 against Nefertiti being behind the north wall, or 4–1 if we consider the Turin study as three independent ones. The Supreme Council of Antiquities issued a statement that the Italian survey demonstrated "with a high level of confidence that Reeves' theory concerning the existence of hidden chambers adjacent to Tutankhamun's tomb is not supported by the GPR data."

Reeves, still believing in his theory, published a second paper in 2019 arguing that Nefertiti was indeed behind the wall.[6] His argument in this paper had two prongs. One prong was aimed at countering the negative results of the geophysical surveys. This took the form of an appendix to Reeves's paper by George Ballard, an expert on geotechnics at Cambridge University. Ballard didn't do any further tests, but rather reviewed all the data generated by the previous surveys. His conclusion was that none of the previous studies confirmed Reeves's theory, but there were some anomalies that might be investigated in the future. The problem here is that if there really is a burial behind the wall, one of the previous surveys should have detected it.

Reeves's new evidence in the 2019 paper comes from his detailed analysis of the paintings on the walls of the tomb. Here he makes some really interesting observations and even a couple of discoveries that everyone else had missed. One of his observations involves how the ancient Egyptian artists painted tombs.

Perhaps the most remarkable thing about ancient Egyptian art is how little it changed during Egypt's three thousand years of glory. To the average visitor in a museum, it doesn't matter if a statue was carved in 2500 BC, 1500 BC, or 500 BC; it all looks like "ancient Egyptian art." Compare that with other civilizations' art. There's quite a difference between medieval and Renaissance art. And how about the difference between the Impressionists and modern art, where we are only talking about one century's difference? Why did Egyptian art stay the same while everyone else's changed? There is an answer.

For the most part, when it came to art, Egypt did not reward creativity. If it wasn't broke, don't fix it. If a temple needed a new statue of the god, the old one was brought out and copied. This was eternal art, unchanging art. Even in tomb paintings, there was a standardization of the art. Before any painting of the walls began, a craftsman laid out a grid on the wall; sometimes this was done with a string coated with red powder, and sometimes the grid was painted right on the wall with thin black lines. The idea was that the grid would guide the artists in their proportions. If the head is three squares, then the shoulders are five and the distance between the shoulder and the waist is four and a half squares. The Egyptians reduced art to paint-by-numbers, and that's why it all looks the same. Except not all of the walls in Tutankhamun's tomb have the same grid structure.

Usually the Egyptian grid was eighteen squares high. However, years before Reeves's theory, Dr. Gay Robins, an expert on Egyptian proportions, noticed that while the other three walls in the burial chamber were the traditional eighteen-square grids, the north wall, the one with all the interesting scenes, used a grid of twenty squares. Why? It all had to do with Tut's heretic father, Akhenaten, who changed the religion and everything else, even the art. During Akhenaten's reign, his artists used the twenty-square grid. So why the eighteen-square grid for three walls and the twenty-square grid for the north wall? Robins's answer is that the walls were being simultaneously painted by different teams of artists. While one team was working on the west wall, another team was working on the north wall. The north wall team was composed of older holdovers from the Akhenaten days and were using the twenty-square grid, with which they were familiar. Nick Reeves disagrees, and here we have his first bit of artistic evidence for Nefertiti being behind the wall.

Reeves believes that the north wall's twenty-square grid shows that it was painted before the return to the eighteen-square grid. In Reeves's scenario, soon after the return to Thebes, Nefertiti is buried in the Valley of the Kings. The artists are from Amarna and use their twenty-square grid. The north wall is thus painted for Nefertiti's burial. Later, when Tutankhamun unexpectedly dies, the north wall is repainted for his burial, and the other three walls are painted for him as well. Because some time has passed since the initial painting of the north wall, the eighteen-square grid has been returned to favor and thus the three walls are all done with those proportions.

The grid is not the only difference between the north wall and the other three. Before all the discussion of Nefertiti behind the wall began, the Getty Conservation Institute did a study of the tomb to document the condition of the walls. They noted that only the north wall's painting was laid down on an "overall gray preparatory layer" that does not appear on the other three walls. Further, a yellow background has been painted around the preexisting painted figures, a feature not present on the other three walls. So both Gay Robins and the Getty agree that different painting techniques were used for the north wall than for the east, west, and south walls. Why the differences? Reeves's answer is that they were done at completely different times.

Reeves's analysis of the paintings on the north wall is fascinating. Some of his conclusions are in the eye of the beholder, but some are undeniable.

The traditional interpretation of the north wall is that there are three distinct scenes relating to Tutankhamen that read from right to left. The first is perhaps the most important. We see two figures, Tutankhamun, now deceased, in the cloak of Osiris, the god of the next world (see Color Plate 19). On his right, King Aye, his successor, is performing the Opening of the Mouth ceremony. Aye, wearing the leopard skin of a high priest, touches a ritual instrument to the mouth of Tutankhamun, which ensures that the deceased pharaoh will have breath and life in the next world. We can be sure who's who because their names are written in cartouches above their heads. This is the explanation that has been given for this scene by everyone for the last hundred years. Indeed, this is the interpretation Reeves gave in *The Complete Tutankhamun*, written twenty-five years before his new theory.[7] But now the new theory asserts that the scene, originally painted for Nefertiti's burial, shows not Aye but rather Tutankhamun performing the Opening of the Mouth ceremony, and he is performing it on the mummy of the recently buried Nefertiti. To support this interpretation, Reeves points out that features of Tutankhamun as Osiris really better match those of Nefertiti. For example, the pronounced creases at the corners of the mouth (the oromental fold) are typical of Nefertiti in later life. Further, Reeves observes that the shape of the body is more appropriate for a woman. As to Aye, he points out that the body of the supposed Aye is of a young man, and at the time of Tutankhamun's death Aye would have been quite old. So on art historical grounds, Reeves feels it is clear that the Opening of the Mouth scene was originally painted for Tutankhamun performing the ritual on Nefertiti.

But what about the cartouches that identify them as Aye and Tutankhamun? That's not a matter of art interpretation. Here we have something that we can all agree on. Reeves points out that if we look closely at the cartouche with Aye's name we can make out faint traces of a hieroglyph that has been painted over (see Color Plate 20). There is no doubt about this. Just beneath the first hieroglyph on the top left is the faint but certain trace of the "reed-leaf" hieroglyph. ⌠ This hieroglyph represents the sound *i* or *a* and is the first letter in Tutankhamun's name. (You may be thinking that the name Tutankhamun doesn't begin with either an *i* or an *a*. The answer is that it doesn't when you say it, but it does when it is written. Recall from Chapter 1 that the "Amun" part is written first because it is the name of a god and gods come first.) Reeves interprets the ghost reed-leaf as indicating that

Tutankhamun's name had originally been in the cartouche and was later painted over with the name Aye. But there is an alternative explanation. There are no traces of any other letters from Tutankhamun's name beneath Aye's name. Further, Aye's name has three reed-leaves in it. It is perhaps more likely that the artist made the mistake of beginning with one of the reed-leaves, saw he made a mistake, and then painted over the one letter.

So far, it is not clear that Nefertiti is buried behind the north wall in Tutankhamun's tomb. Four out of five geophysical surveys found no evidence of a hidden tomb. The art analysis is far from certain. The discovery that the technique used to paint the north wall is different (grid and background) doesn't prove the walls were painted at different times. While Reeves's stylistic arguments are fascinating, they are subjective. Not everyone sees what Reeves sees. But there is still one more argument to be considered and I think, in some ways, it is the most interesting. It involves the third scene on the north wall.

The last scene on the wall shows three figures, two of whom are Tutankhamun (see Color Plate 21). On the extreme left, we have Osiris, the god of the dead, wrapped as a mummy who is welcoming Tutankhamun into the next world. Behind Tutankhamun is his soul or spiritual double, the *ka*. They will be united in the next world and join Osiris. What Reeves has noticed in this scene is truly remarkable. If we look at an early photo of the *ka* figure, taken relatively soon after the tomb was discovered, we see that he is wearing a kilt. If we count the number of pleats, it comes to twenty-four indicated by twenty-four diagonal stripes. Now for the fun. There is a photo taken around 1936 by the University of Chicago's Oriental Institute that also shows the kilt. What Reeves noticed is that there are now twenty-seven stripes on the kilt, and it has remained that way till today (Figure 15.1). What's going on? Sometime after the discovery and before 1936, someone repainted the kilt. Who and why? Who is the easier question to answer—almost certainly it was Howard Carter. He had unique access to the tomb, and was a skilled artist who began his career in Egyptology by copying tomb paintings. He was intimately acquainted with the techniques of Egyptian ancient artists, knew the colors they used and even their brushstrokes. But Carter went even further than just repainting the kilt; he even painted false mold on the kilt.

When the tomb was first opened it was immediately noticed that there was mold on the walls of the burial chamber that had been there since

Figure 15.1. Detail of Tutankhamun's kilt as it is today with twenty-seven pleats. (Photo by Pat Remler.)

ancient times. When the boy-king was hastily buried, the painted walls had not had time to dry, so when the tomb was sealed, mold began to grow on the walls. When the tomb dried completely, the mold on the walls dried and remained there till the tomb's discovery. When Carter repainted the kilt, he added false mold (brown paint) on top of it in the hope that the repainting would blend in with the rest of the paintings. Clearly he wasn't working from earlier photographs, or he would have seen that there was hardly any mold on the original kilt. Carter's version has much more mold than there ever was on the original. So why did Carter repaint the kilt and even add mold to cover his tracks? Reeves's answer to this question is that Carter, like Reeves, wondered if the tomb might continue past the north wall and did a bit of exploration, damaging the wall. After Carter found nothing, he repainted to cover his tracks. This is possible, but there is a simpler explanation of why Carter repainted, one that doesn't involve looking for a hidden tomb.

The most difficult part of excavating the tomb was clearing the burial chamber, because the large nested shrines almost completely filled the burial chamber. Removing the shrines from the tomb was very difficult work, and Carter recorded, "We bumped our heads, nipped our fingers, we had to squeeze in and out like weasels, and work in all kinds of embarrassing positions."[8] During the removal of the shrines, the walls of the burial chamber were scratched, damaging the painted surfaces. This damage was noted by the Getty Conservation Institute, as was the overpainting Carter did to restore the original appearance. The overpainting of the kilt wasn't an attempt to cover up a secret search for a hidden tomb. Carter had no thought that Nefertiti was behind the north wall. He was simply repairing damage he had done to the walls.

Still, many people were unconvinced. Some suggested a small hole should be drilled in the wall, where there were no paintings, to see if there was a void behind the wall. Dr. Zahi Hawass, former director of the Supreme Council of Antiquities, argued that the vibration might damage the painting. The solution was to do another GPR scan. In 2020, Terravision conducted yet another study, this time aiming the radar downward from above the tomb. The findings were never published, but were reported in *Nature* as news. The article said, "A new survey hints at a previously unknown space beyond Tutankhamun's burial chamber."[9] The big question is, how much beyond the burial chamber? There are natural voids within the Valley floor. Is this one of them? In a recent analysis of this study David Lightbody, an Egyptologist with a specialty in GPR, raised an important point about this study.[10] From the diagrams supplied in the *Nature* article, it would be impossible to detect a hidden chamber by GPR from above. The floor of the burial chamber in Tutankhamun's tomb is at least eight meters below the Valley floor. The limit of GPR through limestone is about five meters. So if the Terravision team did find a void, it can't be behind the north wall; it would have to be much closer to the surface. So, once again, a study suggests there is no void. The score was now 5–1 against Nefertiti's burial behind the wall.

So, where does all this leave us with respect to Nefertiti being behind the north wall? As far as the Supreme Council of Antiquities is concerned, the issue is settled. The fact that the three last geophysical surveys failed to detect a tomb is convincing for them. There will be no drilling of holes, no more GPR studies, Nefertiti is simply not there. For Reeves, the fact that the north wall has been repainted, combined with the stylistic details that suggested to him that Nefertiti was on the north wall, is enough to convince him that further investigation is needed. It would be wonderful if Reeves's theory were true. Imagine what fun it would be to follow the excavation of another tomb packed with royal treasures. Think of all the answers the new tomb might provide about the end of the Amarna period and Tutankhamun's role in it. But it just doesn't look as if Nefertiti is behind the north wall. So, for now, the correct answer to the trivia question about how many human mummies were in Tutankhamen's tomb is still three.

16

It Came from Outer Space

One of the research projects that resulted from Tutankhamun's treasures being moved to the new Grand Egyptian Museum focused on Tutankhamun's famous dagger. Actually, two well-known daggers were found in the tomb, both within the wrappings of the mummy, so they must have been very special. Both daggers were of extraordinary workmanship, each with a highly ornamented gold sheath. One was clearly ceremonial; its blade was solid gold. It was a thing of beauty, but not very practical. The second dagger caused all the excitement. This one had a beautiful rock crystal pommel, but what made it doubly special was its blade; it was iron, which raises an interesting question. Where did the iron come from? You see, the Egyptians didn't have iron during Tutankhamun's time. There were no iron deposits that they mined.

Iron was more difficult to work than gold, copper, or bronze. It required a higher temperature to melt out of the ore, creating what was called a "bloom." This then had to be heated and hammered to extract the pure metal, which could be beaten into shape, forming wrought iron. The wrought iron could then be hardened by heating it on a bed of charcoal and then quenching it in water or oil. Around Tutankhamun's day, the Hittites had discovered how to work iron, but kept it a closely guarded secret.

So when it was discovered that Tutankhamun was buried with an iron dagger, it was a big deal. When the artist Winifred Brunton did her series of portraits of the kings of Egypt, she painted Tutankhamun holding the iron dagger (see Color Plate 22).[1] But where did the iron come from? Carter and others thought it had somehow come from the Hittites. Others suggested that the iron in the dagger might be meteoritic, though no scientific tests were published.[2] Recently, X-ray fluorescence spectrometry (XRF) has made nondestructive testing of iron objects possible. With XRF, the object tested is bombarded with X-rays, which excite the surface and cause the metal to fluoresce. The atoms given off by the metal are the metal's fingerprint. The great thing about XRF is that it gives a near-complete profile of the metal, including elements present in relatively small quantities. Meteorites, because of their high nickel content, have fingerprints different from any rocks formed on earth.

When XRF was applied to the iron dagger blade, it showed that the metal had a nickel content of about 11 percent, which indicates that the iron was almost certainly of extraterrestrial origin.[3] Did the Egyptians of Tutankhamun's time know that the iron came from outer space? The answer is yes. Much before Tutankhamun's time the word *bia* meant "copper," but it could also be used to mean just "metal." The Egyptian word for iron was *bia-m-pet,* which literally means "copper from the sky" or "metal from the sky," but is used specifically to designate iron.[4] It is likely that they saw a meteor shower deposit small iron-containing meteorites on the ground or saw a large meteorite entering Earth's atmosphere and crash in the desert. Indeed, ancient Egyptians believed the sky was a giant iron table from which the stars hung.

Another new research tool recently supplied another piece to the iron dagger puzzle. In recent times, Google Earth has been used by archaeologists around the world to locate promising sites for future excavations. In 2010 a group of Italian earth scientists used it to discover a forty-five-meter impact crater in the remote southeastern corner of Egypt's desert. From the satellite photos, the site looked pristine, with no tire tracks or any other signs of it having been disturbed. This was the find of a lifetime, and they responded quickly, organizing an expedition of seven researchers to the site. When they arrived, they were delighted to find that the site was untouched. They were able to survey the crater, plot the distribution of meteor fragments around it, and return with more than a thousand kilograms of samples. They named the site Gebel Kamil, after the nearest prominent geographical feature, a small mountain.[5]

From their survey, the team was able to determine that the impact took place less than five thousand years ago, well within recorded Egyptian history, so this could indeed have been the event that led the Egyptians to call iron "metal from the sky." It was not, however, the source of the meteoritic iron for Tutankhamun's dagger, for its nickel content (20 percent) was far too high. So we are still left with the question of where the meteoritic iron for the dagger came from. There is one remote possibility: the nickel content of Tutankhamun's dagger blade is similar to that in a small individual meteorite found in the Kharga Oasis in 2000, so that area may be the source.[6] However, there is yet another possibility outside of Egypt.

In the late nineteenth century an archive of foreign correspondence was found at Tel el Amarna, Akhenaten's holy city in the desert. The city's foreign office was receiving letters from distant lands written on little clay tablets baked hard as rocks. The tablets, ranging in width from 2½ to 3½ inches and in length from 2½ to 9 inches, were covered with small wedge-shaped writing, quite different from hieroglyphs. They were written in Akkadian, the international language of the day. Many of the letters had been sent to Egypt from kings of other countries. One letter, written by King Tushratta of Mitanni, discusses the marriage of one of his daughters to Amenhotep III, Tutankhamun's grandfather. Among the items in the dowry that Tushratta sends is a dagger with a blade of *habalkinu*, a Hittite word that can be translated as "steel."[7] It is tempting to think that Tutankhamun's iron dagger could be this very dagger, an heirloom from his grandfather.[8]

Two other meteoritic objects were placed on Tutankhamun's body, and both were magical. One was an Eye of Horus amulet. The Eye of Horus was a stylized rendering of the markings around the eye of a falcon. In a sense, Tutankhamun's Eye of Horus amulet completes the story of Isis and Osiris begun on his shrines. We left the myth of Isis and Osiris with the resurrection of Osiris-Tutankhamun. While this seems like a perfect ending, there is more to the story. When Isis, in the form of a bird, hovered over Osiris, she became pregnant with their son, Horus. When Horus grew up, he avenged the death of his father by battling his evil uncle, Set, and of course wins. However, in the struggle, Horus's eye was torn to pieces. But by magic, Toth, the god of writing, reassembled the pieces. Each element of the Eye of Horus represented a fraction to the Egyptians (Figure 16.1): ½, ◁ ¼, and so on. The total comes to $^{63}/_{64}$, and the missing $^{1}/_{64}$ was supplied magically by Toth. The amulet was called *udjat*, or "sound eye," because Toth made the eye complete. Eye of Horus amulets were perhaps the most common of all ancient Egyptian amulets and were worn to ensure good health. In the late Middle Ages, when the Eye of Horus symbol was brought back to Europe by early travelers to Egypt, it also entered into our culture. The dominant theory among Egyptologists is that the sign of

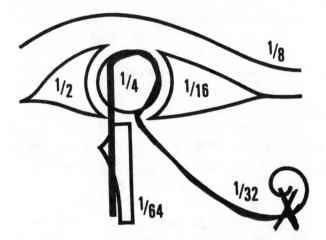

Figure 16.1. Parts of the Eye of Horus became the Egyptian hieroglyphs for fractions. In the Middle Ages they became the pharmacist's Rx (indicated in dark black).

the pharmacist, Rx, is a corruption of three portions of the ancient Eye of Horus: ¼, ⅟₃₂, and ⅟₆₄.

The other meteoritic amulet on Tutankhamun's body was a miniature headrest found behind the pharaoh's neck, inside the gold mask. The amulet had been broken and repaired, indicating that the rarity of the material was recognized. The amulet's purpose was to assist the deceased in lifting his head up in the next world. There is even a spell in the Book of the Dead that explains its function:

> Awake! Thy sufferings are allayed. Thou art awakened when thy head is above the horizon. Stand up, thou art triumphant. . . . Thy head will never be taken from thee. . . . Thy head will never be carried away.[9]

So the priests who buried Tutankhamun chose three meteoritic objects to be placed on their dead king's body. The objects had already made their journey through the heavens. Tutankhamun was yet to make his.

We can understand why Tutankhamun would want the dagger, the headrest amulet, and the Eye of Horus in the tomb with him. But there was one last group of iron objects in the tomb, a set of sixteen chisels. For Carter, these were the most puzzling objects in the tomb (Figure 16.2). They were found in an undecorated box in the Treasury. The box had already been ransacked by tomb robbers, so we can't be certain the set of tools was originally

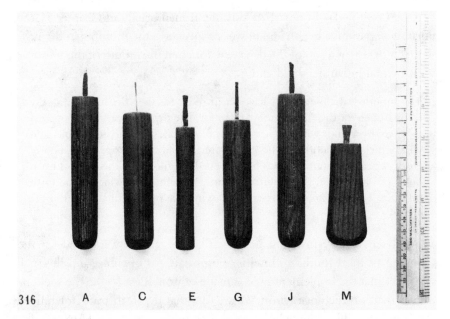

Figure 16.2. The function of these iron chisels found in the tomb is not clear, especially since they are not well made. (Griffith Institute p1052.)

in the box, but the big question is, why were they in the tomb at all? Almost all the objects in the tomb were there either because Tutankhamun wanted to use them in the next world (the dagger) or because they would help him resurrect (the headrest amulet). Why the chisels? Was he an amateur craftsman wanting to take his tools with him? I don't think so. They weren't beautiful; Carter called them "crude," and he was right. They weren't going to be used in the next world by a pharaoh. That leaves ritual objects, and that's what G. A. Wainwright suggested in the 1930s. He believed the tools were used in a ritual.[10] Wainwright first presented a fascinating survey of how meteoritic iron has been used throughout the ages and around the world. His description of how the Eskimo people of Canada, Greenland, and Siberia made hundred-mile pilgrimages to a large meteorite to pound off pieces of it to use in tools is riveting. It shows just how special meteorites could be.

After his survey, Wainwright suggested that the chisels were used in the Opening of the Mouth ceremony, a ritual depicted on the wall of Tutankhamun's tomb. This ceremony was performed on the mummy of the deceased on the day of burial. As was mentioned briefly in Chapter 15, the purpose was to give breath and power of speech to the mummy in the next world. A priest, or a son of the deceased, touched the mouth of the mummy with a ritual instrument and said:

> Thy mouth was closed, but I have set in order for thee thy mouth and thy teeth. I open for thee thy mouth, I open for thee thy two eyes. I have opened for thee thy mouth with the instrument of Anubis, with the iron implement with which the mouths of the gods were opened. Horus open the mouth! Horus open the mouth! Horus hath opened the mouth of the dead, as he in times of old opened the mouth of Osiris, with the iron which came forth from Set, with the iron instrument with which he opened the mouths of the gods.[11]

We can see why Wainwright is suggesting the chisels were used for the Opening of the Mouth. A chisel is appropriate for opening, and the spell stipulates that the implement used is made of iron. Even better, the spell indicates that it is meteoritic iron. We are told that the iron "came forth from Set," Osiris's evil brother, who was defeated but not killed by Horus. In the end, Set was banished to the heavens by a tribunal of gods with the epithet "And he shall thunder in the sky." We are back to "iron from the sky," meteoritic iron. So Wainwright had good reasons for suggesting that the chisels were used for the Opening of the Mouth. But I don't think he was right. Nor did Carter, and he said so:

> Such objects seem to be out of place among ritualistic material belonging to a funeral cult of a king, nor is it conceivable that so large a chest could have contained only these small implements. Their frail and somewhat flimsy make suggests them to be models and not actual tools for use.[12]

Carter rejects Wainwright's idea because the chisels are flimsy, not fit for a king, and he is right, but there are other reasons for rejecting them as having been used for the Opening of the Mouth ceremony. First, there are sixteen chisels, and only two implements were used in the ritual. Second, we know what the implements looked like, and it's not chisels. Third, we can see the implements used for Tutankhamun's Opening of the Mouth; they are painted right there on the wall of his tomb (see Color Plate 19). Tutankhamun, on the left, is standing upright in the form of the mummified Osiris, Lord of the West. Hieroglyphs above his head make it clear that the figure is Tutankhamun, King of Upper and Lower Egypt, not Osiris.

On the right is a figure wearing a leopard skin, indicating he is the high priest. He also wears the crown of the pharaoh. Tutankhamun's successor is performing the ritual. Above his head we have his name, Aye. Aye is in the act of raising the Opening of the Mouth implement toward Tutankhamun's mouth, which will give Tutankhamun breath and speech in the next world. This is what the traditional implement looks like. It is a model of an adz. On the table between them is a second adz used in the ceremony. It looks nothing like the chisels, and as far as anyone knows, nothing like the chisels were ever used ritually.

Carter was fascinated by these tools. In the final volume of his three-volume account of the excavation, he devoted four pages to ruminating about them, but never came to a solid final conclusion. So we are still left with the unanswered question of why they were in the tomb. These were the only iron objects in the tomb with signs of rust, which made it difficult to confirm by that they were made of meteoritic iron. However, a recent infrasound array test indicated a nickel content of between 6 and 13 percent, high enough to indicate a meteoritic origin.[13] As far as we can tell, this is the only thing special about the tools, and may be why they were buried with Tutankhamun.

While there are deposits of iron ore in Egypt's Eastern and Western Deserts, the Egyptians were slow to adopt the use of the metal. I think it was because the Egyptians were so conservative; they just didn't like change. For two thousand years Egypt was top dog in the region, and the pharaoh's army went virtually undefeated, so why change? It was the same with art. They just didn't want change. They were slow to pick up other technological advances from other civilizations. They never fully embraced the wheel, using it primarily for chariots. They didn't use beasts of burden to haul heavy loads. They simply weren't into new things. Iron production did not become common in Egypt until around 500 BC, long after it had become the metal of choice in the rest of the Near East.

Desert Glass

There was one more object in Tutankhamun's tomb that had an extraterrestrial connection, but it wasn't made of iron. One of the most elaborate pieces of Tutankhamun's jewelry was found on his mummy—a densely decorated pectoral. It combines many elements of Egyptian iconography intended to protect the young king in the next world. There's the Eye of Horus, seven protective cobras with solar disks on their heads, and more, but the star of the show is a winged scarab right in the middle of everything. The scarab was the symbol of continued existence because, as we have seen, the ancient Egyptian word *kheper* meant both "exist" and "beetle." So a scarab pectoral is certainly appropriate for a mummy.

The body of the scarab is made of yellow-green glass, while the wings and legs are gold inlaid with semiprecious stones and ceramics. In the winged scarab's talons are *shen* signs, symbols of eternity. The stone that forms the body of the scarab is unique in ancient Egypt; nothing like it appears anywhere else. Howard Carter called it chalcedony, but he was wrong. It was a very special glass, desert glass.

An early reference to such glass comes from a well-known explorer. On December 29, 1933, Colonel P. A. Clayton was exploring Egypt's Great Sand Sea, mapping it for the Egyptian Geological Survey, where he found hundreds of pieces of this mysterious glass covering an area of several square miles.[14] Most natural glass, such as obsidian, is volcanic and contains about 75 percent silica, but there were no volcanoes in the area. Clayton returned a few days later with L. J. Spencer, keeper of minerals in the British Museum. The desert glass was 98 percent pure silica, definitely not volcanic; Spencer suggested an extraterrestrial connection. The glass had perhaps been formed when a red-hot meteor struck the sand, fusing the silica into chunks of desert glass.[15] Spencer's theory was at least a possibility; it explained how nonvolcanic glass formed in the desert. The problem was that there was no impact crater. In recent times, satellite surveys using ground-penetrating radar looked for the crater, but none has been found. Most geologists who have studied this type of glass, called Libyan desert glass (LDG), agree that the glass was not formed by a meteorite impact. So what did form the chunk of glass in Tutankhamun's pectoral? The answer may be found at two very different sites, one in America and one in Siberia. First Siberia.

On the morning of June 30, 1908, an explosion took place in the remote Tunguska region of Siberia that was picked up on seismographs thousands of miles away. Because of the area's remoteness, for years geologists thought it was just an earthquake, but eventually reports reached scientists that along with the tremors had come heat so intense that it burned people in a village forty miles away, and a bright light had been seen in the morning sky. The thought among the scientific community was that a large meteor had struck Tunguska, an event certainly worth investigating. But because of its remoteness, and also because of the limited finances in the Soviet Union at the time, a scientific expedition didn't reach the Tunguska site till 1927, after days of trekking through the Siberian wilderness. They were shocked by what they found.

For as far as they could see, and for miles beyond that, trees had been scorched and blown over by some tremendous wind. (A later estimate would put the damage at eighty million trees.) What they found was consistent with a meteorite impact, but what they did not find was an impact crater, nor the remains of the meteorite. With food running out, they were forced to hike back to civilization. The leader of the investigation, Leonid Kulik, was convinced this was the site of a meteor strike and later organized several better-equipped expeditions that returned to search for the crater and the meteorite. As with those who investigated the desert glass, they never found either.[16]

Today, because of computer modeling, it is generally accepted that there was no direct impact with Earth. Rather, an asteroid exploded approximately eight kilometers above Earth, sending fire and shock waves downward, knocking down trees, scorching them, and stripping the branches, over an area of approximately 830 square miles.[17] The heat at Tunguska was extreme, so if a similar event took place over the Great Sand Sea, would it have been sufficient to fuse the sand and create the desert glass? For the answer to this, we can go to our second site, Alamogordo, New Mexico, where the first atomic bomb was tested in 1945.

After the first test, scientists walking the ground found green glass created by the blast. They named it trinitite after the code name for the test site, Trinity. The heat of the A-bomb had fused the New Mexico sands to form an artificial desert glass. If we combine what was learned from both Tunguska and Trinity, it seems as if something similar to Tunguska happened in the Egyptian desert, creating the desert glass. It is generally agreed that the force of the asteroid that must have exploded over the Egyptian desert was far greater than an A-bomb, and could have easily created the temperature of 1,800 degrees Celsius needed to form the LDG. A recent expedition to the southwestern desert of Egypt has filled in some answers to the questions about the LDG's outer space connection.[18]

From some of the radioactive trace elements in the LDG, it has been possible to calculate when the glass was created—about 28 million years ago. So we know how and when the glass for the scarab in Tutankhamun's pectoral was created, but there is still one mystery. How did it get into the hands of an Egyptian craftsman who carved it into the shape of a beetle for the pectoral? There were no camel caravans in the time of Tutankhamun (indeed, there were no camels in Egypt then), so the remote site would have been nearly impossible to reach. As far as we know, it is unique in all of ancient Egypt. Even today, with four-wheel-drive vehicles, the LDG site takes days to reach. But somehow one piece made its way to Tutankhamun's workshop and eventually into his tomb.

17

CSI Thebes: The Case of the Missing Pectoral

Not all research on Tutankhamun involves new high-tech science or holding an object in your hand for close inspection. Sometimes archives and auction catalogues produce remarkable results. Dr. Marc Gabolde, a French expert on Tutankhamun, had wondered for a long time what happened to the pectoral that was stolen from the mummy of Tutankhamun. In 2015, he spotted a necklace at auction at Christie's in London (see Color Plate 23).[1] The necklace consisted of twenty pairs of teardrop-shaped gold beads interspersed with gold sequins. It looked both familiar and not quite right to Gabolde. The "not quite right" part was easy to understand. The Egyptians never strung teardrop-shaped beads in pairs; it just doesn't look good because of the shape of the beads. Gabolde concluded that the beads were ancient but had been restrung in modern times. This is a common practice. Often antiquity dealers have beads from ancient jewelry where the threads have broken and all that is left is a pile of beads and amulets, so they have them restrung to make them saleable. So this necklace wasn't strung in an Egyptian manner.

The "familiar" part is far more interesting. Gabolde recognized that the gold teardrops and sequins in the necklace for sale at Christie's were identical to the ones in the Tutankhamun pectoral that somehow disappeared from the mummy. We can see some of them in Harry Burton's photograph of the mummy (Figure 17.1). Had Gabolde found the remains of the pectoral that had been taken off the mummy? The answer seems to be no. There are forty teardrops in the necklace for sale, but not nearly that many were left embedded on the body. If they were not from the stolen pectoral, where did they come from?

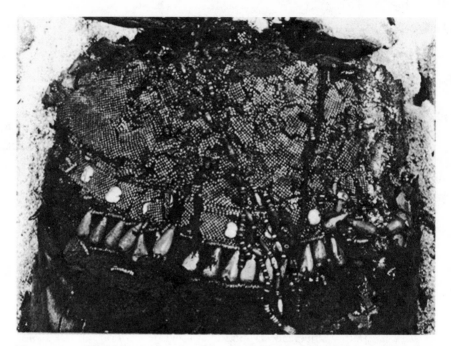

Figure 17.1. Tutankhamun's pectoral has beads identical to the ones auctioned at Christie's. (Griffith Institute p1561.)

When Carter originally saw the pectoral stuck to the mummy, he gave it a number, 256ttt, and drew it on his record cards (Figure 17.2). In addition to the beads stuck in the resin, there was an accumulation of beads that had fallen off the pectoral and were loose in the coffin. Carter took these out, probably for later restringing. So there were really two pieces to the pectoral. There's the part of it that was in pieces at the bottom of the coffin, and there was also the part that was stuck to the body and later stolen. Gabolde had found a modern-strung necklace made from the beads that Carter took out of the coffin.

This is plausible because we know those beads never made it to the Egyptian Museum in Cairo. When the objects were being removed from the tomb and still in the Valley of the Kings, Carter assigned a number to each artifact so he could keep track of everything. Then, when the items were sent to Cairo, the museum logged them into its system, and each object was given a museum number. This was, of course, before computers, so all entries were written by hand in the *journal d'entrée*. By looking at the museum's ledger, we can see that there

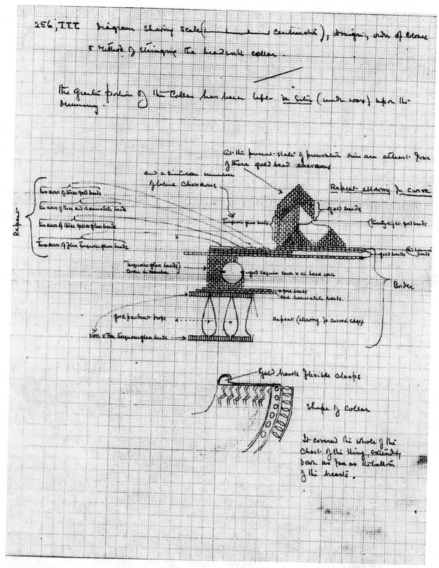

Figure 17.2. Carter's drawing of the pectoral shows the Horus clasps. (Griffith Institute 256ttt.)

is no entry for 256ttt. So somehow the beads Carter removed from the coffin made their way onto the antiquities market. How did this happen? Gabolde found out when he tracked down another possible piece of the pectoral.

The pectoral would have had clasps where it fastened at the back. In his records for 256ttt Carter described them as "flexible gold hawk-headed clasps." Like the beads, these clasps never made it to the Cairo museum. They now reside in America, at the Nelson-Atkins Museum of Art in Kansas City (Figure 17.3). The pieces were sold to the Nelson-Atkins by Spink & Son, the respected antiquities firm that was assisting in the disposal of Carter's estate after his death. According to a letter from Spink:

> The pieces were given by a member of the Carter family to a surgeon who was an amateur Egyptologist, and who attended Mr. Carter. . . . It came to our notice at the time of purchase that the rest of the necklace, which consists mainly of faience beads and other gold ankh signs, was given by a niece of Mr. Carter to a museum in this country [the United Kingdom] who have not displayed them for private reasons.[2]

The letter indicates there are more bits of Tutankhamun jewelry outside Egypt than just the pectoral. Indeed, the necklace and the clasps are not the only beadwork pieces from the tomb that can be connected with Carter. There is a headdress that has a remarkably similar story. Carter assigned the number 547a to a headdress decorated with beads and amulets sewn to

Figure 17.3. The Horus clasps in the Nelson-Atkins Museum seem to have come from Tutankhamun's tomb. (Nelson-Atkins Museum.)

linen. It was in fragmentary condition but was photographed by Burton. This too never reached the Egyptian Museum in Cairo and thus was never entered in the *journal d'entrée*. The fragments of the headdress may also be in America, at the St. Louis Art Museum. It was sold by Spink & Son from the Carter collection when they were liquidating his estate (Figure 17.4). This too seems to be a modern confection made from ancient elements. All the elements included in the modern stringing are in Burton's photo.

One more beadwork piece is worth mentioning. Carter recorded finding a

> small group of round gold and lapis blue glass beads of uncertain use. They do not seem to belong to any of the objects found upon the King—i.e. as far as is humanly possibl[e] to judge. Possibly a short Necklace. Strung alternate gold and glass.[3]

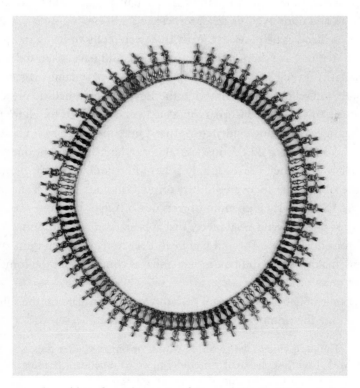

Figure 17.4. A necklace from the estate of Howard Carter. (St. Louis Art Museum.)

Carter gave the group the number 256y, but they too never reached the museum. The British Museum owns a necklace that fits Carter's description of the beads, even restrung as he suggested. It was obtained in 1964 from a private collector and is described by the British Museum as "once belonging to Howard Carter." A pattern seems to be emerging.

Tutankhamun's tomb contained many beadwork pieces, ranging from pectorals to skullcaps to sandals. Many of these were painstakingly restored by Lucas and Mace using their technique of stabilizing the object with wax so it could be restrung. Some items were in such poor condition that they couldn't be restrung—like the pectoral, which was partly stuck to the mummy and partly fallen apart in the coffin. It appears as if Carter may have brought the loose beads to London, perhaps for later restringing. When he died, they were in his estate and were sold by Spink & Son.

The beadwork pieces illustrate something discussed earlier—Carter's proprietary attitude toward Tutankhamun. He had discovered the tomb, excavated it, and conserved its treasures. He thought he could do with these "minor" artifacts as he pleased. Clearly, they weren't his to bring to England. If he wanted to have them restrung there, he could have asked for permission. What is also clear is that he had no intention of stealing artifacts from the tomb and selling them. Although the Egyptian nationalistic press often intimated that Carter and Carnarvon were stealing artifacts to sell for profit, there has never been any evidence for that. Quite the contrary. If Carter had wanted to steal the gold falcon clasps, he wouldn't have mentioned them in his records. Rather, Carter simply believed he could do what he wanted with the objects he discovered in the tomb. Gabolde's research shows that there are far more Tutankhamun objects out of Egypt than one would expect. Most of the Carter bead pieces that appeared on the antiquities market came from his London flat and had been later restrung in modern configurations, making them difficult to recognize as coming from the tomb. This was not always the case.

On November 11, 1925, Carter found two broad collars on the mummy. He gave one the number 256o and described it as a

collar of minute violet faience beads, woven or threaded after the fashion of mat-work, having semi-circular shoulder pieces and pendant border. . . . This collar has not yet been restrung.[4]

This piece, like the others mentioned above, never made it to the Egyptian Museum in Cairo. After Carter's death, a collar resembling his description entered the collection of the Metropolitan Museum of Art in New York. Unlike the other bead pieces, this one did not come from the antiquities market; it came from Howard Carter.

As we saw in Chapter 6, in his will Carter left his house in Luxor and its contents to the Metropolitan Museum of Art, whose staff had helped Carter so much during the excavation of the tomb. Carter had designated Harry Burton, a photographer working for the Metropolitan, as one of his executors, and when Carter died, Burton went to Luxor House (Castle Carter) and packed up the contents he thought the Metropolitan would want. Unfortunately, Burton died soon after, and because of the war, the items he packed weren't shipped to New York till 1948. The Metropolitan's broad collar was among the items (Color Plate 24). For more than fifty years it was on display at the museum, and then in 2011 the Metropolitan returned it to Cairo, as their curators had determined that it almost certainly came from Tutankhamun's tomb. Along with the broad collar, the Metropolitan also returned more than a dozen other items, including gold and silver nails from the coffins, as well as minor fragments of textiles, a fragment of the innermost shrine, and a piece of the quartzite sarcophagus.[5] This list gives an idea of how cavalierly Carter was treating objects from the tomb. Carter's work in the tomb was completed by 1933, but these pieces remained in his house for years.

The objects discussed above don't have Tutankhamun's name on them, so they don't scream Tutankhamun, but some found in Carter's estate do, and they help fill out the picture of how so many Tutankhamun objects came to be outside Egypt. Recall that when Carter died, the objects in his possession with Tutankhamun's name were not part of the estate sale, which was conducted by Spink & Son, a well-established firm selling Egyptian and other antiquities, with whom Carter had worked earlier; these are the pieces that were returned to the Egyptian museum after the war via King Farouk. We can't be 100 percent sure how they had ended up in Carter's flat in London, but there is a chance their first home in England was in Lord Carnarvon's collection at Highclere Castle. We know that when Carnarvon died, Lady Carnarvon asked Carter to assist with the sale of Carnarvon's collection, and Carter, protecting the reputation of his deceased patron, held back the items with Tutankhamun's name on them. So it is possible that these obvious Tutankhamun pieces came from Carnarvon.

In his research through archives, Gabolde was able to reconstruct what these objects were, and the list is shocking. These aren't just souvenir nails from Tutankhamun's coffin (there were some of those too); they included spectacular openwork gold plaques of Tutankhamun as a sphinx and riding in his chariot. These are museum-quality pieces. There were also three ushabti figures with Tutankhamun's name. What was Carter and Carnarvon's intention when they took them? What did they imagine was going to happen with these objects? Perhaps they just weren't thinking.

The kindest interpretation is that at the time when Carnarvon returned to England with them, he was still expecting a division of the finds. The ushabtis were the best bet to be in his share, because there were so many of them, with many duplicates. But how was that going to work? If he did get a division of the finds, was he going to then say, "Oh, I already have three at Highclere"? It is difficult to envision a scenario that doesn't end in disaster. It is almost as if the only possible way out is if they both died before the "theft" was discovered.

The three ushabtis that were in Carter's estate were not the only ones that left Egypt. One has been hiding in plain sight. For many years the Louvre has had a Tutankhamun ushabti on display in their Egyptian galleries. When I asked a curator how they acquired it, he replied that it was a bit of a mystery. It was bought in 1946 "from the estate of Howard Carter's secretary," but as far as we know, Carter never had a secretary.

There may be more items missing from Tutankhamun's tomb. About twenty years ago, a television producer in London took my wife and me to his club, the Saville Club. Over dinner he mentioned that Carter had been a member after he completed his work on the tomb, and that he had left a trunk of his belongings at the club with the instruction that the contents be sold for the benefit of the club, but his name was not to be attached to the sale. I have often wondered what was in that trunk.

The research into the Tut items found outside Egypt didn't shed more light on how they were used in Egypt during the Eighteenth Dynasty; we knew that already. But the research did tell us something about the sociology of the discovery in the early twentieth century, a time when the English ruled, and when they thought they owned Tutankhamun's treasures.

PART III

Tutankhamun's Legacy

He gave his life for tourism.

—Steve Martin

18

Tutankhamun as Activist

Tutankhamun would play a part in two major changes in Egypt: the end of colonialism and the end of the Egyptian antiquities trade. Both had long histories. In this chapter we discuss how colonialism began in Egypt and Tutankhamun's role in ending it.

When Carter and Carnarvon discovered the tomb of Tutankhamun, Egypt's finances and administration were controlled by England, and the country's Antiquities Service was run by France. What was going on? Why were there English judges in Egyptian courts? Couldn't the Egyptians decide for themselves what should happen to their heritage? Unfortunately for Carter and Carnarvon, around the time they discovered the tomb Egyptians were asking these same questions. As we have seen, a growing nationalist movement was making things difficult for Carter and Carnarvon, and their insensitivity to the situation wasn't helping matters. In the decades that followed the excavation of the tomb, Egypt would change radically. The British would leave, Egyptians would take control of the Antiquities Service, and Egypt would be ruled by Egyptians. It would be a long and difficult path for Egypt. A king would be sent into exile, a president would be assassinated, and there would be a revolution by people wanting to remove a dictator and rule themselves. Tut didn't cause all these changes, but he did play a role, and that role is part of his legacy. To understand the situation in Egypt at the time of the discovery of Tutankhamun's tomb, let's first look briefly at Egypt's history of colonial rule.

Bonaparte in Egypt

Bonaparte's invasion of Egypt in 1798 is famous not because of its political consequences, which were minimal. Bonaparte lost and went home; it was a failed attempt to colonize Egypt. The reason it is so often trotted out is that it is an easy story to tell. Bonaparte had no right to invade Egypt, so it is a clear-cut narrative. Another reason it is told so often is the glamour and exoticism. Bonaparte was the dashing *enfant terrible*, and his antics were set against the backdrop of the pyramids of Egypt. What could be better?

When Bonaparte invaded Egypt with his army of fifty thousand, he proclaimed that he was coming to free the Egyptians from the tyrannical rule of the Mamelukes, the warrior class that had run Egypt for centuries. No one believed him.[1] He had come to colonize. He intended to take over Egypt for the same reason other foreign powers were interested in Egypt—it was strategically situated between East and West. Egypt was England's land route to India, and England was France's enemy. If Bonaparte could cut off England's trade with India, it would be a severe blow to Britain's economy.[2] Bonaparte wasn't there to free the Egyptians from oppressors and then go home; he intended to stay.

Along with his fifty thousand soldiers, he brought a corps of 150 savants—engineers, architects, scientists, naturalists, and scholars—to map Egypt and its monuments. Their mission was to study and describe both modern and ancient Egypt. Many of the savants were distinguished members of France's National Institute. The group included Jean-Baptiste Fourier, the mathematician for whom the Fourier equations are named; Deodat de Dolomieu, the mineralogist after whom the Dolomite Mountains are named; and Étienne Geoffroy Saint-Hillaire, a brilliant young naturalist who would later bring the first giraffe to Paris.[3] There were also artists such as Vivant Denon, who later became the first director of the Louvre.[4]

Bonaparte was a military man first, but he was also interested in history and culture, and on August 21, 1798, he founded the Institut d'Égypte, the world's first Egyptological society. The Institut had four sections: mathematics, physics, political economy, and literature and art. Bonaparte headed the mathematics section and took an active part in the meetings of the Institut, which took place in the recently vacated palace of Qassim Bey, who had fled south. Napoleon proposed very specific, practical problems to the Institut's members: What was the best method of purifying the Nile water that the army was drinking? Were the materials for making gunpower to be found in Egypt? Could ovens for baking good French bread be built?[5] The scientists were also free to investigate topics of their own choice. They could explore Egypt.

It was a disastrous military campaign for the French. First their fleet anchored at Abukir Bay was sunk by England's Horatio Nelson, and then their army was decimated by the plague. After three years in Egypt, the French army surrendered to the British, who had assisted the Egyptians in ousting Bonaparte.[6] It was his first defeat, but for the scientists who accompanied the military campaign, there was glory. When the savants returned to France, they published the *Description de l'Égypte*, the largest publication in the world at that time. It took more than twenty years to publish, but when the *Description* was finally completed in 1821, five massive volumes of engravings depicted the antiquities, three volumes told of the natural history, and two presented modern Egypt. It was a sensation. There were also nine very large volumes of scholarly articles by the savants, but no one read them; everyone just looked at the fabulous illustrations. Here were hundreds and hundreds of accurate drawings of the temples and tombs of Egypt. This is how Europe learned about ancient Egypt. It was the beginning of Orientalism, and Egyptomania swept the continent. In a sense, this was early publicity for the discovery of Tutankhamun. Bonaparte's failed attempt at colonizing Egypt didn't have long-lasting political consequences. The important effects were cultural.

Bonaparte had no way of knowing it, but his failed expedition made Egypt even more vulnerable to foreign exploitation. Before Bonaparte's expedition, travelers to Egypt rarely went south to Upper Egypt. They conducted business in Alexandria or Cairo and returned home. Now, with the publication of the *Description de l'Égypte*, Europeans were aware of the fabulous temples of Dendera, Karnak, and Luxor in the south. Then there was the Valley of the Kings, where treasures might be found. By alerting Europe to the monuments of Egypt, Bonaparte created a market for antiquities. Wealthy Europeans were suddenly willing to pay handsomely for a piece of ancient Egypt.

The fifty years that followed Bonaparte's hasty exit from Egypt was the Wild West of the antiquities trade. There were no regulations; no one cared what you took. If you could get it out of Egypt, it was yours. Egypt was ruled by Mohamed Ali, the Ottoman Empire's man in Egypt, whose descendants would rule Egypt for more than a century. He was born in Macedonia and was an ethnic Albanian; Egypt wasn't his heritage. To him the monuments were "just stones." At one point he gave away five obelisks to curry favor with European powers.[7] Adventurers poured into Egypt in search of ancient stones.

The Italian Giovanni Belzoni specialized in bringing back large antiquities: the alabaster sarcophagus of Seti I (now at Sir John Soane's Museum in London); a colossal head of Ramses the Great (now in the British Museum); an obelisk from the island of Philae (now on the estate of William Bankes in Dorset, England). Belzoni bragged of his exploits in a popular book he published, held exhibitions of his treasures, and even created a replica of the tomb of Seti I.[8] All this encouraged other adventurers to follow his example. So many treasures were removed from Egypt during the nineteenth century that when Brian Fagan published his extremely readable history of the period he titled it *Rape of the Nile*.[9] But it wasn't the quest for antiquities that would lead to England's control over Egypt. It was a canal. There is a curious connection between this canal and Napoleon Bonaparte's failed expedition to Egypt.

When General Bonaparte set sail for Egypt, one of his missions was to determine if a canal between the Mediterranean and the Red Sea was possible. Most of the trade from Europe to India went around the Cape of Good Hope. A canal would permit ships to sail across the Mediterranean to Alexandria, then through the canal to Suez, into the Red Sea, and on to India. If the French could control such a canal, it would be a great economic advantage for France and a financial defeat for their enemy England.

There had been a canal in pharaonic times, and Bonaparte was determined to find its remains. In late December 1798, he rode out to explore the Isthmus of Suez with his chief engineer and a few of the savants. After several days of searching, Bonaparte found the canal and traced it for fifteen miles.[10] Excited by his discovery, Bonaparte instructed the chief engineer, Jacques-Marie Le Père, to return with a team to survey the entire isthmus to determine if a canal was possible. Le Père and his team made three expeditions to the isthmus, surveying under challenging conditions. Constantly harassed by Bedouins, they had difficulty obtaining food and supplies and slept out in the cold. They finally completed the survey in 1800 and sent the report to Bonaparte, who was back in Paris by then. Le

Père reported that because the Red Sea at high tide was thirty feet higher than the Mediterranean, digging a canal would produce flooding in Egypt. He was wrong. Some of his fellow savants, including Fourier and mathematician Pierre-Simon Laplace, correctly understood that sea level is sea level everywhere, and there was no danger of flooding. Still, the plan for the canal was abandoned and not raised again for fifty years. When in the 1850s Ferdinand de Lesseps revived the idea of a canal, he unknowingly opened the pathway the English would use to control Egypt.

The Canal

De Lesseps was an idealistic engineer with almost superhuman energy and optimism. He envisioned the Suez Canal as a promoter of peace. The canal would benefit world trade by lowering shipping costs for everyone, and because it would benefit all the nations of the world, everyone would come together to both build and maintain it. Unlike Bonaparte, de Lesseps had no intention of maintaining control of the canal; it would be an international venture. Further, it would increase Egypt's standing in the world. In addition to having the canal on Egyptian soil, Egypt would levy taxes on all the goods transported through the canal and finally achieve economic stability. Everyone would win. In 1856 he presented his detailed proposal to the viceroy of Egypt, Said Pasha, a descendant of Mohamed Ali.

An international canal company would be formed, with shares in the company sold to the nations of the world. Egypt would supply the land and the labor to build the canal and would thus earn its equity in the canal. De Lesseps was well aware that the pashas of Egypt were accustomed to using the *corvée*, basically calling up the peasants to do forced labor. So his proposal stipulated:

> Workers will be paid a third more than they would normally receive in Egypt. In addition to their pay, workers are entitled to food, accommodation, medical and other welfare services.[11]

Said Pasha agreed, and the public offering of the Canal Company's stock appeared in 1859. It was a great success, with more than half of the shares selling in the first three days of the offer. The big surprise for de Lesseps was that England, which stood to gain the most from using the canal, wasn't buying. Rather, the British were doing everything possible to sabotage the project. They spread rumors that the company was bankrupt, that conscripted labor was going to be used, et cetera, et cetera. They viewed the canal as the French attempting to gain control of the region. The English could have bought shares and had influence, but they feared that sometime in the future they might be drawn into military action to protect their interests, and they weren't willing to do that. Fortunately, de Lesseps didn't need the support of the British, and proceeded full steam ahead.

When work on the canal was in its early stages, Said Pasha died and was replaced by Ismail Pasha, who convinced the Ottoman sultan to grant him the title of khedive, which to him sounded more independent than being a viceroy. It wasn't, but now Egypt was ruled by a khedive.

The political situation was now more complex than when de Lesseps had begun building the canal. Egypt was under the control of the Ottoman Empire, and the Ottoman sultan had power over the viceroy/khedive of Egypt. The Sublime Porte (the central Ottoman government, located in Constantinople) was nearly bankrupt, so England had power over the sultan. Soon politics would threaten the canal's completion. But for the moment, Khedive Ismail was on board with the canal project, and he bought Said's shares in the canal, so the digging should have proceeded as before.[12] Up to this point, all the laborers had been paid by the khedive. But he was running out of money just as the project needed more workers, and the *corvée* would have to be used. But the British, still thinking they could sabotage the project, used their influence over the Sultan to have him declare that the *corvee* was illegal in Egypt. So now Ismail could not provide the labor he was contracted to supply. With the shortage of manual laborers, de Lesseps used huge steam-powered dredgers to continue digging the canal.

Because Ismail's equity in the Canal Company was based on supplying labor and land, he had to pay to the company an amount equivalent to what he would have spent on labor, but he didn't have it. He was broke. Ismail had always been extravagant, building palaces for friends and relatives throughout Egypt. In preparation for the opening ceremonies for the canal, he invited six thousand foreign royals and dignitaries to the festivities, paying for their accommodations. He built a palace for Empress Eugenie of France so that she would be comfortable during her visit (it is now a hotel). He also built a road from her palace to the Giza pyramids so that the empress could visit the pyramids in in the comfort of her carriage. So when it was time for Khedive Ismail to pay his share of building the canal, he couldn't. His solution was to sell his shares in the canal to England. By now it was clear that England could not stop construction of the canal, so the British became a partner rather than be shut out. Because Egypt had sold its shares in the Suez Canal, the government no longer had any control over the canal, which was being now being administered by foreigners.

Rising nationalism in Egypt was causing riots, and there were calls for foreigners to be expelled. Ismail sailed off to exile, leaving the new khedive, Tewfik, to solve the unsolvable. The nationalists, led by the military commander Ahmed Orabi, successfully rebelled against Tewfik, took control of Alexandria, and began fortifying the city, intending to take control of both the government and the canal. The foreigners in Alexandria were now in danger, so the British, saying they were coming to rescue British citizens, and also to support Tewfik, sent more than a dozen of their ironclad fighting ships into Alexandria's harbor and started shelling Orabi's position. The bombardment of Alexandria lasted for ten hours, and in the end, much of the city was reduced to rubble (Figure 18.1).[13] The British landed marines, and Egypt became an unofficial British protectorate; it would remain one for more than half a century. Such was the political situation Carter and Carnarvon encountered forty years later.

When Howard Carter discovered the tomb of Tutankhamun, the country was administered by the British. De Lesseps, of course, could never have foreseen such consequences of his canal and was only very indirectly responsible for England's control over Egypt. He was, however, directly responsible for France's control of the Antiquities Service.

The Antiquities Service's First Director

When the canal was first being built, de Lesseps became a close friend of the viceroy, Said Pasha. De Lesseps, always the idealist, was concerned about the protection of Egypt's antiquities. On June 1, 1858, the viceroy created the Antiquities Service and on the recommendation of de Lesseps appointed a Frenchman, August Mariette, as its first director, beginning a long tradition of the French running the Antiquities Service. As a young man, Mariette had been sent to Egypt in 1850 by the Louvre to purchase Coptic

HARPER'S WEEKLY.

JOURNAL OF CIVILIZATION.

Vol. XXVI.—No. 1335.
Copyright, 1882, by Harper & Brothers.

NEW YORK, SATURDAY, JULY 22, 1882.

TEN CENTS A COPY.
$4.00 PER YEAR, IN ADVANCE.

THE BOMBARDMENT OF ALEXANDRIA.—[See Page 456.]

Figure 18.1. In 1881 the British bombarded Alexandria and later took control of Egypt. (Photo Pat Remler.)

and Syriac manuscripts from the patriarchs of the Coptic Church. His experiences give us an idea of the trade in antiquities in Egypt at the time.

When his negotiations for papyri bogged down, Mariette began visiting the antiquities dealers of Cairo. He saw several large stone sphinxes in the shops, and when he asked where they came from, the reply was always Saqqara. He decided to investigate, and on October 18, 1850, he hired donkeys and mules, bought provisions, and procured a tent. Nine days later he was excavating in the sands of Saqqara. It was as simple as that.

He stumbled on a sphinx's head much like those in the Cairo antiquities shops. Clearing the sand, he uncovered fifteen sphinxes. He recalled a description by Strabo, the ancient geographer, of a place called the Serapeum, where the sacred Apis bulls were buried. Strabo said it was preceded by an avenue of sphinxes.[14]

The name Serapeum is a corruption of the names of two gods, Osiris and Apis. In ancient Egyptian, Osiris's name was pronounced as "Usir"; Osiris is the Egyptian word with a Greek ending tacked on. In Egyptian, the name of the other god was pronounced as "Ap," but was pronounced as "Apis" by the Greeks. During the Greek period, the two gods merged to become Usir-Ap; then the Romans added the ending -eum to indicate that this was the place of Usir-Ap, the Serapeum.

The sacred Apis bull was worshipped by the Egyptians and mummified when it died. According to one account, the Apis was born when a bolt of lightning came down from the heavens and impregnated the mother of the Apis. The Apis calf had special markings—it was black with a white diamond on its forehead, a falcon on its back, and a scarab under its tongue, and its tail hairs were split. Mariette was determined to find the Apis bulls. By November, Mariette had taken all the money he had been given to buy manuscripts and spent it on hiring thirty workmen in his search for the Serapeum.[15]

He discovered a small temple built by Nectanebo II, the last native Egyptian king. Inscriptions indicated the temple was dedicated to the Apis. Mariette thought the entrance to the tombs might lie beneath the paving stones of the temple and pried them up. He was wrong about the entrance but found hundreds of small bronze and ceramic amulets of various gods. Word soon spread of Mariette's discovery, but as is usual in Egypt, it was wildly exaggerated and the trove became "thousands of gold statues." The Egyptian government ordered Mariette to cease all excavations, but after prolonged negotiations, he was permitted to continue. In November 1852, after removing tons of debris, Mariette finally found the entrance to the Serapeum, and became the first person in modern times to enter the burial place of the Apis bulls.

He entered a high, spacious corridor about an eighth of a mile long, lined on both sides with twenty-four open chambers. They contained huge granite sarcophagi carved to receive the mummies of the Apis bulls that died between the beginning of the Twenty-Sixth Dynasty (663 BC) and the end of the Greek Period (30 BC). More galleries contained the bulls from earlier periods.[16] In the middle of one gallery stood a huge rock too heavy for his workmen to budge, so Mariette blasted it with explosives, discovering the burial of a man with a gold mask covering his face. Two jasper amulets suspended from a gold chain hung on his neck. They bore the inscription Kah-em-Waset, indicating that he was one of the many sons of Ramses the Great.

Mariette's excavations ended in 1853, but he shipped more than two hundred crates of antiquities back to the Louvre. His discovery of the Serapeum was the high point of his new career as an excavator, and when he was offered the position as director of the Antiquities Service he quickly accepted. Under Mariette, foreigners would have a great deal of freedom and were permitted to take many important antiquities out of Egypt. Mariette retained his position till his death in 1881, when he was succeeded by Gaston Maspero, another Frenchman. After England took control of Egypt, this tradition was formalized in the Entente Cordiale of April 8, 1904, between England and France. It stipulated that "the post of Director-General of Antiquities in Egypt shall continue, as in the past, to be entrusted to a French *savant*."[17] So we had the British determining that the French would be in control of Egypt's patrimony. This is why when Carter discovered the tomb, he was under the supervision of a Frenchman, Pierre Lacau. But as we have seen, times were changing.

Egyptian nationalism was on the rise. England had just formally given up control of Egypt, and Egyptians had elected a parliament. The leader of Parliament was Saad Zaghloul, a staunch nationalist who was not new to politics or British rule. After World War I, the European powers met to reorganize the defeated Ottoman Empire. Led by Zaghloul, the Egyptians formed their own delegation to attend the discussions that would be vital to their future, but they never got to participate. The British didn't permit the delegates to travel, and Zaghloul was arrested and exiled to Malta. After returning from exile in 1923, Zaghloul became leader of the nationalist Wafd Party and became prime minister after the elections of January 12, 1924. Now, when Carter was excavating, Zaghloul and his Wafd Party were leading Parliament.

With this as background, the behavior of Carter and Carnarvon seems almost inconceivable. To sell the exclusive rights of the Tutankhamun story to a British newspaper, cutting out the Egyptians, seems almost suicidal, but it gives us an idea of just how out of touch Carnarvon was with Egyptian sensibilities. He never considered how the Egyptians would feel about his exclusive deal with the *Times*. He was an Englishman and had grown up with British colonialism.

The Egyptians were quick to express how *they* felt:

> There in . . . the Valley of the Kings, an absolute despotic government has arisen on the ruins of the ancient Pharao[n]ic, and of the modern Egyptian government. That Government is the Government of Lord Carnarvon and Mr. Carter Limited. Does anybody dare to dispute it within the boundaries of that Valley? . . . The Carnarvon Government permits and explains, and prevents and grants, it invites the Ministers of Egypt, out of courtesy and generosity, to see the Kings of Egypt. . . . Lord Carnarvon is exploiting the moral remains of our ancient fathers before our eyes, and he fails to give the grandchildren any information about their forefathers. What era do we live in and to which government do we submit?[18]

There was even a series of postcards showing objects being removed from the tomb. The captions for all the cards were the same: "Exploitation of Tout-Ankh-Amon's Tomb" (Figure 18.2). Weigall had it right when he warned Carter about how the Egyptians felt and how times had changed, but Carter didn't want to hear it. True, the agreement for the selling of the Tutankhamun rights to the *Times* was Carnarvon's idea, but Carter had his own ideas, which made the situation even worse.

When Carter was locked out of the tomb by the minister of public works, Murqus Hanny, he hired F. M. Maxwell to represent him in court. It was a terrible choice of lawyer. When Maxwell had been a British prosecutor, he had argued for the death penalty for Hanny in a treason case. Why hire him when Hanny was overseeing your expedition? Carter couldn't seem to understand the Egyptians' new nationalism. He was colonial through and through.

Exploitation of Tout-Ankh-Amon's Tomb

Figure 18.2. A series of postcards were produced with the caption "Exploitation of Tout-Ankh-Amon's Tomb."

Indeed, the reason he had been locked out was that he wanted to admit the wives of his colleagues to the tomb for a special showing. When the undersecretary of state in the Ministry of Public Works heard about this, he refused permission and asked Carter if any of his colleagues were Muslims. Carter didn't get it, and asked what he meant. The reply was, "I wouldn't begrudge you the visits of twenty-two ladies over and above your sixteen men if there was at least one among them who was Muslim."[19]

When the mummy of Tutankhamun was examined, two men were in charge, Dr. Douglas Derry and Dr. Hamdy Bey. When the final report was published, Bey was acknowledged, but only Derry's name was on it.[20] It might have been a useful gesture to have him as co-author.

Although Carter didn't see the cultural gap between himself and the Egyptians as a problem, the Egyptians certainly did, and Tutankhamun became intertwined with the quest for self-rule. One poet, Ahmad Shawqi, repeatedly linked Tutankhamun with independence:

He traveled forty centuries, considering them, until he came home, and found there . . .
　　England and its army and its lord, brandishing its Indian sword, protecting its India.[21]

In a different poem Tutankhamun becomes the rallying cry.

> Pharaoh, the time of self-rule is in effect, and the dynasty of arrogant lords has passed.
> Now the foreign tyrants in every land must relinquish their rule over their subjects.[22]

To be fair to Carter, we must make it clear that there is absolutely no evidence that he was a racist, holding anything against people because they were darker than he. To the contrary, recall that during the Saqqara incident, he strongly took the side of his native guards, as opposed to the French, who demanded an apology. In his will, he remembered his faithful Egyptian overseer for his excavation and left 150 Egyptian pounds to Abd el-Ahmed.[23] Upon Carter's death, his niece, Phyllis Walker, received a handwritten letter of condolence from two of the *gaffirs* who had worked on the excavation. It would not have been easy for them to have written and mailed such a letter, a clear sign Carter had formed a close bond with his workmen.

Carter's colonial views were not personal; they were cultural, shared by the majority of his countrymen. We should remember that the only Egypt Carter ever knew was ruled by the British. When he was first sent to Egypt as a teenage artist, Egypt was ruled by the British, and when he discovered the tomb, it was still ruled by the British. Timothy Mitchell, in his book *Colonising Egypt*, discusses the mechanisms by which colonialism is established. He presents the Paris World Exhibition of 1889 as an example of how subtle some of those mechanisms can be. The Egyptian exhibit had been built by the French and recreated a Cairo street, complete with overhanging latticed windows and the Mosque of Qait Bey. In addition, they imported fifty Egyptian donkeys with their drivers to give visitors rides down the street. In contrast to the other exhibits with their straight, orderly streets, it was chaos.[24] And when visitors entered the mosque, they found themselves in a coffee shop with dancing girls. This is how the French presented Egypt to the world. It was a world in need of colonizing.

Keys to the Kingdom

Throughout the ten years of excavating in Tutankhamun's tomb, Carter never acknowledged the colonial problem. By the beginning of 1930, the tomb was practically empty, with just the shrines to be moved. Carter told Lady Carnarvon that there was no need to renew the concession, as they were nearly done. But now, with no concession, Carter had no official connection with the tomb, and Egypt was full of nationalists ready to flex their muscles. Carter was told it was "forbidden by law to hand over keys of any government property to any individual who was not on the permanent staff of the Egyptian Government."[25] Carter was incensed; he felt that this was his tomb. The government still wanted Carter to complete the work on the tomb and presented what should have been a workable solution: a permanent government official would have charge of the keys but would be entirely under Carter's orders and would be available to Carter whenever he wanted the keys. This wasn't acceptable to Carter, and he fumed for a year about the loss of his keys, but eventually the work was completed.

In the first volume of *The Tomb of Tut.Ankh.Amen*, published in 1923, Carter described all the security measures he took to protect the tomb from thefts—the numerous guards placed outside the tomb, a heavy wooden grille at the entrance and a massive steel gate at the inner doorway, each secured by four padlocks. "And that there might never be any mistake about these latter," he wrote, "the keys were in the permanent charge of one particular member of the European staff." The message was clear: no Egyptian is going to be entrusted with the treasures of Tutankhamun. So in 1930, even when the tomb was cleared, Carter didn't like the idea of an Egyptian holding the keys.

In his thoughtful book *Complicated Antiquities*, Elliott Colla makes a very interesting philosophical/sociological point about how Carter treated the objects he found. By treating Tutankhamun's treasures as artifacts, things to be studied scientifically, conserved, and curated, rather than as cultural heritage, Europeans found it easier to claim that they were better custodians for the objects.[26] Egyptians claimed that they, as descendants of Tutankhamun, were uniquely entitled to be the caretakers of Tutankhamun's tomb. Carter had turned the "wonderful things" described in the first volume of *The Tomb of Tut.Ankh.Amen* into artifacts to be treated scientifically, making his (European) claim to curate and control them stronger. Indeed, the last two volumes of Carter's three-volume work don't read nearly so well as the first, and I wonder if this is because there is more emotion ("wonderful things") in volume I. In volumes II and III Carter had gone into scientist mode. As Colla put it, "arguments in favor of Egyptian management of the Tutankhamen excavation site were explicit analogues to arguments for Egyptian self-rule."[27]

As the excavation progressed and nationalism grew, the divide between Carter and the Egyptians grew wider and wider. The newspapers were full of outrage:

> My young king, they are going to transport you to the museum and set you next to Qasr al-Nil Barracks, to add insult to injury? So that my free king, you might look out over your occupied country?[28]

But Carter didn't want to hear it.

Once in a while the literary gazettes had humorous pieces connecting Tutankhamun to self-rule, but they were no less pointed. One involves a conversation between the Sphinx and Tut that begins in Arabic, but soon switches to English:

Sphinx: Hey Amun! Amun!

Tutankhamun: Who's that calling my name?

Sphinx: It's me!

Tut: Is that you Sphinx? [In English] How are you, old fellow?

Sphinx: What's this my son, you're speaking English now?

Tut: Yes, but that's because in my tomb I hear nothing but English.

Sphinx: Aren't you ashamed to let yourself be colored English? Where has your true patriotism gone? . . . Aren't you ashamed of how you got rid of those noble men?

Tut: Who are you calling noble? If those people were noble, they wouldn't set foot in other people's tombs. [Normally] when someone yanks something from the hand of a dead person, it's called stealing. But when they snatch it after a thousand years have passed, they call it great archaeological discovery and all honor goes to the one who committed the crime.[29]

In the Egyptian mind, Tutankhamun would remain linked to the struggle for self-governance and the need to throw off colonial rule.

To the very end, Carter seems to have thought that he owned everything related to Tutankhamun; Tutankhamun was his proprietary right. We saw this throughout the ten years he worked in the tomb. First Carter went along with Carnarvon selling the newspaper rights to Tutankhamun. Then in 1924, when the British Empire Exhibition planned to include a replica of the tomb among its exhibits, Carter objected and started legal proceedings (and lost). Later, when Carter heard that the Egyptian Museum in Cairo intended to include a description of objects from the tomb in the museum's new catalogue, he complained; how could they be sure the objects were theirs?

The Purloined Amulet

At the very end, after the tomb was cleared, this notion that he owned everything caused a break in his friendship with Sir Alan Gardiner. In the 1930s Carter gave Gardiner what is called a *whm* amulet. *Whm* is ancient Egyptian for the hoof and leg of a bovine, and the amulet was a miniature of that. These amulets were used as food offerings for the dead and were usually placed in tombs. The amulet's origin goes back to the Opening of the Mouth ceremony, when the foreleg of a calf was amputated while the animal was still alive. A common vignette in the *Book of the Dead* shows a shaven-headed butcher-priest cutting the leg while the animal is still standing, with the mother behind in obvious distress. In the ceremony, the priest touches the amputated leg to the mouth of the mummy, giving him life. Then the priest again touches the mouth of the mummy, this time with an *adz*, giving him speech and breath (see Color Plate 19).

When Carter gave Gardiner the *whm* amulet, he assured him that it didn't come from the tomb. Gardiner showed it to Reginald Engelbach, the British director of the Egyptian Museum. Suffice it to say that Engelbach's letter to Gardiner begins with "The *whm* amulet you showed me has been stolen from the tomb of Tutankhamen."[30] Several of these amulets had been sent by Carter from the tomb to the Egyptian Museum, and Engelbach realized that Gardiner's amulet had been made from the same mold. Things got worse from there. Gardiner wrote to Carter and enclosed Engelbach's letter, saying, "I deeply regret having been placed in so awkward a position."[31]

Gardiner then revealed to Engelbach that he had been given other things from the tomb. In a letter to Engelbach dated October 23, 1934, Gardiner says:

> In order that my personal position may be entirely clear, I wish to tell you that
> (1) I possess a tiny fragment of linen wrapping from the tomb, given to me at

the time by Carter, and (2) I took away with me, with Carter's permission, a lump of plaster bearing some sealings from the doorway to the sarcophagus chamber. This was being thrown away with other debris and I took it home to give to my younger son, then a schoolboy, and I believe he still possesses it.[32]

The point is not the value of the objects nor why they were being given away; the problem is that Carter believed he had the right to do with them as he pleased. As we now know, far more significant objects from Tutankhamun's tomb left Egypt via Carter.

Part of Tutankhamun's legacy is that the excavation of his tomb raised the question of ownership of Egypt's heritage. The Egyptian nationalists were not reacting against foreigners excavating in their country; rather, they were protesting how they were being treated and how the foreigners were behaving. If Carter and Carnarvon had acted as guests of a foreign country, if it had occurred to either of them to ask about or discuss removing items from the tomb, their relationship with the Egyptians would have been much smoother. But they didn't, and they treated the tomb as if they owned it.

With England receding from the picture, the Americans saw an opportunity to fill the colonial void. After all, the Egyptians didn't resent Americans the way they did the English. So James Henry Breasted, from the University of Chicago, proposed that a Rockefeller-funded, Western-controlled museum be built in Cairo. Egypt turned it down. They had had enough of colonialism. It is worth noting that for more than thirty years after the Tutankhamun excavation was completed, not one Tutankhamun exhibition had been sent abroad. Tutankhamun was Egypt's, and Egypt's alone.

In 1952 Egypt's government suddenly changed when the military seized power and King Farouk was sent into exile. Now, for the first time in nearly a hundred years, the Antiquities Service would no longer be under a Frenchman. The last Frenchman to hold the position of director, Fr. Étienne Drioton, resigned and returned home. From then on, an Egyptian would hold that position. It had been a long, hard road to freedom from foreign rule, but the struggle was not yet over. A king had been sent into exile, and in coming years a president would be assassinated; later still, people would bravely gather in Tahrir Square, next to the Egyptian Museum and Tutankhamun's treasures, to protest a dictator. Tutankhamun's part in the drama had ended, but as late as 1956 the French and English had not given up their colonial aspirations toward Egypt, and they invaded Egypt in an attempt to regain control of the Suez Canal. The plan failed, and England would not be permitted to excavate again in Egypt till 1964.[33]

Intertwined with colonialism and the struggle to throw off foreign control was the question of how to care for Egypt's heritage. Part of Tutankhamun's legacy are the laws that govern Egyptian antiquities today. When it was finally decided that no Tutankhamun antiquities would leave Egypt, an important precedent was set. As we will see, it would be broadened in the years that followed.

19

Who Owns Tutankhamun?

In the 1980s and 1990s, New York's major auction houses, Christie's and Sotheby's, held at least four major auctions of Egyptian antiquities each year.[1] It was an exciting scene, one in which important private collections were formed and museum acquisitions were made. There were receptions where wealthy collectors could preview the antiquities they would bid on—anything from a New Kingdom coffin to a complete Book of the Dead. Beautiful color catalogues were delivered to collectors around the world, and on the day of the sale the auction room was packed with collectors and curators, with buyers from around the world bidding live by phone. Today there are far fewer auctions of Egyptian antiquities, and a much smaller selection of artifacts. The market is dead. It was a slow death, and to a great extent it was due to a series of decisions, laws, and policies that were set into motion by the discovery of Tutankhamun's tomb.

The Era of Pillage and Plunder

Before Tutankhamun there was a fifty-year period with relatively little regulation of the antiquities market. In the early part of the nineteenth century, adventurers could search for antiquities in Egypt and pretty much bring home what they found. Many foreign museums had agents in Egypt searching for pieces that would form their collections. The French had Bernardino Drovetti, while the British had Henry Salt.[2] Salt created several collections, with one going to the British Museum and another to the Louvre. Antiquities were flowing out of Egypt and into European collections, and no one seemed to care.

Mohamed Ali, who ruled Egypt from 1805 to 1848, is infamous for dismantling ancient temples and reusing the blocks to build his factories. Because of Mohamed Ali's building projects, we no longer have Cleopatra VII's temple at Armant. When Napoleon's savants visited Armant Temple in 1799, they recorded a scene of Cleopatra VII giving birth to Caesarion.[3] It is a good thing they did, for it no longer exists thanks to Mohamed Ali. There just wasn't great concern for preserving the monuments. This is why Claude Lelorrain in 1821 could dynamite out the Dendera Zodiac from the temple's ceiling and bring it back to France.[4]

Antiquities often left Egypt at the hands of adventurers, but there were other routes as well. During Bonaparte's Egyptian campaign (1798–1801) his savants accumulated an impressive collection of antiquities, intending to bring them back to France. However, when the French surrendered to the British in 1801, many of the antiquities were seized as spoils of war by the British. This is why the Rosetta Stone, the key to the decipherment of the ancient Egyptian language, is in the British Museum, not the Louvre.[5] Neither the English nor the French entertained the idea that the Rosetta Stone belonged to Egypt. That was a concept for the future, one that wouldn't be fully articulated till the time of the Tutankhamun excavation.

Surprisingly, one of the earliest laws banning the export of antiquities without official permission occurred under Mohamed Ali's rule. The Ordinance of 1835 contains one of the earliest discussions of patrimony and says that antiquities are a source of national pride.[6] Clearly Mohamed Ali didn't write the ordinance, but it was an important first step in controlling the flow of antiquities out of Egypt. Equally important was the creation of the Antiquities Service in 1858, with Auguste Mariette as its first director. There was still an unofficial trade in antiquities, and some early directors of the Antiquities Service, such as Mariette and Gaston Maspero, resorted to making purchases on this market. The creation of the first permanent museum at Boulaq in 1863 was an important step toward preserving Egypt's heritage. Previously, antiquities were moved from one temporary location to another, and were often given as gifts to visiting dignitaries. With the new museum there was a sense of permanence for a national collection. Mariette lived at the museum with his pet gazelle.

Before becoming director of the Antiquities Service, Mariette had plundered with the best of them, sending two hundred crates of antiquities back to the Louvre. Now, as director, he became a dedicated protector of

Egypt's heritage. When the treasures of Queen Ah-hotep were sent to the International Exposition in Paris in 1867, Empress Eugenie admired the queen's elegant jewelry pieces and told Khedive Ismail she would like to have them. Mariette made sure they stayed in Egypt.[7] Museum collections belonged in museums, and they were not to be given away. Mariette wasn't as successful with Egypt's obelisks. Two left on his watch, one to London and the other to New York.[8]

Later, when the British controlled Egypt, the Antiquities Service and the museum were placed under the jurisdiction of the Ministry of Public Works. An 1883 decree dealing with finds stated that if excavators found duplicates, the excavators could be permitted to keep some pieces. This became known as *partage*, or division of the finds, and the decree formalized this practice for the first time.[9] Under this decree, the Egyptian Museum in Cairo acquired important objects at no expense and foreign museums were able to ensure that they got artifacts from a documented context. Many provenanced antiquities left Egypt via the Egypt Exploration Fund's newly opened excavations in Egypt.[10] Subscribers to the Fund, which was based in Britain, could get a share of what had been divided by the Egyptian government with the Fund, which later became the Egypt Exploration Society. Some of these subscribers were American museums, such as the Museum of Fine Arts in Boston and the Metropolitan Museum of Art in New York. Eventually these museums decided it would be better to initiate their own ambitious excavation programs, and other institutions followed. With all these new excavations and discoveries, Egypt had more antiquities than she could handle. So around this time the Egyptian Museum set up a sales room, where tourists and others could buy items that duplicated pieces already in the museum's collection. If the museum already had three hundred Third Intermediate Period coffins, why not sell duplicates or examples that were damaged? Buyers were given export licenses and sales receipts attesting to the authenticity of the purchase. It was a sensible policy. If excavators could keep duplicates of what they found, this would encourage more excavations and more discoveries. Duplicates could be sold to bring in funds to the museum and support the Antiquities Service. Pieces were also sold by licensed antiquities dealers under the supervision of the Antiquities Service. This was a practice that continued until modern times. In the 1970s, students on study tours to Egypt could visit the licensed antiquities dealers of Luxor, who had inexpensive amulets and scarabs that even a student could afford. In addition to picking up souvenirs, it was an excellent learning experience for them.

The practice of foreign excavators keeping duplicates and the Egyptian Museum and licensed antiquities dealers selling duplicates wasn't quite enough to take care of the excess created by the discovery of a very large cache of coffins and other funerary items at Deir el Bahri in 1891.[11] Many of the 153 items found were given away by the khedive as a diplomatic gesture to various nations that had good relations with Egypt. Egyptian antiquities were ambassadors of goodwill as well as a source of income. So at the time of the discovery of Tutankhamun's tomb, it was a well-established practice that antiquities could leave Egypt and excavators received a division of the finds. There were a few exceptions, but they were well defined. The big exception was the Valley of the Kings. If an intact tomb was discovered, everything stayed with the Antiquities Service.

Before the discovery of Tutankhamun's tomb, there had been only one virtually intact tomb found in the Valley—Theodore Davis's discovery of the tomb of Yuya and Tuya, Tutankhamun's maternal grandparents.[12] Although the concession specified that everything would remain in Egypt, Davis was still offered a division of the finds, but he declined, saying it all should remain together in Egypt.[13] Thus, Carter and Carnarvon had every reason to believe they would get a division of the finds. There was the long tradition of division; Tutankhamun's tomb had been robbed twice, so it wasn't intact; and even in the case of Yuya and Tuya, the only intact tomb found in the Valley, a division of the finds had been offered. So why didn't they get a division?

As we know, Carter and Carnarvon discovered the tomb during a time of political upheaval in Egypt, with nationalism at its peak—and the Englishmen did not grasp the situation and they behaved badly (see Chapter 4). After prolonged negotiations, the government's final decision was that all of Tut's treasures would stay in Egypt. In the past, during colonial times, the French directors had been very generous with divisions, but now, with nationalism growing stronger, the Egyptians for the first time imposed a very strict interpretation of the antiquities laws. At this point, we may ask about the rationale for their decision. Why should all of Tutankhamun's treasures stay in Egypt?

One approach to answering the question is legal, and Carter considered going to court in Egypt. His lawyers would have undoubtedly argued that the tomb was not intact, that there was considerable evidence that it had been entered twice, and thus according to the language of the concession, Lord Carnarvon was legally entitled to a division of the finds. This is certainly a defensible position.

The Antiquities Service might have argued that for all practical purposes, the tomb was intact. It might have been "ransacked," but nothing significant was taken; this was not a "looted" tomb. This too is a defensible position, involving the spirit of the law more than the letter of the law. As a matter of fact, this is just what Pierre Lacau was thinking. In December 1922, only a month after the discovery, he was already considering keeping all of Tutankhamun's treasures in Egypt. Writing to the undersecretary of public works, he first explained the legalities of the contract with Lord Carnarvon, and then said:

> By those words "intact tombs" cited in the present contract and in the contract relating to a prior similar concession, it has been expressed specifically and acknowledged by Lord Carnarvon, that "It is fully understood that it does not mean absolutely inviolate, but rather a tomb still containing its contents in a good state and forming a whole."[14]

We don't know what the courts would have decided, but this is just the legal side of the issue. More interesting is, what were both sides thinking? What was the rationale behind the Antiquities Service's decision that all of Tutankhamun's treasures should stay in Egypt? Even if the courts decided in their favor and all of Tutankhamun's treasures were legally theirs, there could still be reasons the Antiquities Service might have wanted to give a *partage* to Lady Carnarvon.

For example, by giving duplicates to excavators, they would encourage future excavations, which would discover new objects at no cost to Egypt and add to knowledge of ancient Egypt. Further, by having Egyptian antiquities in museums around the world, they would foster interest in ancient Egyptian civilization, add to Egypt's prestige, increase tourism, and so on. These are obvious arguments and certainly must have been considered by the officials making their decisions. After all, there were duplicates. With more than four hundred ushabtis found in Tutankhamun's tomb, a few could have been spared. We know that at one point, after Lady Carnarvon had willingly signed away any rights she might have had to a division of the finds, Carter was assured she would still be given some duplicate objects. But when the final decision was made, she wasn't given anything.

Foreign excavation teams expected a division of the finds, and they saw it as a matter of life and death. Would their museums' trustees vote to give funds to support expeditions that wouldn't be bringing back anything? They didn't think so. They saw their futures as in danger and were solidly behind Carter. Indeed, the Metropolitan Museum's expedition canceled their 1924–1925 season:

> In consequence of the radical changes made by the Director-General of Antiquities at Cairo [Pierre Lacau], in the regulations governing archaeological fieldwork in Egypt which went into effect on November 1, 1924, a decision was reached at that time by our trustees to suspend the excavations of the Metropolitan's Egyptian expedition, to await the outcome of negotiations seeking adequate assurance under the new regulations as to the fair and equitable conditions of further work.[15]

Not everyone was against Lacau. The chief inspector at Saqqara, an Englishman named Cecil Firth, wrote a letter to both the minister of public works and the undersecretary of public works in support of Lacau (Lacau was, of course, his boss, as were the minister and undersecretary):

> I wished to bring to the notice of the Minister what I believed to be the underlying causes of the dispute—namely hostility to the Egyptian government, by one or more Foreign Societies whose interests threatened by M. Lacau's work on behalf of the county he serves. I wished the Minister to know that M. Lacaus views are shared by at least one of his colleagues in the Service des Antiquite's. Personally I consider the Metropolitan Museum of New York always cherished a hope that some considerable share of the contents of the tomb of Tutankhamon would naturally fall to it. . . . You will not have failed to notice that in the account of the opening of the sarcophagus published in the "Times" Mr. Harkness's name [Harkness was a trustee of and donor to the museum] is mentioned before that of M. Lacau and the fullest possible advertisement is given to the share of the Metropolitan Museum in Mr. Carters work.[16]

Aside from his difficulty with his native language, Firth didn't seem to realize that Carter might simply be grateful to the Metropolitan for having supplied four crucial members of his excavation team and wanted to give them credit whenever he could. Still, in the end, the Antiquities Service decided not to give anything to Lady Carnarvon.

I think it is fair to conclude that the decision was partly political. With the nationalists screaming "This is our tomb!" it was difficult to "give away" Egypt's heritage. In the heat of the battle, the point of view shifted from "this is ours" to "this stays here," which are two different things. Eventually the position would become even stronger and change from "this stays here" to "everything stays here." It is a position tied to nationalism, and we can see its seeds in the arguments over Tutankhamun's treasures and how the Egyptians viewed them.

The final game changer was Egyptian Law No. 117, enacted on August 6, 1983 (and often referred to as the Law of 1983). It ended the export of Egyptian antiquities, put licensed antiquities dealers out of business, and severely curtailed the legal antiquities trade. Article 6 of the law asserts that all antiquities are the property of Egypt ("All antiquities are strictly regulated and considered to be the property of the state"). Article 8 makes even owning an antiquity illegal ("The possession of antiquities shall be prohibited"). Article 9 prevents any antiquities from leaving Egypt ("[Disposition of antiquities may not] result in the removal of the antiquity outside the country").

The law was not retroactive, so any antiquities taken out of Egypt legally before 1983 are still legal to own. So today, if Christie's or Sotheby's wants to sell an antiquity, the object must have a provenance proving it was legally obtained prior to 1983. The antiquities market is now made up of "old pieces" that circulate from owner to owner and are getting harder and harder to find. It all started with the patrimony issues raised during the excavation of Tutankhamun's tomb, and this is probably a good thing for archaeology.

20

Tutankhamun Superstar

From the very beginning of the tomb's discovery, people were fascinated with Tutankhamun. Here was someone from the distant past, a mysterious king who was somehow involved in a religious revolution, and now his tomb had been discovered and it might be packed with fabulous treasures. Who wouldn't be excited? Even before the tomb was opened, newspaper artists were drawing what they imagined the tomb would be like (see Color Plate 6). Then, when the tomb was opened, almost every day a new treasure was being taken out of the tomb. Each week the *Illustrated London News* reported what artifacts had been removed that week, illustrated by Harry Burton's wonderful photographs. In France *L'Illustration* did the same to keep the Tut frenzy up. Children and adults kept scrapbooks of the newspaper accounts of the excavation. This was big history, and they knew it.

Hotels in Luxor filled with tourists who were happy to stand tomb-side in the hot Egyptian sun, waiting for a glimpse of the next treasure brought out by Carter and his team. Enterprising photographers took pictures as the objects were being transported to the laboratory, and they quickly converted these photographs to postcards to be sold to the tourists who could write home, "I was there!" These action postcards catch the immediacy of the moment.

Some of the earliest Tut souvenirs were created for these early pilgrims to Tutankhamun's tomb. In Cairo's Khan el Khalili bazaar you could visit Ahmed Souliman's shop and pick up a bottle of Touth-Ankh-Amon perfume to bring home to your sweetie (see Color Plate 25). And when you got home, you could buy a beautifully crafted Tutankhamun penknife, based on the guardian statues (see Color Plate 26). If you didn't want any more Tut tchotchkes, there were plenty of songs you could dance to, many written before it was known that Tutankhamun was a boy-king. "Old King Tut Was a Wise Old Nut" contained this lyric:

> He got into his royal bed
> Three thousand years B.C.
> And left a call for twelve o'clock
> In nineteen twenty three.[1]

Some songs intended for vaudeville contained far more slapstick than history. The team of Murray and Alan came up with "3000 Years Ago," which mixed cultures and made no sense:

> They [two mummies] told me all about King Tut and everything he knew,
> And all the things they spoke about I'll now translate for you ...
> Then every woman wore a veil to hide her face from view.
> I saw a lot of girls today who ought to wear them too.
> The ladies would salaam the men or else they'd get the sack.
> If you salaam the girls today you bet they'd slam you back.[2]

It doesn't get much worse than that.

Someone who benefited greatly from Tutmania was Charles Joseph Carter (no relation to Howard). Charles was already a well-established magician when the tomb was discovered, and he quickly capitalized on his name and printed fabulous posters advertising himself as "Carter the Great," showing himself on a camel in front of the Sphinx (see Color Plate 27). We are told he "sweeps the secrets of the sphinx and marvels of the tomb of old King Tut to the modern world." There are two tip-offs that the poster was rushed into print. First, we have "old King Tut"; Carter hadn't yet discovered that Tutankhamun was a teenager. Second, the verb sweep doesn't really work; *reveals* would have been much better. Clearly a rush job. In 2001 Glenn David Gould wrote an excellent novel about Carter the Great that captured the magic scene during the Roaring Twenties.[3] It is worth reading.

The first novel devoted to Tutankhamun, *The Kiss of Pharaoh: The Love Story of Tut-Anch-Amen*, appeared in 1923, soon after the discovery of the tomb.[4] The jacket proclaims:

> Those who have read of the finding and opening of Tutankhamen's luxuriously appointed tomb or who have seen newspaper pictures of the treasures will especially enjoy this novel of the young pharaoh's brilliant reign and of his death. When all of Thebes stretched out across the desert in colorful procession of the magnificent procession in the Valley of the Kings.

When the book was published, very little was known about Tutankhamun, not even his queen's name, Ankhesenamen. In the book, Tutankhamun is married to Rana, but only after considerable trials and tribulations. At the end of the novel, a soothsayer prophesies that Tutankhamun shall rule for only seven years and that three thousand years after his death, a foreign race would come and plunder his tomb.

While *The Kiss of Tut-Anch-Amun* is the first novel written after the tomb's discovery, it may not be the first one written about the discovery of the tomb. A novel written more than fifty years *before* the discovery, Théophile Gautier's 1857 *Romance of a Mummy*, is remarkably accurate in predicting Carter and Carnarvon's finds: "'I have a presentment that we shall find a tomb intact in the Valley of Biban-el-Molook' said a young Englishman of haughty mien to an individual of much more humble appearance."[5] The humble individual has been hired by the lord as his archaeologist.

In the prologue to the novel, Lord Evandale, a wealthy Englishman, discovers the intact tomb of an Egyptian queen, Tahoser. When unwrapped, the mummy is discovered to be remarkably well preserved:

> As he stood beside the dead beauty, the young lord experienced that retrospective longing often inspired by the sight of a marble or a painting representing a woman of past time celebrated for her charms: It seemed to him that he might have loved her if he had lived three thousand five hundred years ago, this fair being that the grave had left untouched.[6]

When the mummy and the rest of the tomb's contents are transported to England, the excavators find a papyrus in the sarcophagus that tells the story of the beautiful Tahoser. The daughter of a high priest during the time of the Exodus, Tahoser adored an Israelite who did not return her love. She is, however, loved by Egypt's pharaoh and must marry him. When the Israelite's true love, Rachel, learns of Tahoser's love for her fiancé, she suggests, in true biblical style, that he marry both of them. This cozy arrangement was not to be; the Exodus, with its plagues and curses, intervenes, and Tahoser is left behind. Of course, the pharaoh never returns from the parted Red Sea, so Queen Tahoser becomes ruler of Egypt. Soon she dies and is entombed, only to be found three thousand years later by Lord Evansdale. At the end of *Romance of a Mummy* we are told:

> As for Lord Evandale, he has never cared to marry although he is the last of his race. The young ladies cannot understand his coldness towards the fair sex, but would they in all likelihood ever imagine that Lord Evandale is in love

retrospectively with Tahoser, daughter of the highpriest Petamounoph, who died three thousand five hundred years ago?[7]

The First Tutankhamun Exhibition

While everyone was hastily cranking out Tut novels, perfumes, and songs to sell, the first Tutankhamun exhibition was being prepared for the 1924 British Empire Exhibition at Wembley. This was the exhibition that Carter unsuccessfully tried to stop by claiming they were using Harry Burton's photos to make their replicas of the objects found in Tutankhamun's tomb. The replicas were made by William Aumonier, a well-known sculptor from Hull who had created several public monuments. Working with a team of assistants, in only eight months they sculpted, painted, and gilded replicas of the three funerary couches, a chariot, the gilded throne, guardian statues, and alabaster vases found in the tomb, and quite a few other artifacts (Figure 20.1). In spite of Weigall's claim that the replicas were produced only from non-Burton photos, it is difficult to believe that Aumonier didn't look at the Burton photographs that were appearing regularly in the *Illustrated London News*. It is interesting that not only did the *Illustrated London News* cover the discovery of the Tutankhamun objects, it also covered Aumonier's creation of the replicas. Aumonier may have been a good artist, but he was certainly not a historian: he said that when Tutankhamun went for his daily chariot ride, he shot slaves with his bow and arrows for amusement.[8]

The exhibition was a success, and even the Pathé newsreels, which were shown in movie theaters along with the feature film, showed the replicas being carved and gilded in the workshop.[9] Although the replicas were widely touted for their accuracy, they look much better from a distance. Up close, they have the feel of reproductions for tourists. To be fair to Aumonier, he was producing three-dimensional objects from two-dimensional photographs, without the benefit of measurements. Further, there were very few color photographs available, so it was difficult to get the colors right. Arthur Weigall was the exhibition's expert consultant. He had seen the real thing and would certainly have known the replicas were not quite right. I wonder what he thought of the exhibition.

Figure 20.1. An exhibition of replicas was quickly assembled in Wembley, England, to cash in on Tutmania. (Photo courtesy Peggy Joy Library.)

You can decide for yourself how accurate the Wembley replicas are; they still exist. After the exhibition, they were bought by Albert Reckitt, a local businessman, and were given to the city of Hull in 1936 so all could view them. They were put in storage during World War II and survived the bombing of Hull, and were next exhibited in 1972 to coincide with the British Museum's "Treasures of Tutankhamun" exhibition. Today they are on permanent display in Hull's Hands on History Museum, where thousands get to see this wonderful piece of vintage Tutmania.

The Wembley exhibition was a great success, but the idea of a traveling Tutankhamun exhibition was decades in the future. Everyone should have seen it coming. When Carnarvon sold the rights to the Tutankhamun story to the *Times*, it was the beginning of the monetization of Egyptian archae-ology. Carter made enough from his Tutankhamun lectures and books to retire. Tutankhamun was big business for a time, and then it wasn't; once the treasures had been moved to the Cairo Museum, the public far from Egypt lost interest. But when Egypt's monuments were in danger, Tutankhamun was called upon to help rescue them, and the Tut exhibition was born.

Tut's Baby Exhibition

In the 1960s, Egypt began planning to build the High Dam at Aswan.[10] Egypt's growing population was desperate for hydroelectric power, but the water that would back up behind the dam, creating Lake Nasser, the largest artificially created body of water in the world, would submerge some of Egypt's greatest monuments. With the help of UNESCO, a massive salvage campaign was launched to save Egypt's Nubian monuments. The project was forcing Egypt out of her nationalistic cocoon and onto the world stage.

Various countries would take responsibility for different endangered monuments. Under Sweden's leadership, the rock-cut temple of Abu Simbel was to be sawn into pieces and reassembled on higher ground.[11] The temple of Philae was dismantled and moved block by block to a higher island.[12] Smaller temples were dismantled and moved farther inland so they would be on the shore of Lake Nasser, not under it.[13] It would take more than a decade to save Egypt's monuments, requiring vast international cooper-ation. To raise awareness of the plight of Egypt's monuments and enlist help, a modest exhibition of Tutankhamun objects was sent on an international tour in 1961. Tutankhamun's role had changed from activist to ambassador.

It was the first time the Antiquities Service had sent Tutankhamun ob-jects out of the country on tour, and no one really knew how to do it. The blockbuster exhibition hadn't been invented yet, and publicity was modest, but still the exhibition was a success. It toured eighteen cities in the United States, and six in Canada; when it went to Japan, three million people saw the boy-king's treasures. Part of its success was due to logistics. It was a small show of only thirty-four objects, featuring Tutankhamun's jewelry; everything could fit into one van, and it could travel easily. Awareness of the plight of Egypt's monuments was heightened, various countries came on board, and funds were raised. Even France, which had controlled the

Antiquities Service for so long, joined the cause to save the monuments. As a reward, the Louvre got a Tutankhamun exhibition in 1967.[14] It too was very successful and provided the first inkling of how a Tutankhamun exhibition could help a museum generate income. It was a long way from the blockbuster; that would have to wait for the P. T. Barnum of the museum world.

The concept of a museum blockbuster exhibition is really due to two men: Tutankhamun and Dr. Thomas Hoving. In one decade, Hoving, the flamboyant director of New York's Metropolitan Museum of Art, transformed the museum from a stuffy repository of art to a vibrant museum that became the place to be seen. Hoving pioneered extraordinary, vigorously marketed loan exhibitions, complete with huge circus-type banners draped on the front of the museum. Hoving wanted to do for the Met what *Jesus Christ Superstar* did for the Bible. He was going to bring art to a new audience, and like on Broadway, he measured success by reviews, attendance, and box office receipts. By all three measures, his exhibitions were hits. One of his first was "Harlem on My Mind" (1969) designed to draw new populations into the museum. Then came "Scythian Gold" (1975), a striking exhibition of gold combs, necklaces, and bracelets that had been crafted circa 400 BC in Russia's frozen Altai and Pasyryk Mountains by a little-known civilization.[15] In exchange for "Scythian Gold," the Met loaned some of their masterpiece paintings to Russia for an exhibition.

"Scythian Gold" enjoyed record-breaking crowds coming to see ancient gold treasures created by a mysterious culture. The success wasn't just cultural; it was financial as well, due primarily to the beautiful color catalogue and replicas of the jewelry that were sold in the enlarged gift shop. This exhibition was followed by "Russian Costumes" (1976), for which Hoving went to Moscow with Jackie Onassis to help select garments worn by the tsars and tsarinas. With these winning exhibitions, Hoving proved to the museum world that a well-publicized exhibition and a vibrant gift shop could be a major source of income.

Although Hoving's early exhibitions were successful, they were nothing like today's blockbusters. One crucial piece of the puzzle was missing: insurance. The objects loaned by foreign museums had to be insured, and insurance costs money. For the early exhibitions, when the total value of the works displayed was in the millions of dollars, the Met could afford to insure everything, but when Hoving started thinking bigger, there were real problems. How much is the gold mask of Tutankhamun worth? A hundred million dollars? More? How about his gold jewelry? No, when values are placed on items such as these, the cost of insurance became too much, even for the Metropolitan Museum of Art.

The solution to the problem came from a little-known government practice intended to assist American businesses that operated abroad. The U.S. government indemnified businesses situated offshore for 90 percent of their value. Hoving lobbied to have the practice cover American museums. After all, they were "doing business" with foreign museums when they brought works of art from abroad to the United States. His idea worked; the bill quickly passed in both the Congress and the Senate and was signed into law by President Gerald R. Ford. The path to a blockbuster was now smoother. In his tell-all autobiography of his days at the Met, Hoving describes how as soon as the bill was passed, he went into a flurry of activity planning blockbusters.[16] But someone had beaten him to Tutankhamun.

In 1972, to celebrate the fiftieth anniversary of the discovery of the tomb, the British Museum negotiated an agreement with Egypt to send a larger Tutankhamun exhibition—fifty objects, including the famous gold mask. The exhibition was going to travel to other countries, but it premiered at the British Museum.[17] Finally, England got Tutankhamun.

The British exhibition set records for attendance in England, and then the exhibition went on to other countries. Hoving desperately wanted to get the exhibition for the Metropolitan Museum, as he knew its potential if it was marketed properly, but at first he failed. Then he got lucky: President Richard Nixon stepped in. While the exhibition was in Russia, Nixon asked Egypt's president, Anwar Sadat, if the show could come to the United States, and Sadat, wanting to cement good relations with America, agreed.[18] But, in a sense, Hoving was beaten by someone else. Carter Brown, director of the National Gallery of Art in Washington, DC, had earlier realized the possibility of the Tut exhibit and had already made the deal.[19] The exhibition was to go to five American cities, and would open at the National Gallery, much to Hoving's chagrin. Still, the agreement was that the Metropolitan Museum of Art would be responsible for organizing the tour. This created the perfect storm for the invention of the blockbuster. Tutankhamun would provide the star power and Hoving the marketing skills. He would select five or so additional Tut objects to make the exhibition special, would produce the catalogue, and, perhaps more important, would select items to be reproduced and sold in the gift shop. P. T. Barnum had his Jumbo the elephant, and Hoving had his King Tut. It was all very exciting, but Hoving had no idea how difficult dealing with the Egyptians could be.

His first problem was getting an appointment with Dr. Gamal Mokhtar, the director of the Egyptian Antiquities Organization. Although President Sadat had decreed that the United States would get the exhibition, Mokhtar would have the final say on which additional objects could be included, what the financial arrangements would be, and how long each city would have the exhibition. When Hoving went for his appointment with Mokhtar, he was shocked by the mayhem in the director's office. Hoving's description may seem exaggerated, but I have been in that office when Mokhtar was head of antiquities, and I can attest that it is spot-on.

The office was a very large room with no privacy, and everyone heard each person plead his case. Mokhtar's two phones were ringing constantly. Hoving arrived at 11:00 a.m. and was finally able to talk to the director around 1:00 p.m. The meeting lasted less than a minute: when Mokhtar saw Hoving, he said, "Dr. Hoving, meet me at the Sheraton tonight. Everything will be settled then."

All kinds of details for the exhibition had to be worked out, and Mokhtar was not a decisive man. When Hoving gave Mokhtar a list of the additional objects he wanted in the exhibition, Mokhtar said he would consider it. When Mokhtar asked how much admission the Metropolitan was going to charge, Hoving explained that the Metropolitan Museum did not charge admission. This convinced Mokhtar that there could be no exhibition. Where would the money for the Egyptian Antiquities Organization come from? The blockbuster had not yet been invented. No one knew yet that there was a fortune in gift shop sales, catalogues, and sponsors who wanted to be associated with the glamour of Tutankhamun.

Hoving explained that items such as Hermès scarves with a Tutankhamun design could raise thousands and thousands of dollars. In the end Hoving said that he was sure he could contribute $1.4 million to the Antiquities Organization for their cooperation. Mokhtar said he would consider it, and suggested Hoving should return in a month.

When Hoving returned, there were more nocturnal meetings, this time with some progress. Hoving had just concluded agreements with the Franklin Mint and Boehm Porcelains to produce souvenirs that would bring in millions of dollars. Mokhtar was thrilled. Hoving explained that he would have to return to Cairo with a team to photograph the objects for the catalogue, make molds for the replicas that would be sold in the gift shop, and take careful measurements so the display cases could be constructed. As was often the case in those days, there was no electricity in the museum just then, and they would need to set up lights for photography. No problem, Mokhtar assured Hoving; the electricity would be on when he returned.

Hoving and his team returned three months later, in January 1975. Still no electricity, but he was assured it was expected in three months. The director of the Metropolitan Museum of Art hit the ceiling. After his anger subsided, it was replaced by fear, and then finally by a plan. Fortunately, on a previous trip Hoving had met Fuad el-Orabi, perhaps the only man in Egypt who had the knowledge and power to solve the problem. He called him immediately. El-Orabi was director of the sound and light operation at the Great Pyramid. Each night thousands of tourists bought tickets to sit on folding chairs on the Giza Plateau to watch colored lights flash on the pyramids while a narrator told of the pyramids' age and mystery. The show is dramatic and tourists love it, and for decades it has been a financial success. Hoving figured that the show required a great deal of electricity and the know-how to keep it running flawlessly. He offered El-Orabi a paid position on the Met's team as an electrical consultant. El-Orabi told Hoving to meet him outside the back wall of the Egyptian Museum at eleven-thirty that night.

At the specified time a truck pulled up to the deserted street and el-Orabi, two technicians, and a huge spool of electrical cable emerged. The men began digging at the foot of a streetlight. They were going to splice into the Cairo lighting system, run the cable over the museum wall up to the museum roof, through a broken skylight, and into the room in which the Met team had set up their studio. When Hoving expressed concerns about splicing into the live high-voltage wires of the Cairo lighting system, el-Orabi looked at his watch and simply said, "Be patient, Dr. Hoving." Soon the lights for several blocks around the museum began to dim and then went out. The next morning museum officials were amazed to find Hoving's team, lights ablaze, photographing Tutankhamun's treasures.

The quest to obtain the exhibition "Treasures of Tutankhamun" was a constant struggle, but sometimes it was a funny struggle. Among the extra five objects Hoving wanted for Tutankhamen's American tour was the statue of Selket, one of the four goddesses who protected the shrine containing the boy-king's internal organs. She would go on to become a bestseller in the gift shop, but not without difficulty. Tut's organs were placed inside a beautiful alabaster chest, and this was encased in a gilded wood shrine surrounded by the four goddesses. It was a spectacular ensemble, and Hoving wanted the statue of Selket, the goddess with the scorpion on her head, indicating how powerful she was.

When Hoving explained that he wanted the Selket statue for the exhibition, he was quickly rebuffed—the four statues and the base they rested on were all carved from one piece of wood and couldn't be separated. This was nonsense, and Hoving knew it. He had studied the 1920s photographs of the excavation and had seen the statues being carried out separately from the tomb. He offered his Egyptian colleagues a bet they couldn't refuse: if he could lift the Selket statue out of the base, he could have it for the show—and he would buy everyone dinner at Cairo's best restaurant. If he couldn't lift it, he would buy them two dinners at the restaurant. It was a win-win for the Egyptians, so Hoving donned his white curatorial gloves, walked over to the shrine, grasped the Selket statue, and lifted. No problem—it came right out. Later, the Selket statue would be reproduced in three sizes, with the largest selling in the gift shop for more than $1,500. These replicas are still available in the gift shop today, nearly fifty years later (see Color Plate 28).

The back-and-forth trips to Egypt, the endless negotiations with Egyptian authorities, and the scheduling of the exhibition for five cities all took a toll on Hoving. His Egyptian adventure was not something he remembered fondly. When I met him for the first time, at a dinner at my university, he had just returned from Egypt and was shell-shocked. I was the only Egyptologist on campus, so it was an obvious choice for university officials to seat me next to Hoving.

Although still exhausted from his Egyptian ordeals, Hoving was very excited that the exhibition was finally going to happen and said to me, "You had better call Christine if you want to book tickets for your students." Christine Lilyquist was the curator of the Met's Egyptian collection and a friend, but what did he mean? Tickets for an exhibition at the Metropolitan Museum of Art? It was a fabulous old museum with many important collections, but it was never crowded. You never needed tickets for an exhibition.

When I asked how much tickets would cost, the whole thing became even more puzzling. They were free. Hoving explained that because the Met received considerable amounts of money from New York City, their charter stipulated that they couldn't charge admission. The tickets weren't for revenue, they were for crowd control. So many people were expected to visit the exhibition that they would need to obtain timed tickets issued in advance, to avoid massive crowding. If the Met was paying millions to get the exhibition and the tickets were free, how would they get their money back? In the gift shop, Hoving told me.[20] Again, I didn't get it. This was before gift shops were fashionable places to shop, before they stocked designer scarves and high-priced souvenirs.

The day tickets were first available, I went with my two young daughters on an adventure to get tickets. We arrived at the museum around 5:30 a.m. to get ours, and there was already a long line stretching down Fifth Avenue. There was a party atmosphere, with everyone talking to everyone else, giant Tutankhamun banners flying from the top of the Met's façade, and everyone excited to be part of history. When the museum opened, the line moved surprisingly quickly. Each person was allowed four tickets, and you could choose the date for when you saw the exhibition.

When we finally went to see the show, it was not disappointing. Each item was beautifully displayed and the timed ticketing system worked; it was crowded, but not too crowded. You could see everything, and you had the feeling you were part of a very special cultural event. The place that was crowded was the gift shop. Everyone wanted souvenirs, and there were high-ticket items the likes of which had not been seen in museum gift shops before. Hoving had pulled it off. Tutankhamun was a success, a very big success. Exxon produced and supplied a teacher's handbook for use in New York City classrooms, so Tutankhamun became part of the curriculum.[21] The handbook was an elaborate kit, and included replicas of Carter's handwritten cards recording objects, cardboard cutouts of the golden shrine that surrounded the sarcophagus, and basic hieroglyph lessons.

Tutankhamun was so successful that on April 22, 1978, he made an appearance on *Saturday Night Live* when Steve Martin sang his now famous "King Tut." Those who remember the skit probably recall the unforgettable lines "Born in Arizona, moved to Babylonia, King Tut." But few remember that the lyrics are mostly about the museum exhibition.

> Now when he was a young man,
> He never thought he'd see,

> People stand in line to see the boy king . . .
> (King Tut) Now if I'd known
> They'd line up to see him,
> I'd taken all my money
> And bought me a museum (King Tut).

Hoving must have been thrilled.

In the end, the Egyptian Antiquities Organization received $11 million as their share of the proceeds, and the Metropolitan Museum made money and increased its membership. But even with the exhibition's success, Hoving's struggles with Egypt were not yet over. When everything was done and all the objects had been packed and safely returned, Hoving went back to Egypt to thank President Sadat for his help and present him with the large and very expensive reproduction of the Selket statue.

When he arrived at the Cairo airport, a customs inspector saw the wood crate containing the Selket and asked that it be opened. When the lid was removed, the inspector was greeted by the gilded statue of the goddess with her open arms. Astounded, he gasped, "Impound it!" Hoving explained it was a replica and a gift for President Sadat, but that made no difference. It was going to be confiscated. He asked the inspector if he had ever caught people smuggling antiquities out of Egypt. Yes, he had, many. Had he ever caught anyone smuggling antiquities *into* Egypt? "A *very* good point. But I have to impound it anyway."[22] And he did.

So, empty-handed, Hoving went to thank President Sadat for his cooperation in obtaining the exhibition for America. He told the president of Egypt about the statue being confiscated. Sadat laughed and said, "That's the perfect image of Egypt! The Selket will never show up again." He was right.

Soon after "Treasures of Tutankhamun," Hoving left the Metropolitan Museum. During his tenure there, he totally revitalized the place. He increased attendance, convinced wealthy collectors to give their collections to the museum, and with the help of Tutankhamun, invented the blockbuster exhibit.

Hoving's blockbuster Tut exhibition created a whole new generation of Tut tchotchkes. Remember Ahmed Souliman in the Cairo bazaar who was selling Touth-Ankh-Amon perfume? Well, now you could buy King Tut Men's Cologne, made in Brooklyn (see Color Plate 29). Or you could nosh on King Tut's Party Mix, which came in a pyramid box featuring a dancing pharaoh (see Color Plate 30). For pure, authentic Tutmania there were cookies that came in a tin showing Tutankhamun's treasures. The small print

Figure 20.2. The *Tut Times* was handed out to those who attended a replica exhibit in New York in 2016.

says: "Tutankhamun Treasures. Circa 1338 BC. Cookies by Infamous Circa 1978 AD."

In the 1990s a new kind of Tutankhamun blockbuster was created—the replica exhibition. With the advent of laser scanning and 3D printing, it became possible to make very accurate replicas of both the tomb and its contents. But would people pay to see replicas? The answer was a resounding yes. There have been several traveling replica exhibitions, and almost all have been great successes. One held November 21, 2015–May 1, 2016, near Times Square in New York was, I thought, superb. The replicas and the tomb were extremely accurate, but the exhibition was also able to do some things that an exhibition of the real things couldn't. For example, they re-created the tomb's Antechamber as it was when first discovered, packed with the treasures. The attendees loved it. Then, using a second set of replicas, they displayed the various objects up close.

This exhibition was well publicized and drew large crowds. Their handout, *The Tut Times*, was a lighthearted history of both Tutmania and the history of exhibitions and was worth keeping (Figure 20.2). These second-generation replica exhibitions may be the future of Tutankhamun exhibitions. At some point it may be decided that Tutankhamun's treasures are too precious to travel. When that happens, Tutankhamun will step into the limelight once again through the replica exhibitions.

21

The Best Excavation Ever

One of Tutankhamun's greatest legacies is the standard his tomb set for all future excavations. As soon as the tomb was discovered, Carter realized the magnitude of what he had found, and understood that he would need a team of specialists to help him. He sought out a photographer, a conservator, two draftsmen, an engineer, and a philologist. It wasn't just that he knew he needed experts; he knew how to best use their special skills.

First, Photograph

Harry Burton was a gifted photographer. However, photographing every single item in situ was unheard of, and it wasn't going to be easy. Often a chest contained four or five layers of fragile objects inside it, and Carter wanted a record of each layer, so he would know what had been put in first and what next. Burton would photograph the top layer, then Carter and Mace would remove that layer, take it to the laboratory set up in another tomb, and then call in Burton to photograph the next layer. Sometimes it took days to record the contents of a single box. Later, Burton's photos were used by restorers to help reconstruct the elaborate bead pieces and other objects that were falling apart because of disintegrating threads. Some of Burton's detailed photos were recently used in the reconstruction of Tutankhamun's armor (see Chapter 12).

In addition to all the in-situ photographs, Burton produced a record of the individual items before conservation. Today they are the only records of the original condition of the treasures. And besides recording the objects, Burton recorded important moments in the history of the excavation. Everyone knew they were participating in history, the likes of which archaeology might not see again, and Carter realized the importance of documenting every step. So Burton produced a series of dramatic, well-lit photographs of the team taking down the first wall, opening the burial chamber, revealing the golden shrines (see Figure 4.1), lifting the sarcophagus lid—every important step of the excavation.[1] Nothing like this had ever been done before.

Then, Record

The Metropolitan Museum of Art also loaned Carter two architectural draftsmen, Walter Hauser and Lindsey Hall, who created architectural plans of the tomb and indicated the find spots of the larger items. In addition to Harry Burton's photos and Hauser and Hall's plans, Carter, because he was an artist, was able to add still another layer of recording. He kept meticulous records for most objects in the tomb on index cards. Many of these cards have images beautifully drawn in meticulous detail, sometimes showing the pattern of beads strung on a necklace, sometimes the granulation on a gold object (see Figure 17.2).

Carter was exhibiting a kind of thoroughness that no one had ever seen in an archaeological excavation. It was so remarkable that only a month after they began the excavation, Pierre Lacau, the director of the Antiquities Service, realizing what an incredible job Carter was doing, wrote to the undersecretary of state:

> In this sense, it could serve as an example. Egypt and Egyptology owe their thanks to Lord Carnarvon and Mr. Carter. Thanks to their method and persistence, they are obtaining results that surpass anything we have seen with previous archaeologists.[2]

This is strong praise when we consider how many excavations Lacau had seen, and that he did not like Carter. There was never any doubt in Lacau's mind that Carter was the right man for the job. Even when Carter was locked out of the tomb over the disagreement about visitors and working conditions, the Antiquities Service still wanted to find a way for him to return to work. He alone had the patience and skills for such a massive undertaking.

When Lacau said no previous archaeologist had ever done anything like the excavation of Tutankhamun's tomb, he was right. There had been spectacular finds in Egypt, but none had ever been recorded or preserved in the way Carter was proceeding. One spectacular find that comes to mind first is Ernesto Schiaparelli's discovery of the tomb of Kha and Merit in 1906. Kha was the royal architect for several pharaohs, including Amenhotep II and Tuthmosis IV, just a few generations before Tutankhamun's time. Schiaparelli discovered the intact tomb of Kha and his wife, Merit, on the west bank of Luxor at Deir el Medineh. It was intact, packed with all the objects the architect and his wife wanted to take with them to the next world. Like Tutankhamun, the noble couple were still in their coffins, their jewelry still on them. The treasures of the tomb included one of the earliest and most beautiful Books of the Dead ever found. There were beautifully decorated chests containing their clothing and all the objects they would need in the afterlife. Kha had taken with him his gold-covered cubit stick, given to him by the pharaoh, just in case he had to do some work in the next world. Today, the tomb's treasures are beautifully displayed in the Turin Archaeological Museum and are considered the finest example of what daily life in the next world was expected to be like. It is such an important find that many Egyptologists still wonder how the Antiquities Service could have permitted such a unique treasure to leave Egypt. But the point is not why or how the tomb's contents left Egypt. What is important is that it shows that Lacau was right when he said Carter was excavating in a way never seen in Egypt before.

Schiaparelli's primary goal in excavating was to bring the objects back to Italy for the museum. The tomb was cleared in a matter of a month, as if Schiaparelli was eager to get the items out of the tomb before they were stolen or something else happened to them. Schiaparelli is notorious in Egyptology for not publishing the results of his excavations (some are still unpublished). The report of the tomb of Kha and Merit did not appear until more than twenty years after the discovery, when it was included in a survey of Schiaparelli's work for the period 1902–1926.[3] The hasty excavation and minimal recording is a great loss to archaeology. It would be wonderful to have a series of detailed photos of the tomb when it was first discovered and as it was being cleared, but we don't. The Schiaparelli excavation was so poorly executed and recorded that in her masterly summary of Italian Egyptology, Patrizia Piacentini devotes only one sentence to the discovery of the tomb of Kha and Merit.[4]

Schiaparelli was not alone in neglecting to photograph his remarkable find in situ. When Theodore Davis discovered the nearly intact tomb of

Yuya and Tuya, he too did not photograph objects in situ (see Chapter 2). In his publication of the excavation, all we have are the photographs of the objects taken in the Egyptian Museum in Cairo, after they had been removed from the tomb. One specific comparison between the photographing of Tutankhamun's tomb with that of Yuya and Tuya is the taking down of the walls blocking the burial chambers. We have already talked about how Carter waited for Carnarvon to arrive before removing the wall, and we have Burton's photographs of the process, with the seals carefully recorded. In contrast, we have Davis's account of his removal of the wall he found: "It was very slow work. . . . However, in the course of an hour or so, the doorway was cleared."[5] It would have been nice to have had a few photographs.

The lack of photographs of important tombs as they were discovered is not limited to tombs before Tutankhamun. Although it is frequently asserted that Tutankhamun's tomb is the only pharaoh's tomb ever found intact, that is not true. The French Egyptologist Pierre Montet had been excavating at Tanis for nearly ten years when he made a spectacular find. During the 1939 season, an anomaly caught Montet's attention. At the site's southwest corner, an enclosure wall did not parallel the wall of the temple it encircled. Investigating the reason for the irregularity in the wall, Montet cleared a group of mud-brick structures and found a limestone tomb beneath them. Paintings on the walls indicated that it was the tomb of Osorkon II of the Twenty-Second Dynasty, who ruled more than three centuries after Tutankhamun. The tomb consisted of several rooms, one of which contained the remains of Osorkon's son and successor, Taklot II. Another room contained the funerary equipment of his other son, Prince Hor-Nakht. Although these tombs had been plundered, what was left behind by the robbers was of such high quality that conceptions of the wealth of the northern Twenty-First and Twenty-Second dynasties had to be revised.

Once the rooms had been cleared, Montet found an adjacent tomb that had never been disturbed. He realized that this could be a discovery of the magnitude of Tutankhamun's tomb. When he was finally able to enter the tomb, the wall reliefs indicated that he had found the tomb of Pseusennes I, the founder of the Twenty-First Dynasty. There were hundreds of ushabti figures and bronze vessels, but the object that dominated the burial chamber was a solid silver coffin, similar in style to Tutankhamun's gold coffin, but with a falcon's head rather than the face of the king. When the coffin was opened on March 23, 1939, in the presence of King Farouk, a gold mask was revealed, covering the long-dead pharaoh. But the inscriptions indicated he was a previously unknown king, Sheshonq II. The spectacular gold mask and jewelry rivaled Tutankhamun's, and another similarity was four miniature silver coffins holding the king's internal organs. It was a remarkable find, but no photographs were taken of the finds in situ.

If Sheshonq II was buried in a tomb originally intended for Pseusennes I, where was Pseusennes? Given the riches of the pharaoh he just found, Montet couldn't help but wonder what the tomb of Pseusennes I would reveal. One year later he found out. After clearing the tomb of Sheshonq II, Montet realized that the west wall actually contained two cleverly hidden doorways. He dismantled one and found a corridor with a large granite plug still in place. There was just enough room between the block and the wall for Montet to see into the chamber. He had found the intact tomb of Pseusennes I.

It took six days to remove the granite plug. Unlike Howard Carter, when Montet entered the burial chamber, he brought along no distinguished visitors, no press—World War II was raging then. The burial chamber was dominated by a massive pink granite sarcophagus. All around were canopic jars, ushabti figures, and gold and silver vessels. On February 21, 1940, Montet raised the lid of the sarcophagus. Inside was an anthropoid black granite sarcophagus that recalled the nested coffins of Tutankhamun. When the lid to the second sarcophagus was raised, a solid silver coffin was revealed. The silver coffin contained a beautiful gold mask and a fantastic array of jewelry, again rivaling Tutankhamun's. The king's fingers and toes had been encased in gold stalls, and like Tutankhamun, he had been buried with gold sandals on his feet.[6] It took two weeks to remove the jewelry from the coffin.

It was a fantastic discovery of royal burials with royal treasures. Today they are exhibited in a special Treasury Room on the second floor of the Egyptian Museum in Cairo. It would have been wonderful if Montet had had a Harry Burton to photograph the treasures as they were found. The few photographs that document the underground discovery have a slightly amateurish, out-of-focus quality, but we must remember that it was wartime and Montet was working under great pressure. I honestly believe that to this day there has been no expedition or discovery that has been photographed as thoroughly or as well as Tutankhamun's.

Then, Conserve

As Carter was setting standards for photographing and recording an excavation, he was also leading the way in conservation. Many of the objects, especially those involving linen or leather, were in an extremely fragile state. Carter realized he would need a full-time conservation team and laboratory. As we have seen, the laboratory was established in KV-11 and Alfred Lucas was in charge of conservation. Lucas had a broad scientific education, attending both the London School of Mines and the Royal College of Science.[7] Lucas first went to Egypt because of weak lungs and stayed for nearly fifty years, holding various government positions, eventually becoming a chemist for the Antiquities Service. When Carter discovered the tomb, the Antiquities Service loaned Lucas to him and they worked together for nearly ten years, till the tomb was fully cleared.

It is remarkable that Lucas could assist Carter for so long, not only setting standards for conservation of objects in the 1920s but also pioneering new techniques and publishing them for all to use in the future. From Carter's reports it might sound as if the same technique was used over and over—coat wood objects with paraffin before removing to the conservation lab—but for each material, Lucas was working out different treatments. Iron was different from copper, which was different from bronze, and linen was different from leather. These were not trivial trial-and-error home remedies. Lucas was well grounded in the sciences and understood the physical principles behind conservation. During the excavation, Lucas published what became the bible for many of us, *Ancient Egyptian Materials and Industries*.[8] It is far more than a conservation handbook. It describes how ancient bronze was made, what percentage was copper (88 percent) and what percentage tin (9 percent). It discusses how glass was made. It tells where the different quarries were located for the different stones used in building. *Ancient Egyptian Materials and Industries* is so important as a conservation guide that it has never gone out of print, going through three editions in Lucas's long life and then being revised by others.[9] So not only did the excavation of Tutankhamun's tomb give us new standards of conservation, it also gave us a periodically updated, science-based manual for conservation of materials of all kinds.

The Boy-King's Legacy

As we have seen, the discovery of Tutankhamun's tomb did far more than provide the world with spectacular artifacts. His was a tomb that had far-reaching effects throughout the world and in some ways changed it forever. On the most limited level, it set the standards for how a tomb should be excavated. The team of conservators and specialists that Carter put together became a model for how it should be done—if you had the funds. The idea of a single archaeologist, like Flinders Petrie, assisted by a few graduate students and Egyptian diggers was over. Tutankhamun had changed the concept of archaeological excavations forever.

On a wider scope, the tomb played a significant role in changing the political landscape of Egypt. When Carter and Carnarvon made that ill-fated decision to sell the exclusive newspaper rights to the *Times* of London, they unknowingly assisted Egypt on a course toward independence. Both the tomb and the boy-king became rallying points for Egyptian nationalists, and their efforts eventually led to the end of British rule of Egypt. This is perhaps the greatest gift that Tutankhamun has given to Egypt, but there is one more change related to nationalism that should not be forgotten.

Before Tutankhamun, the practice in excavation was division of the finds. Excavators almost always got to bring artifacts home. With the discovery of Tutankhamun's tomb, the discussion began to focus on who owned Egypt's patrimony, and whether any excavated objects should be given to foreign excavators. Ultimately, the decision was made that all Egyptian antiquities should remain in Egypt, and that is still the case today. Contrary to the fear that it would end excavations in Egypt, there are more foreign excavators from universities and museums working in Egypt than ever before. And as we have seen from our survey of Tutankhamun research, more has been learned about Tutankhamun and the objects he intended to take with him to the next world *after* the laws forbidding export of antiquities were put in place than *before* the laws. Tutankhamun research is alive and well.

One more far-reaching effect of the tomb's discovery is that it changed the museum world forever. "Treasures of Tutankhamun," the first true blockbuster exhibition, showed the world's museums that people would flock to exhibitions if beautiful objects were displayed in such a way that they told an interesting story. Much of the popularity and financial viability of today's museums is based on the model begun with Tutankhamun's first world tour.

Tutankhamun and his tomb changed the world in ways the boy-king could never have imagined. His sole purpose in packing all those treasures in his tomb was to ensure that he would live forever. In a sense, he succeeded. To say the name of the dead is to make him live again.

Epilogue

The last one hundred years have been remarkable for both Tutankhamun and the research about him. He has gone from an obscure minor king of Egypt to the most famous pharaoh of all, and as we have seen, this fame has had significant consequences. Egyptian antiquities are viewed quite differently from when the tomb was first discovered. It is hard to believe that during the first years of the excavation of Tutankhamun's tomb, the Egyptian Museum in Cairo was selling Egyptian antiquities in their sale room. Now, what's found in Egypt stays in Egypt.

For the museum world, the discovery of Tutankhamun has rewritten the playbook. The museum blockbuster exhibition phenomenon and the financial importance of gift shops to a museum's bottom line were an indirect result of the discovery of Tutankhamun's tomb and his treasures.

The last hundred years have seen tremendous changes in Tutankhamun research, which has had its ups and downs. Shortly after the tomb's discovery, there was hardly any research and then there was a great thaw that led to a flood of research. On opposite ends of the spectrum, we saw remarkable efforts to conserve and preserve the tomb's treasures, but the mummy of Tutankhamun was literally torn apart by researchers who should have known better. What happened to Tutankhamun could never happen today. Now it is nearly impossible to get a single hair of Tutankhamun's for study. The move toward "nondestructive" tests has been overwhelming. Now objects are routinely CT-scanned before conservation measures are applied. Carter should have X-rayed Tutankhamun rather than just turning him over to Dr. Derry. He could have known what was inside before unwrapping and that could have guided the procedure. Thankfully, Egyptology has changed with the times; we are far less destructive. But not all changes have been Egyptological. The boy king has also been instrumental in political change.

With "Tutankhamun" as a rallying cry, Egypt began to take control of its patrimony, telling foreigners that they were quite capable of making their own decision about what happens to their heritage. As this nationalism was unfolding, Egypt was inching toward democracy. I wonder what the young pharaoh would have thought about that. It has been an eventful one hundred years for Tutankhamun. What might we expect in the next hundred years?

We can expect great advances in research for two reasons. First, new scientific techniques are going to make things easier. As we saw in Chapter 10, the DNA work done so far has been inconclusive. Scientists could not agree on what the results were or what they meant. Part of the reason was the state of DNA sequencing at the time. When Craig Ventnor published his groundbreaking "Sequence of the Human Genome" in the journal *Science* in 2001,[1] there were gaps and errors. By the time of Tutankhamun's sequencing, techniques were better, but not radically so. Today, things have advanced so dramatically that all the ambiguities of the early Tutankhamun DNA studies may soon be resolved. In 2022, *Science* published an entire section devoted to the vast improvements in DNA technology.[2] Now smaller samples are required to achieve far less ambiguous results. There is little doubt that in the future all the questions about Tutankhamun's family tree will be answered. We will know with near certainty who his mother was, if the body in Tomb 55 was his father, and what diseases the boy-king had.

And there are still discoveries to be made. A vast majority of blocks from Tutankhamun's mortuary temple are missing. Frequently such blocks were used as filler in later pharaohs' pylons, and sometimes they were used to build the medieval buildings of Luxor. As reconstruction at Karnak Temple continues and as new building within the city of Luxor expands, undoubtedly blocks bearing Tutankhamun inscriptions will emerge, and they will help fill in pieces of the puzzle. For example, we may soon learn if Tutankhamun was, indeed, a warrior.

Other discoveries involve objects from the tomb that have gone missing. Surely, Tutankhamun's internal organs that were taken out during the king's mummification will be located, and using modern forensic techniques we may learn a great deal about his death. On a more speculative level, there is still the mystery of what happened to Tutankhamun's young widow, Ankhesenamun. No trace of her tomb has ever been found. If she did have a tomb, and if it is discovered, think about what new treasures it might contain and how much might be learned. The second hundred years of Tutankhamun research may be even more exciting than the first.

Notes

INTRODUCTION

1. Hawass and Saleem, *Scanning*.
2. Carter and Mace, *The Tomb*.
3. Brier, *The Murder*.
4. Gardiner, *Egyptian Grammar*, 71–76.

CHAPTER 1

1. Breasted, *Ancient Records*, 2:43.
2. Diodorus Siculus, *Library*, 165.
3. Pococke, *Description*, I:98.
4. Gillespie and Dewachter, *Monuments*, 10.
5. Schneider, *Shabtis*, I:9–32.
6. Gillespie and Dewachter, *Monuments*, II, notes to pl. 77–81.
7. Gillespie and Dewachter, *Monuments*, II, notes to pl. 77–81.
8. *Description de l'Égypte*, II, pl. 77.
9. Fakhry, *The Pyramids*, 137–138.
10. Belzoni, *Narrative*, 156–157.
11. Hornung, *Tomb of Seti I*.
12. Hornung, *Tomb of Seti I*, 158.
13. Graefe and Balova, *Royal Cache*, 13.
14. Maspero, *Trouvaille*; Maspero, *Les Momies*.
15. Edwards, "Recent Discovery."
16. Reeves, *Complete Valley*, 194.
17. Cerny, "Chronology," 24–30.
18. Breasted, *Ancient Records*, 4:322–325.
19. Smith, *Royal Mummies*, 32–36.
20. Romer, *Valley of the Kings*, 161–162.
21. Brier, "The Mummy," 33–38.
22. Quoted in Romer, *Valley of the Kings*, 161–162.
23. Breasted, *Ancient Records*, 2:313–315.
24. Clayton, *Chronicles*, 11–12.
25. Redford, *Akhenaten*.

26. Aldred, *Akhenaten and Nefertiti*, 28–31.
27. Murnane, "Nature," 33–40.
28. Kemp, *Amarna Reports.*
29. Cohen, "Intelligence," 91–98.
30. Eaton-Kraus, *The Unknown Tutankhamun*, 4.

CHAPTER 2

1. Reeves and Taylor, *Howard Carter*, 22.
2. Newberry, *Beni Hasan*, Part I, x.
3. Newberry, *El Bersheh*, Part I, plate 15.
4. Petrie, *Seventy Years*, 152.
5. Naville, *Temple of Deir el Bahri*, Parts I–VI.
6. Caminos and Fischer, *Ancient Egyptian Epigraphy*, 7.
7. Naville, *Temple of Deir el Bahari*, Part II, preface.
8. Minter, *The Well-Connected Gardener.*
9. Amherst, *History of Gardening.*
10. Carter, "Report," 115–121.
11. Adams, *The Millionaire and the Mummies.*
12. Davis, *Tomb of Thoutmosis IV.*
13. Howard Carter, letter to Lady Amherst, March 18, 1904, Dahesh Museum, Greenwich, CT.
14. Davis, *The Tomb of Hatshopsitu.*
15. Adams, *The Millionaire and the Mummies*, 60.
16. Smith. *Temples, Tombs*, 25–42.
17. Davis, *The Funeral Papyrus.*
18. Hankey, "Arthur Weigall and the Tomb," 42–43.
19. Blankenberg-Van Delden, *Large Commemorative Scarabs,* 16.
20. I say "were" because they have recently been moved to the new Grand Egyptian Museum which is scheduled to open in 2023.
21. Adams, *The Millionaire and the Mummies.*
22. Reeves and Taylor, *Howard Carter*, 80–85.
23. Smith, *Tombs, Temples*, 56.
24. Reeves and Wilkinson, *The Complete Valley*, 120.
25. For a clear, recent analysis of the bones, see Filer, "Anatomy."
26. Smith, *Royal Mummies*, 1–56.
27. Davis, *Tomb of Queen Tiyi.*
28. Davis, *Tombs of Haramhabi and Touatankhamanmou*, 20.
29. "The Egyptian Expedition," 40–43.
30. Winlock, *Materials.*
31. Davis, *Tombs of Harmhabi and Touatankhamanmou,* 3.
32. Griffith, "Carnarvon Tablets," 36–37.
33. Gardiner, "The Defeat of the Hyksos," 95–110.

34. Carnarvon and Carter, *Five Years*.

CHAPTER 3

1. *Le Pèlerin*, back page, January 14, 1923.
2. Carter and Mace, *The Tomb*, 95–96, Vol. I.
3. Winlock, *The Tomb of Senebtisi*.
4. Lee, *The Grand Piano*.
5. Johnson, "Painting with Light," 65.
6. Lucas, *Ancient Egyptian Materials*.
7. Gardiner, *Egyptian Grammar*.
8. Breasted, *Pioneer to the Past*, 133–134.
9. Breasted, *Ancient Records*, 2:417–427.
10. Breasted, *History of Egypt*, 133–134.
11. James, *Howard Carter*, 238–239.
12. Cohen and Westbrook, *Amarna Diplomacy*.
13. Cohen and Westbrook, *Amarna Diplomacy*.
14. I say "was" because in 2021 the treasures of Tutankhamun were moved to the new Grand Egyptian Museum scheduled to open at the end of 2022 in conjunction with the one-hundredth anniversary of the discovery of Tutankhamun's tomb.
15. Eaton-Krauss, *The Small Golden Shrine*.
16. For the evidence of this break-in, see James, *Howard Carter*, 225–228.
17. Wynne, *Behind the Mask*, 114–115.
18. Carter and Mace, *The Tomb*, I:178.
19. Carter and Mace, *The Tomb*, I:46.

CHAPTER 4

1. James, *Howard Carter*, 242.
2. Carter and Mace, *The Tomb*, II:51–52.
3. Carter, *The Tomb of Tut.ankh.amen. Statement*.
4. Carter and Mace, *The Tomb*, I:94, 102.
5. Daressy, *A Brief Description*.
6. Carter and Mace, *The Tomb*, I:73–74.
7. James, *Howard Carter*, 311.
8. James, *Howard Carter*, 338–340.

CHAPTER 5

1. Carter, *The Tomb*, II:75.
2. James, *Howard Carter*, 345.
3. Carter, *The Tomb*, II:82.

4. Carter, *The Tomb*, II:155.
5. Leek, *Human Remains*, 17–18.

CHAPTER 6

1. Leek, *The Human Remains*, 9.
2. Brier and Wade, "Surgical Procedures," 89–97.
3. Carter, *The Tomb*, III:83.
4. Alan Gardiner to Heddie Gardiner, February 17, 1923, Griffith Institute Archive, Oxford, UK.
5. Maspero, *Les Momies Royales*, 525–526.
6. Lesko, *King Tut's Wine Cellar*, 22.
7. Carter, *The Tomb*, III:105–106.
8. Reeves, *The Complete Tutankhamun*, 101.
9. James, *Howard Carter*, 380.
10. James, *Howard Carter*, 407. For a listing of Carter's antiquities prepared by Spink and Son for probate, see Reeves, "Howard Carter's Collection," 242–247.

CHAPTER 7

1. Piankoff, *The Pyramid*, 18.
2. Piankoff, *The Tomb of Ramses VI*.
3. Piankoff, *Shrines*, 59.
4. Piankoff, *Shrines*, 65.
5. Piankoff, *Shrines*, 74.
6. Reeves, *The Complete Tutankhamun*, 147.

CHAPTER 8

1. Bierbrier, *Who Was Who*, 332–333.
2. Dawson, "Pettigrew's Demonstrations," 171–172.
3. Dawson, "Pettigrew's Demonstrations," 173.
4. Pettigrew, *History*.
5. Dawson, "Pettigrew's Demonstrations," 181.
6. Smith, *Royal Mummies*, 1912.
7. Ruffer, *Studies,* 1921.
8. Letter dated February 6, 1932. Collection of Anthony Marks.
9. Harrison and Abdalla, "Remains of Tutankhamun," 8–14.
10. Harer, "An Explanation," 83–88.
11. Harer, "Was Tutankhamun Killed," 50–54.
12. Harer, "New Evidence," 225–232.
13. Hawass and Saleem, *Scanning the Pharaohs,* 272n22.
14. Forbes, Ikram, and Kamrin, "Tutankhamun's Ribs," 50–56.

15. Harrison and Abdalla, "Remains of Tutankhamun," 8–14.
16. *Tutankhamun's Post-Mortem* (television documentary), BBC, 1969.
17. In 1978 Dr. James Harris, a professor of orthodontics at the University of Michigan, was given permission to X-ray the skull of Tutankhamun. Harris had already carried out pioneering work on X-raying the Royal Mummies in the Egyptian Museum in Cairo and felt Harrison's X-ray of Tutankhamun's skull hadn't been adequate. He too never published his findings adequately, but did observe that Tutankhamun's right ear was missing.
18. Leek, *Human Remains*.
19. Leek, *Human Remains*, 23.

CHAPTER 9

1. For an interesting history of the early days of mummy studies, see Pringle, *The Mummy Congress*. Pringle attended an early Mummy Congress intending to write an article for a journal and ended up writing a book about it.
2. Hawass and Saleem, *Scanning*.
3. Hawass and Saleem, *Scanning*, 98.
4. Brier, *The Murder*.
5. Guterbock, "The Deeds," 94.
6. Guterbock, "The Deeds," 94–95.
7. Nib-hururiya is the Hittite transliteration for Neb-Kheperu-Re.
8. Guterbock, "Deeds," 97–98.
9. Gillam and Brier, "Can Orthopaedic Knowledge," 8–9.
10. Hawass and Saleem, *Scanning,* 97.
11. Corthals, "The King Is Dead," 170.

CHAPTER 10

1. Watson, *The Double Helix*.
2. Jones, *The Molecule Hunt*, 14–15.
3. Pääbo, "Molecular Cloning," 644–645.
4. Woodward et al., "DNA Sequence."
5. Hedges and Schweitzer, "Detecting," 1190–1192.
6. Ventnor et al., "The Sequence."
7. Hawass et al., "Ancestry and Pathology."
8. Smith, *Royal Mummies*, 51–56.
9. Harrison, "An Anatomical Examination."
10. Filer, "Anatomy of a Mummy," 26–29.
11. Hawass and Saleem, *Scanning,* 84.
12. Harris and Wente, "Mummy of the 'Elder Lady.'"
13. Rühli and Ikram, "Purported."
14. Hawass et al., "Ancestry and Pathology."

15. Lalanne, "Suffering from Malaria," 279.
16. Lorenzen and Willerslev, "King Tutankhamun's Family."
17. Gabolde, "The Chromosomes."
18. Timmann, "King Tutankhamun's Family."

CHAPTER 11

1. Breasted, *Ancient Records*, III:163–174.
2. Clayton, *Chronicles*, 95.
3. See Littauer and Crouwel, *Chariots*, n. 1.
4. Lichtheim, *Ancient Egyptian Literature*, II:70.
5. Crouwel, "Studying the Six Chariots," 75.
6. Guidotti, *Il Carro*.
7. Davis, *The Tomb of Iouiya*, 35.
8. Davis, *The Tomb of Iouiya*.
9. Carter and Mace, *The Tomb*, I:121.
10. Murray and Nutall, *A Handlist*.
11. Murray and Nutall, *A Handlist*, vii.
12. E.g., McLeod, *Composite Bows*; Manniche, *Musical Instruments*; Tait, *Game-Boxes*.
13. Littauer and Crouwel, *Chariots*.
14. Crouwel, "Studying the Six Chariots," 83.
15. Crouwel, "Studying the Six Chariots," 21, 14.
16. Carter and Mace, *The Tomb*, II:54–63.
17. Carter and Mace, *The Tomb*, II:61.
18. Crouwel, "Studying the Six Chariots," 82–84.
19. Crouwel, "Studying the Six Chariots," 83.
20. Carter and Mace, *The Tomb*, III:34.
21. Littauer and Crouwel, *Chariots*, 104.
22. Reginald Engelbach to Howard Carter, January 4, 1934, collection of Anthony Marks.
23. "Building Pharaoh's Chariot" (television documentary), *Nova*, PBS, 2016.
24. Brock, "A Possible Chariot Canopy."
25. Brock, "A Possible Chariot Canopy," 33.
26. Kawai, "Ceremonial Canopied Chariot."

CHAPTER 12

1. Veldmeijer et al., "Tutankhamun's Cuirass," 4.
2. Veldmeijer et al., "Tutankhamun's Cuirass," 14.
3. Veldmeijer et al., "Tutankhamun's Cuirass," 11.
4. McLeod, *Composite Bows*.
5. Carter and Mace, *The Tomb*, I:113.
6. McLeod, *Composite Bows*, 11.

7. McLeod, *Self Bows,* 1.
8. Reeves, *The Complete Tutankhamun,* 179.
9. Epigraphic Survey, *Reliefs and Inscriptions, Volume 1*; Epigraphic Survey, *Reliefs and Inscriptions, Volume 2.*
10. Johnson. *An Asiatic Battle Scene.*
11. Johnson, "Tutankhamen-Period Battle."
12. Eaton-Kraus, *The Small Golden Shrine,* 37.
13. Smith-Sangster. "Personal Experience."
14. Johnson, "A Royal Fishing and Fowling," 47.

CHAPTER 13

1. Veldmeijer, *Tutankhamun's Footwear.*
2. Morshed and Veldmeijer, "Conserving," 103–104.
3. Hawass and Saleem, *Scanning,* 98.
4. Veldmeijer, *Tutankhamun's Footwear,* 139.
5. Veldmeijer, *Tutankhamun's Footwear,* 138–139.
6. Veldmeijer, *Tutankhamun's Footwear,* 138.
7. Veldmeijer and Ikram, "Tutankhamun's Sticks," 8–12.
8. Gardiner, *Egyptian Grammar.*
9. Veldmeijer and Ikram, "Tutankhamun's Sticks," 12.
10. Smith-Sangster, "Personal Experience," 40–49.

CHAPTER 14

1. Eaton-Krauss, *The Sarcophagus,* 19–22.
2. Lichtheim, *Ancient Egyptian,* II:28.
3. Allen, *The Egyptian,* 282.
4. Reeves, *The Complete Tutankhamun,* 23.
5. Reeves, *The Complete Tutankhamun,* 122.
6. Carter and Mace, *The Tomb,* II:90.

CHAPTER 15

1. Factum Arte, *The Authorized Facsimile.*
2. Reeves, *The Burial.*
3. Fahim, "Scans."
4. Hammond, "Why Valley."
5. Sambuellia et al., "The Third," 288–296.
6. Reeves, *The Decorated.*
7. Reeves, *The Complete Tutankhamun,* 72–73.
8. Quoted in Reeves, *The Complete Tutankhamun,* 100.
9. Marchant, *Is This Nefertiti's Tomb?*

10. Lightbody, "The Tutankhamun-Nefertiti Burial," 95.

CHAPTER 16

1. Brunton, *Kings and Queens.*
2. Bjorkman, "Meteors and Meteorites," 91–130.
3. Comelli et al., "The Meteoritic Origin," 1301–1309.
4. Almansa-Villatoro, "Cultural Indexicality," 74.
5. D'Orazio et al., "Gebel Kamil."
6. Comeli, "The Meteoritic Origin," 1306.
7. Johnson and Tyldesley, "Iron from the Sky," 4.
8. Eaton-Krauss, "Tutankhamun's Iron Dagger," 32.
9. Petrie, *Amulets,* 15.
10. Wainwright, "Iron in Egypt."
11. Budge, *Egyptian Magic,* 195–196.
12. Carter and Mace, *The Tomb,* III:90.
13. Broschat et al., *Iron from Tutankhamun's Tomb,* 28.
14. Clayton, *Desert Explorer.*
15. Spencer, "Tektites."
16. For a popular account of the investigations and eyewitness accounts, see Baxter and Atkins, *The Fire.*
17. Verma, *The Tunguska Fireball,* 93–94.
18. For a documentary on the expedition, see LGI Media, "The Fireball."

CHAPTER 17

1. Gabolde, "An Egyptian Gold Necklace."
2. Gabolde, "An Egyptian Gold Necklace," 7.
3. Howard Carter, note on gold and lapis beads, item 256y, 1925, Griffith Institute Archives, Oxford.
4. Howard Carter, note on bead collars, item 256o, March 11, 1925, Griffith Institute Archives, Oxford.
5. Gabolde, "An Egyptian Gold Necklace," 21n71.

CHAPTER 18

1. Moreh, *Al-Jabarti's,* 31.
2. Symcox, "Geopolitics."
3. Burleigh, *Mirage*; Allin, *Zafra.*
4. Denon, *Voyage.*
5. Gillespie and Dewachter, *Monuments,* 10.
6. Mackesy, *British Victory.*
7. Brier, *Cleopatra's Needles,* 104–105.

8. Belzoni, *Narrative.*

9. Fagan, *Rape.*

10. Herold, *Bonaparte,* 220–223.

11. Beatty, *De Lesseps,* 144.

12. "Suez Canal."

13. "Bombardment," 1–26.

14. Lauer, *Saqqara,* 21–28.

15. Fagan, *Rape,* 274–278.

16. "Tombs Recently Discovered at Sakkara," 283–284.

17. Mainterot, "France," 82.

18. *Egyptian Gazette,* February 21, 1923, quoted in Reid, "Remembering," 161–162.

19. Colla, *Conflicted,* 205.

20. Carter and Mace, *The Tomb,* III:167–169.

21. Colla. *Conflicted,* 220.

22. Colla, *Conflicted,* 220.

23. James, *Howard Carter,* 407.

24. Mitchell, *Colonising Egypt,* 1.

25. Percy Newberry to Howard Carter, January 11, 1930, collection of Anthony Marks.

26. Colla, *Conflicted,* 175–176.

27. Colla, *Conflicted,* 176.

28. Fikri Abaza, "Illa Tutankhamun," *Al-Ahram,* February 20, 1924, quoted in Colla, *Conflicted,* 73.

29. Colla, *Conflicted,* 222–223.

30. Reginald Engelbach to Alan H. Gardiner, October 14, 1934, collection of Anthony Marks.

31. Alan Gardiner to Howard Carter, November 17, 1934, collection of Anthony Marks.

32. Alan Gardiner to Reginald Engelbach, October 23, 1934, collection of Anthony Marks.

33. Dodson, "The British Isles," 128.

CHAPTER 19

1. Sotheby's, *Egyptian*; Sotheby's, *Antiquities.*

2. Fagan, *Rape,* 85–93.

3. *Description de l'Égypte, Antiquities,* vol. I, plate 96.

4. Greco and Buchwald, *The Zodiac.*

5. Parkinson, *Cracking Codes.*

6. Khater, *Le régime,* 271.

7. Reeves, *Ancient Egypt,* 51–52.

8. Gorringe, *Egyptian Obelisks*; Hayward, *Cleopatra's Needles.*

9. Bednarski et al., *A History*, 35.

10. Naville, *The Temple*; Naville, *Bubastis*.

11. Reeves, *Ancient Egypt*, 81–82.

12. Davis, *The Tomb of Iouiya*.

13. Adams, *The Millionaire*, 108–109.

14. Pierre Lacau to Undersecretary of Public Works, December 19, 1922, collection of Anthony Marks.

15. Metropolitan, *Museum Bulletins*, 3.

16. Cecil Firth to Minister of Public Works, March 6, 1924, collection of Anthony Marks.

CHAPTER 20

1. Lewis, "Old King Tut."

2. Gerber, "3000 Years."

3. Gold, *Carter Beats*.

4. Goyne, *The Kiss*.

5. Gauthier, *Romance*, 3.

6. Gauthier, *Romance*, 50.

7. Gauthier, *Romance*, 245.

8. Sheppard, "Treasures," 4.

9. Pathé News, "Luxor at Wembley," March 3, 1924.

10. Amr, *Aswan*.

11. *The Salvage of Abu Simbel Temples*.

12. *Report on the Safe-guarding of the Philae Monuments*.

13. Keating, *Nubian Rescue*.

14. Desroches-Noblecourt, *Toutankhamon*.

15. Piotrovsky, *From the Lands*.

16. Hoving, *Making*, 346–347.

17. Zaki, "Tutankhamun Exhibition," 79–88.

18. For a different version of the origin of the exhibition, see Ancient Egyptian Heritage and Archaeology Foundation interview with Dr. Christine Lilyquist, https://www.ancientegyptarchaeologyfund.com/project/oral-history-project/, May 4, 2018.

19. Kamp, "The King of New York."

20. Metropolitan Museum of Art, *Treasures of Tutankhamun*.

21. Fineberg and Karlin, *Tutankhamun in the Classroom*.

22. Hoving, *Making*, 412–413.

CHAPTER 21

1. Riggs, *Photographing Tutankhamun*, 141–171.

2. Pierre Lacau to Undersecretary of Public Works, December 19, 1922, collection of Anthony Marks.

3. Schiaparelli, *Relazione*, 17–20.

4. Piacentini, "Italy," 380.
5. Davis, *Tomb of Iouiya,* 4.
6. Montet, *Les constructions.*
7. Dawson et al., *Who Was Who.*
8. Lucas, *Ancient Egyptian Materials.*
9. Lucas, *Ancient Egyptian Materials.*

EPILOGUE

1. Ventnor, "Sequence."
2. Aganezov, "A Complete Reference Genome."

Bibliography

Adams, John. *The Millionaire and the Mummies*. New York: St. Martin's Press, 2013.

Aldred, Cyril. *Akhenaten and Nefertiti*. New York: Viking Press, 1973.

Allen, George Thomas. *The Egyptian Book of the Dead*. Chicago: University of Chicago Press, 1960.

Allin, Michael. *Zafra*. New York: Walker, 1998.

Almansa-Villatoro, M. V. "The Cultural Indexicality of the N41 Sign for *bj3*: The Metal from the Sky and the Sky of Metal." *Journal of Egyptian Archaeology* 105 (2019): 73–82.

Amherst, Alicia. *History of Gardening in England*. London: Bernard Quaritch, 1895.

Amr, Abdel Wahad. *Aswan High Dam Hydro-Electric Scheme*. Cairo: Ministry of Public Works, 1960.

Assad, Hany, and Daniel Kolos. *The Name of the Dead: Tutankhamun Translated*. Mississaugua, ON: Benben Publications, 1979.

Azanezov, Sergey, et al. "A Complete Reference Genome Improves Analysis of Human Genetic Variation." *Science* 376 (2022): 54.

Ballard, George. "A Review of the Geophysical Data." In *The Decorated North Wall in the Tomb of Tutankhamun (KV 62)*, edited by Nicholas Reeves. Tucson, AZ: Amarna Royal Tombs Project, 2019.

Baxter, John, and Thomas Atkins. *The Fire Came By*. London: MacDonald and Jane's, 1966.

Beatty, Charles. *De Lesseps of Suez*. New York: Harper, 1956.

Bednarski, Andrew, et al. *A History of World Egyptology*. Cambridge: Cambridge University Press, 2021.

Belzoni, Giovanni Battista. *Narrative of Operations and Recent Discoveries Within the Pyramids, Temples, Tombs, in Egypt and Nubia*. London: John Murray, 1820.

Bierbrier, M. L. *Who Was Who in Egyptology*. London: Egypt Exploration Society, 1995.

Bjorkman, J. K. "Meteors and Meteorites in the Ancient Near East." *Meteoritics* 8 (1973): 91–130.

Blankenberg-Van Delden, C. *The Large Commemorative Scarabs of Amenhotep III*. Leiden: Brill, 1969.

"The Bombardment of Alexandria." *The Graphic*, July 24, 1882, 1–26.

Breasted, Charles. *Pioneer to the Past: The Story of James H. Breasted*. New York: Scribner's, 1948.

Breasted, James Henry. *Ancient Records of Egypt*. Chicago: University of Chicago Press, 1906.

Breasted, James Henry. *History of Egypt*. New York: Scribner's, 1905.

Brier, Bob. *Cleopatra's Needles*. London: Bloomsbury, 2016.

Brier, Bob. *The Encyclopedia of Mummies*. New York: Facts on File, 1998.

Brier, Bob. "The Mummy of Unknown Man E: A Preliminary Examination." *Bulletin of the Egyptian Museum* 3 (2006): 33–38.

Brier, Bob. *The Murder of Tutankhamen*. New York: Putnam, 1998.

Brier, Bob, and Ronald S. Wade. "Surgical Procedures During Ancient Egyptian Mummification." *Zeitschrift fur Aegyptische Sprache* 126 (1999): 89–97.

Brock, Edwin C. "A Possible Chariot Canopy for Tutankhamun." In *Chasing Chariots*, edited by André Veldmeijer and Salima Ikram, 29–44. Leiden: Sidestone Press, 2013.

Broschat, Katja, et al. *Iron from Tutankhamun's Tomb*. Cairo: AUC Press, 2021.

Brunton, Winifred. *Kings and Queens of Ancient Egypt*. London: Hodder & Stoughton, 1925.

Budge, E. A. Wallis. *Egyptian Magic*. London: Kegan, Paul, 1899.

"Building Pharaoh's Chariot." *Nova*, PBS, 2016.

Burleigh, Nina. *Mirage: Napoleon's Scientists and the Unveiling of Egypt*. New York: HarperCollins, 2007.

Caminos, R. A., and H. G. Fischer. *Ancient Egyptian Epigraphy and Palaeography*. New York: Metropolitan Museum, 1976.

Carnarvon, Earl of, and Howard Carter. *Five Years Explorations at Thebes*. Oxford: Oxford University Press, 1912.

Carter, Howard. "Report on General Work Done in the Southern Inspectorate." *Annales du Service des Antiquities de l'Egypte* (1902): 115–121.

Carter, Howard. *The Tomb of Tut.Ankh.Amen. Statement with Documents as to the Events Which Occurred in Egypt in the Winter of 1923–4, Leading to the Ultimate Break with the Egyptian Government*. London: Cassell, 1924.

Carter, Howard, and Arthur Mace. *The Tomb of Tut.Ankh.Amen*. 3 vols. London: Cassell, 1923– 1932.

Caruthers, William, ed. *Histories of Egyptology*. London: Routledge, 2019.

Cerny, Jaroslav. "Chronology of the Twenty-First Dynasty." *Journal of Egyptian Archaeology* 32 (1946): 24–30.

Cerny, Jaroslav. *Hieratic Inscriptions from the Tomb of Tut'Ankhamun*. Oxford: Griffith Institute, 1965.

Clayton, Peter. *Chronicles of the Pharaohs*. London: Thames & Hudson, 1995.

Clayton, Peter. *Desert Explorer: A Biography of Colonel P. A. Clayton*. London: Zezura Press, 1998.

Cohen, Raymond. "Intelligence in the Amarna Letters." In *Amarna Diplomacy*, edited by Raymond Cohen and Raymond Westbrook, 91–98. Baltimore: Johns Hopkins University Press, 2000.

Cohen, Raymond, and Raymond Westbrook, eds. *Amarna Diplomacy*. Baltimore: Johns Hopkins University Press, 2000.

Cola, Elliott. *Conflicted Antiquities*. Durham, NC: Duke University Press, 2007.

Comelli, Daniela, et al. "The Meteoritic Origin of Tutankhamun's Iron Dagger Blade." *Meteoritic and Planetary Science* 51, no. 7 (2016): 1301–1309.

Connor, Simon, and Dimitri Laboury, eds. *Tutankhamun: Discovering the Forgotten Pharaoh*. Liège: Presses Universitaires de Liège, 2020.

Corthals, Angelique. "The King Is Dead! CSI Baban el-Moluk." In *Tutankhamun: Discovering the Forgotten Pharaoh*, edited by Simon Conor and Dimitri Laboury, 170–171. Liège: Presses Universitaires de Liège, 2020.

Crouwel, Joost. "Studying the Six Chariots from the Tomb of Tutankhamun—An Update." In *Chasing Chariots*, edited by André Veldmeijer and Salima Ikram, 73–94. Leiden: Sidestone Press, 2013.

Curators of the Egyptian Museum. *A Short Description of the Objects from the Tomb of Tutankhamun*. Cairo: Institut Français, 1927.

Daressy, G. *A Brief Description of the Principal Monuments Exhibited in the Egyptian Museum*. Cairo: Press of the French Institute, 1924.

Davies, Nina M. *Tutankhamun's Painted Box*. Oxford: Griffith Institute, 1962.

Davis, Theodore M. *The Funeral Papyrus of Iouiya*. London: Archibald Constable, 1908.

Davis, Theodore M. *The Tomb of Hatshopsitu*. London: Archibald Constable, 1906.

Davis, Theodore M. *The Tomb of Iouiya and Touiyou*. London: Archibald Constable, 1907.

Davis, Theodore M. *The Tomb of Queen Tiyi*. London: Archibald Constable, 1910.

Davis, Theodore M. *The Tomb of Thoutmosis IV*. London: Archibald Constable, 1904.

Davis, Theodore M. *The Tombs of Haramhabi and Touatankhamanmou*. London: Archibald Constable, 1912.

Dawson, Warren R. "Pettigrew's Demonstrations upon Mummies." *Journal of Egyptian Archaeology* 20 (1934): 170–192.

Dawson, Warren R., et al. *Who Was Who in Egyptology*. London: Egypt Exploration Society, 1995.

Denon, Vivant. *Voyage dans la Basse et Haute Egypte*. Paris: Didot, 1802.

Derry, Douglas E. "Report upon the Two Human Foetuses Discovered in the Tomb of Tut.Ankh.Amen." In *The Tomb of Tut.Ankh.Amen*, vol. III, edited by Howard Carter and Arthur Mace, 167–169. London: Cassell, 1933.

Description de l'Égypte, Antiquities. Vol. II. Paris: Imprimerie Imperiale, 1812.

Desroches-Noblecourt, Christiane. *Toutankhamon et son temps*. Paris: Ministère d'État, Affaires Culturelles, 1967.

Diodorus Siculus. *Library of History*. Vol. I. Cambridge, MA: Harvard University Press, 1969.

Dodson, Aidan. "The British Isles." In *History of World Egyptology*, edited by Andrew Bednarski et al., 91–135. Cambridge: Cambridge University Press, 2021.

D'Orazio, Massimo, et al. "Gebel Kamil: The Iron Meteorite That Formed the Kamil Crater (Egypt)." *Meteoritic and Planetary Science* 46, no. 8 (2011): 1179–1196.

Eaton-Krauss, Marianne. "The Burial of Tutankhamen." *KMT* 20, no. 4 (2009–2010): 34–48.

Eaton-Krauss, Marianne. *The Sarcophagus in the Tomb of Tutankhamun*. Oxford: Griffith Institute, 1993.

Eaton-Krauss, Marianne. *The Small Golden Shrine from the Tomb of Tutankhamun*. Oxford: Griffith Institute, 1985.

Eaton-Krauss, Marianne. "Tutankhamun's Iron Dagger: Made From a Meteoroite?" *KMT* 27 (2016): 30–32.

Eaton-Krauss, Marianne. *The Unknown Tutankhamun*. London: Bloomsbury, 2016.

Edwards, Amelia. "Recent Discovery of Royal Mummies and Other Egyptian Antiquities." *London Illustrated News,* February 4, 1882, 113–120.

Edwards, I. E. S. *The Treasures of Tutankhamun*. New York: Viking Press, 1972.

"The Egyptian Expedition." *Bulletin of the Metropolitan Museum of Art*, December 1922, 40–43.

Epigraphic Survey. *Reliefs and Inscriptions at Luxor Temple. Volume 1: The Festival Procession of Opet in the Colonnade Hall*. Chicago: Oriental Institute, 1994.

Epigraphic Survey. *Reliefs and Inscriptions at Luxor Temple. Volume 2: The Façade, Portals, Upper Register Scenes, Columns, Marginalia, and Statuary in the Colonnade Hall*. Chicago: Oriental Institute, 1998.

Essam, Angy. "Egypt's GEM Conservation Center Conserves Tutankhamun's Cuirass Which Will Be Displayed for the 1st Time." *Egypt Today,* September 19, 2020, 1–10.

Factum Arte. *The Authorized Facsimile of the Burial Chamber of Tutankhamun*. Basel: Factum Arte, 2013.

Fagan, Brian. *Rape of the Nile*. New York: Charles Scribner's Sons, 1975.

Fahim, Kareem. "Scans of Tutankhamun's Tomb Hint at a Grander Scale." *New York Times,* March 18, 2015.

Fakhry, Ahmed. *The Pyramids*. Chicago: University of Chicago Press, 1970.

Fern, Tracy. *Howard and the Mummy*. New York: Farrar, Straus & Giroux, 2018.

Filer, Joyce M. "Anatomy of a Mummy." *Archaeology,* March/April 2002, 26–29.

Fineberg, Carol, and Renata Karlin. *Tutankhamun in the Classroom. Teachers' Handbook*. New York: Exxon Corp., 1977.

Fiona, Eighth Countess of Carnarvon. *Carnarvon & Carter*. Dorset, UK: Highclere Enterprises, 2007.

Forbes, Dennis. *The Tomb of Tutankhamun (KV 62)*. Sebastopol: KMT Communications, 2018.

Forbes, Dennis, Salima Ikram, and Janice Kamrin. "Tutankhamun's Ribs: A Proposed Solution to a Problem." *KMT* 18, no. 1 (2007): 50–56.

Frayling, Christopher. *The Face of Tutankhamun*. London: Farber & Farber, 1992.

Gabolde, Marc. "The Chromosomes of Tutankhamun." In *Tutankhamun: Discovering the Forgotten Pharaoh*, edited by Simon Connor and Dimitri Laboury, 276–281. Liège: Presses Universitaires de Liège, 2020.

Gabolde, Marc. "An Egyptian Gold Necklace for Sale: Comparisons with Tutankhamun's Jewellery." HAL Archive, 2019.

Gardiner, Alan. "The Defeat of the Hyksos by Kahmose: The Carnarvon Tablet No. I." *Journal of Egyptian Archaeology* III (1916): 95–110.

Gardiner, Alan. *Egyptian Grammar*. Oxford: Griffith Institute, 1950.

Gauthier, Theophile. *Romance of a Mummy*. Philadelphia: Lippincott, 1892.

Gerber, Alex. *3000 Years Ago*. New York: Irving Berlin, 1923.

Gillam, Michael, and Bob Brier. "Can Orthopaedic Knowledge Solve a 3,000-Year-Old Egyptian Mystery?" *Newsletter of the British Orthopaedic Association* 44 (2010): 8–9.

Gillespie, Charles, and Michel Dewachter. *The Monuments of Egypt*. Princeton, NJ: Princeton Architectural Press, 1987.

Gold, Glen David. *Carter Beats the Devil*. New York: Hyperion, 2001.

Goring, Elizabeth, et al., eds. *Chief of Seers: Egyptian Studies in Memory of Cyril Aldred*. London: Kegan Paul, 1997.

Gorringe, Henry. *Egyptian Obelisks*. London: John C. Nimmo, 1885.

Goyne, Richard. *The Kiss of Pharaoh: The Love Story of Tut-Anch-Amen*. New York: Stokes, 1923.

Graefe, Erhart, and Galina Balova. *The Royal Cache TT 320: A Re-examination*. Cairo: Supreme Council of Antiquities Press, 2010.

Greco, Diane, and Jed Buchwald. *The Zodiac of Paris*. Princeton, NJ: Princeton University Press, 2010.

Griffith, F. L. "Carnarvon Tablets I and II." In *Five Years Explorations at Thebes*, edited by Earl of Carnarvon and Howard Carter, 36–37. Oxford: Oxford University Press, 1912.

Guidotti, Maria Cristine. *Il Carro e le Armi de Museo Egizio di Firenze*. Florence: Giunti, 2002.

Guterbock, Hans Gustav. "The Deeds of Suppiluliliuma as Told by His Son Mursilis II." *Journal of Cuneiform Studies* 10 (1956): 75–98.

Hammond, Norman. "Why Valley of Kings Will Yield More Secrets." *Times* (London), August 15, 2015.

Hankey, J. "Arthur Weigall and the Tomb of Yuya and Tuya." *KMT* 9, no. 2 (1998): 41–45.

Harer, W. B. "An Explanation of King Tutankhamun's Death." *Bulletin of the Egyptian Museum* 3 (2006): 83–88.

Harer, W. B. "New Evidence of King Tutankhamun's Death: His Bizarre Embalming." *Journal of Egyptian Archaeology* 97 (2011): 225–232.

Harer, W. B. "Was Tutankhamun Killed by a Hippo?" *Ancient Egypt* 72 (2012): 50–54.

Harris, J. E., and E. F. Wente. "Mummy of the 'Elder Lady' in the Tomb of Amenhotep II." *Science* 200 (June 9, 1978): 1149–1151.

Harrison, R. G. "An Anatomical Examination of the Pharaonic Remains Purported to Be Akhenaten." *Journal of Egyptian Archaeology* 52 (1966): 95–119.

Harrison, R. G., and A. B. Abdalla. "The Remains of Tutankhamun." *Antiquity* 46 (1972): 8–14.

Hawass, Zahi. *Discovering Tutankhamun: From Howard Carter to DNA*. Cairo: AUC Press, 2003.

Hawass, Zahi, et al. "Ancestry and Pathology in King Tutankhamun's Family." *Journal of the American Medical Association* 303 (2010): 638–647.

Hawass, Zahi, and Sahar Saleem. *Scanning the Pharaohs*. Cairo: AUC Press, 2016.

Hayward, R. *Cleopatra's Needles*. Derbyshire: Moorland, 1978.

Hedges, S. B., and M. H. Schweitzer. "Detecting Dinosaur DNA." *Science* 268 (May 26, 1995): 1191–1192.

Herold, Christopher. *Bonaparte in Egypt*. New York: Harper & Row, 1962.

Hornung, Erik. *The Tomb of Seti I*. Munich: Artemis, 1991.

Hoving, Thomas. *Making the Mummies Dance*. New York: Simon & Schuster, 1993.

Hoving, Thomas. *Tutankhamun the Untold Story*. New York: Simon & Schuster, 1978.

Ikram, Salima. "Some Thoughts on the Mummification of King Tutankhamun." *Études et Travaux* [Academie Polonaise des Sciences] XXVI (2013): 292–301.

James, T. G. H. *Howard Carter: The Path to Tutankhamun*. London: Kegan Paul, 1992.

Johnson, Diane, and Joyce Tyldesley. "Iron from the Sky." *Geoscientist Online*, April 2014.

Johnson, George B. "Painting with Light: The Work of Archaeological Photographer Harry Burton." *KMT* 8, no. 2 (1997): 58–77.

Johnson, W. Raymond. *An Asiatic Battle Scene of Tutankhamun*. Chicago: University of Chicago Press, 1992.

Johnson, W. Raymond. "A Royal Fishing and Fowling Talatat Scene from Amarna." *KMT* 26, no. 4 (2016): 40–51.

Johnson, W. Raymond. "Tutankhamun-Period Battle Narratives at Luxor." *KMT* 20, no. 4 (2009): 20–33.

Jones, Dilwyn. *Model Boats from the Tomb of Tut'Ankhamun*. Oxford: Griffith Institute, 1990.

Jones, Martin. *The Molecule Hunt*. New York: Arcade, 2002.

Kamp, David. "The King of New York." *Vanity Fair* 55 (2013): 158–171.

Kawai, Nozomu. "The Ceremonial Canopied Chariot of Tutankhamun (JE 61990 and JE 60705): A Tentative Virtual Reconstruction." *CIPEG Journal* 4 (2020): 1–11.

Keating, Rex. *Nubian Rescue*. London: Robert Hale, 1975.

Kemp, Barry. *Amarna Reports I–VI*. London: Egypt Exploration Society, 1984–1995.

Khater, Antoine. *Le régime juridique des fouilles et antiquités en Égypte*. Cairo: Institut Français, 1960.

Lalanne, Bernard. "Suffering from Malaria in the Age of Tutankhamun." In *Tutankhamun: Discovering the Forgotten Pharaoh*, edited by Simon Connor and Dimitri Laboury, 273–274. Liège: Presses Universitaires de Liège, 2020.

Lauer, Jean-Philippe. *Saqqara*. New York: Charles Scribner's Sons, 1976.

Lee, Christopher C. *The Grand Piano Came by Camel*. Edinburgh: Mainstream Publishing, 1992.

Leek. F. Filce. *The Human Remains from the Tomb of Tut'Ankhamun*. Oxford: Griffith Institute, 1972.

Lesko, Leonard H. *King Tut's Wine Cellar*. Berkeley, CA: B. C. Scribe Publications, 1977.

Lewis, Roger. "Old King Tut Was a Wise Old Nut" [sheet music]. Kansas City: J. W. Jenkins, 1923.

LGI Media. *The Fireball of Tutankhamun*. BBC Television, 2006.

Lichtheim, Miriam. *Ancient Egyptian Literature*. Vol. II. Berkeley: University of California Press, 1976.

Lightbody, David Ian. "The Tutankhamun-Nefertiti Burial Hypothesis: A Critique." *Journal of Ancient Egyptian Architecture* 5 (2021): 83–99.

Littaur, M. A., and J. H. Crouwel. *Chariots and Related Equipment from the Tomb of Tutankhamun*. Oxford: Griffith Institute, 1985.

Lorenzen, Eline, and Eske Willerslev. "King Tutankhamun's Family and Demise" [comment]. *Journal of the American Medical Association* 303, no. 24 (June 23–30, 2010): 3471.

Lucas, Alfred. *Ancient Egyptian Materials and Industries*. London: Arnold, 1962.

Mackesy, Piers. *British Victory in Egypt, 1801*. London: Routledge, 1995.

Mainterot, Philippe. "France." In *A History of World Archaeology*, edited by Andrew Bednarski et al., 68–90. Cambridge: Cambridge University Press, 2021.

Manniche, Lise. *Musical Instruments from the Tomb of Tut'Ankhamun*. Oxford: Griffith Institute, 1963.

Marchant, Jo. "Is This Nefertiti's Tomb?" *Nature*, February 19, 2020, 497–498.

Marchant, Jo. *The Shadow King*. Boston: Da Capo Press, 2013.

Maspero, Gaston. *Les Momies Royales de Deir-el-Bahri*. Cairo: Mission Archaeologique Française au Caire, 1899.

Maspero, Gaston. *Trouvaille de Deir el-Bahri*. Cairo: F. Moures, 1881.

McLeod, W. *Composite Bows from the Tomb of Tut'Ankhamun*. Oxford: Griffith Institute, 1982.

McLeod, W. *Self Bows and Other Archery Tackle from the Tomb of Tut'Ankhamun*. Oxford: Griffith Institute, 1982.

Metropolitan Museum of Art. *Museum Bulletins 1924–5*. New York: Metropolitan Museum of Art, 1924–1925.

Metropolitan Museum of Art. *Treasures of Tutankhamun*. New York: Metropolitan Museum of Art, 1977.

Ministry of Culture (Cairo). *Official Gazette*. February 14, 2010.

Minter, Sue. *The Well-Connected Gardiner: A Biography of Alicia Amherst*. Sulihull: Great Hay Books, 2010.

Mitchell, Timothy. *Colonising Egypt*. Berkeley: University of California Press, 1991.

Montet, Pierre. *Les constructions et le tombeau de Psousennes à Tanis*. Paris: CNRS, 1951.

Moreh, Shmuel, ed. *Al-Jabarti's Chronicle of the French Occupation*. Princeton, NJ: Weiner, 1993.

Morshed, Nagm El Deen, and André J. Veldmeijer. "Conserving, Reconstructing, and Displaying Tutankhamun's Sandals: The GEM-CC's Procedure." *Ex Orient Lux* 45 (2014–2015): 103–104.

Murnane, William. "Nature of the Aten: Akhenaten and His Gods." *Amarna Letters* 3 (1994): 33–40.

Murray, Hellen, and Mary Nutall. *A Handlist to Howard Carter's Catalogue of Objects in Tut'Ankhamun's Tomb*. Oxford: Griffith Institute, 1963.

Naville, Édouard. *Bubastis*. London: Egypt Exploration Fund, 1891.

Naville, Édouard. *The Temple of Deir el Bahri*. Parts I–VI. London: Egypt Exploration Society, 1895–1906.

Newberry, Percy. *Beni Hasan*. Part I. London: Kegan, Paul, Trench, Trubner, 1893.

Newberry, Percy. *El Bersheh*. Part I. London: Egypt Exploration Fund, 1895.

Pääbo, Svante. "Molecular Cloning of Ancient Egyptian Mummy DNA." *Nature* 314 (1985): 644–645.

Panckoucke, C. L. F., ed. *Description de L'Égypte*. Paris: C. L. F. Panckoucke, 1822.

Parkinson, Richard. *Cracking Codes: The Rosetta Stone*. Berkeley: University of California Press, 1999.

Petrie, W. M. Flinders. *Amulets*. Warminster: Aris & Phillips, 1972.

Petrie, W. M. Flinders. *Seventy Years in Archaeology*. New York: Holt, 1932.

Pettigrew, Thomas. *History of Egyptian Mummies*. Los Angeles: North American Archives, 1985.

Piacentini, Patriza. "Italy." In *A History of World Egyptology*, edited by Andrew Bednarski et al., 369–396. Cambridge: Cambridge University Press, 2021.

Piankoff, Alexandre. *The Pyramid of Unas*. New York: Pantheon Books, 1968.

Piankoff, Alexandre. *The Shrines of Tutankhamun*. New York: Pantheon Books, 1959.

Piankoff, Alexandre. *The Tomb of Ramses VI*. New York: Bollingen Foundation, 1954.

Piotrovsky, Boris. *From the Lands of the Scythians*. New York: Metropolitan Museum of Art, 1974.

Pococke, Richard. *A Description of the East*. London: W. Boyer, 1743.

Pringle, Heather. *The Mummy Congress*. New York: Hyperion Books, 2001.

Redford, Donald B. *Akhenaten the Heretic Pharaoh*. Princeton, NJ: Princeton University Press, 1984.

Reeves, Nicholas. *Ancient Egypt: The Great Discoveries*. London: Thames & Hudson, 2000.

Reeves, Nicholas. *The Burial of Nefertiti?* Tucson, AZ: Amarna Royal Tombs Project, 2015.

Reeves, Nicholas. *The Complete Tutankhamun*. London: Thames & Hudson, 1990.

Reeves, Nicholas. *The Decorated North Wall in the Tomb of Tutankhamun (KV 62)*. Tucson, AZ: Amarna Royal Tombs Project, 2019.

Reeves, Nicholas. "Howard Carter's Collection of Egyptian and Classical Antiquities." In *Chief of Seers: Egyptian Studies in Memory of Cyril Aldred*, edited by Elizabeth Goring et al., 242–250. London: Kegan Paul, 1997.

Reeves, Nicholas. *Into the Mummy's Tomb*. New York: Scholastic, 1992.

Reeves, Nicholas, and John Taylor. *Howard Carter Before Tutankhamun*. London: Abrams, 1993.

Reeves, Nicholas, and Richard Wilkinson. *The Complete Valley of the Kings*. London: Thames & Hudson, 2000.

Reid, Donald M. "Remembering and Forgetting Tutankhamun." In *Histories of World Egyptology*, edited by William Caruthers, 157–173. London: Routledge, 2019.

Report on the Safe-guarding of the Philae Monuments. The Hague: Netherlands Engineering Consulting, 1960.

Riggs, Christina. *Photographing Tutankhamun*. Cairo: AUC Press, 2019.

Riggs, Christina. *Treasured: How Tutankhamun Shaped a Century*. New York: Current Affairs, 2021.

Romer, John. *Valley of the Kings*. New York: William Morrow, 1981.

Ruffer, Armand. *Studies in the Paleopathology of Egypt*. Chicago: University of Chicago Press, 1921.

Rühli, F. J., and S. Ikram. "Purported Medical Diagnoses of Pharaoh Tutankhamun, c. 1325 BC." *Homo: Journal of Comparative Human Biology* 65, no. 1 (2014): 51–63.

Said, Edward. *Orientalism*. New York: Viking Press, 1994.

Sambuellia, Luigi, et al. "The Third KV 62 Radar Scan: Searching for Hidden Chambers Adjacent to Tutankhamun's Tomb." *Journal of Cultural Heritage*, May 2019, 288–296.

The Salvage of Abu Simbel Temples. Stockholm: VBB, 1971.

Schiaparelli, Ernesto. *Relazione sui Lavori della Missione Archeologica Italiana in Egitto, II. La Tomba Intatta dell'Architetto "Cha" Nella Necropoli di Tebe*. Turin: Museo di Antichita, 1927.

Schneider, Hans D. *Shabtis*. Vol. I. Leiden: Rijksmuseum, 1977.

Sheppard, Thomas. "Treasures of Tutankhamun's Tomb." *Ours Magazine* 190 (May 1936).

Silverman, David, Josef Wegner, and Jennifer Houser Wegner. *Akhenaten and Tutankhamun*. Philadelphia: University of Pennsylvania Museum, 2006.

Smith, G. Elliot. *The Royal Mummies*. Cairo: Imprimerie de l'Institut Français, 1912.

Smith, Joseph Lindon. *Temples, Tombs, and Ancient Art*. Norman: University of Oklahoma Press, 1956.

Smith, Stuart Tyson, and Nancy Stone Bernard. *The Valley of the Kings*. Oxford University Press, 2003.

Smith-Sangster, Emily. "Personal Experience or Royal Canon?" *KMT* 32, no. 4 (2021): 40–49.

Sotheby's. *Antiquities and Islamic Art, February 8 and 9, 1985*. New York: Sotheby's, 1985.

Sotheby's. *Egyptian Classical and Near Eastern Antiquities, June 10 and 11, 1983*. New York: Sotheby's, 1983.

Spencer, L. J. "Tektites and Silica-Glass." *Mineralogical Magazine* 25, no. 167 (1939): 425–440.

"Suez Canal." *Illustrated London News*, January 31, 1863, 125–128.

Symcox, Geoffrey. "The Geopolitics of the Egyptian Expedition, 1797–1798." In *Napoleon in Egypt*, edited by Irene Bierman, 13–32. Los Angeles: Ithaca Press, 2003.

Tait, W. J. *Game-Boxes and Accessories from the Tomb of Tut'Ankhamun*. Oxford: Griffith Institute, 1982.

Timmann, Christian. "King Tutankhamun's Family and Demise" [comment]. *Journal of the American Medical Association* 303, no. 24 (June 23–30, 2010): 3473.

"Tombs Recently Discovered at Sakkara." *Illustrated London News,* April 15, 1853, 283–284.

Veldmeijer, André. *Tutankhamun's Footwear*. Leiden: Sidestone Press, 2011.

Veldmeijer, André, et al. "Tutankhamun's Cuirass Reconsidered." *Ex Oriente Lux* 48 (2022): 1–14.

Veldmeijer, André, and Salima Ikram, eds. *Chariots in Ancient Egypt*. Leiden: Sidestone Press, 2018.

Veldmeijer, André, and Salima Ikram, eds. *Chasing Chariots*. Leiden: Sidestone Press, 2013.

Veldmeijer, André, and Salima Ikram. "Tutankhamun's Sticks and Staves." *Scribe,* Spring 2020, 8–12.

Ventnor, Craig, et al. "The Sequence of the Human Genome." *Science* 291 (February 16, 2001): 1304–1351.

Verma, Surema. *The Tungusta Fireball*. Cambridge: Icon Books, 2005.

Wainwright, G. A. "Iron in Egypt." *Journal of Egyptian Archaeology* 18 (1932): 3–15.

Watson, James. *The Double Helix*. New York: Signet, 1969.

Weigall, Arthur. *Tutankhamun and Other Essays*. New York: George H. Doran, 1924.

Weiss, Walter M. *Tutankhamun His Tomb and His Treasures*. Bayreuth: Dieter Semmelmann, 2013.

Wilkinson, John Gardner. *Manners and Customs of the Ancient Egyptians*. 3 vols. London: John Murray, 1837.

Williams, Maynard Owen. "At the Tomb of Tutankhamen." *National Geographic Magazine* XLIII, no. 5 (1923): 461–492.

Winlock, Herbert. *Materials Used at the Embalming of King Tut-Ankh-Amun*. New York: Metropolitan Museum of Art, 1941.

Winlock, Herbert. *The Tomb of Senebtisi at Lisht*. New York: Arno Press, 1977.

Winlock, Herbert. *Tutankhamun's Funeral*. New York: Metropolitan Museum of Art, 2010.

Woodward, Scott, et al. "DNA Sequence from Cretaceous Period Bone Fragments." *Science* 266 (November 18, 1994): 1229–1232.

Wynne, Barry. *Behind the Mask of Tutankhamen*. New York: Taplinger Publishing, 1972.

Zaki, A. A. "Tutankhamun Exhibition at the British Museum in 1972." *Journal of Tourism and Research* 3, no. 2 (2017): 79–88.

Index

For the benefit of digital users, indexed terms that span two pages (e.g., 52–53) may, on occasion, appear on only one of those pages.

The letter *f* following a page locator denotes a figure.